STRATEGIC
SURVEY
1989-1990

Published by **Brassey's** for

**THE INTERNATIONAL
INSTITUTE FOR
STRATEGIC STUDIES**
23 Tavistock Street
London WC2E 7NQ

STRATEGIC SURVEY 1989–1990

Published by Brassey's for
The International Institute for Strategic Studies
23 Tavistock Street, London WC2E 7NQ

Director
François Heisbourg

Editor
Sidney Bearman

This publication has been prepared by the Director of the Institute and his Staff, who accept full responsibility for its contents, which describe and analyse events up to late March 1990. These do not, and indeed cannot, represent a consensus of views among the world-wide membership of the Institute as a whole.

First published May 1990

ISBN 0 08 040369 7 (Flexi)
ISSN 0459-7230

Printed and bound in Great Britain by Nuffield Press, Hollow Way, Cowley, Oxford OX4 2PH

CONTENTS

Perspectives

During the past twelve months, the basis of the world's geopolitical structure has been radically transformed. Within an incredibly short time successive revolutions in Eastern Europe wrested one country after another from the grip of communist rulers, and national and social tensions frayed the fabric of the Soviet empire. These momentous events overturned the political and security arrangements that have existed since the end of the Second World War and brought into prospect a real moderation of, if not yet an end to, the East–West confrontation.

Although the 'revolution of 89' occurred principally in Eastern Europe, its shock waves are global in reach and their effect is far from spent; indeed, some areas, such as North-east Asia, have yet to feel the full brunt of the tremors. The framework that lent predictability to existing alliance relationships, both in the East and the West, has crumbled leaving an instability that will not be easy to overcome, for the speed with which events are racing towards a but dimly discernible culmination makes understanding difficult and prediction impossible. The only certainty is that of continuing uncertainty, from which a new form of international relations will eventually emerge.

The greatest instability of all is in the Soviet Union. The revolution from above, which General Secretary Gorbachev launched five years ago in an effort to transform Soviet social, political and economic life, threatens to turn into a revolution from below which might have the same effect in the USSR as similar ones had in Eastern Europe. Conservative forces would clearly like to turn Gorbachev out of office, slow the economic reforms, and call a halt to the political changes now under way. That conservatives have not yet tried to do so may be partly because they cannot agree on an alternative programme with any more chance of success than the one Gorbachev is valiantly trying to put into place.

While the Western Alliance does not face the same burden of problems, it must adjust, with greater rapidity than its members would like, to the changes that have at least called into question and arguably undermined its previous *raison d'être*. The Warsaw Pact has ceased to exist as a functioning military alliance, and it is doubtful whether as an institution it will long survive the departure of East Germany from its ranks. Even before elections in Hungary and Czechoslovakia brought truly democratic regimes to power, each country had asked for a withdrawal of all Soviet forces and each had received assurances from Moscow that they would be gone before the middle of 1991. Were it not for its fear of the impact of the integration of West and East Germany into a unified state, Poland, too, would ask for the removal of Soviet troops. The ebbing of the threat from the East and the imminence of the unification of Germany, require an immediate adjustment in the security arrangements that exist in Europe today. Fortunately, all Western governments have recognized this, for without that recognition the difficult task of agreeing on and developing mechanisms to replace those that have been so successful for the last 40 years would be an impossible one.

Many Questions, Few Answers

There is little question that the Soviet Union remains the key to the adjustments that will have to be made. One major difficulty, however, is that events in the USSR have spun so far out of control that there can be no certainty of what the country will look like when, and if, it finally stabilizes. But whatever the end result, the profound changes now under way are certain to last many years, and will oblige the country to continue to look predominantly inwards. Present Soviet willingness to compromise on arms-control matters, and even on the fundamentally important German question, clearly points to a recognition by Soviet leaders that they must not only avoid confrontation with the West, but must actually reach out for Western support. With the future of Germany (and hence of Europe) as well as the future of the USSR in full flux, we are left with many unanswered questions.

Will Gorbachev be able to ride the tiger he has unchained? Can he speed up political and economic change sufficiently to keep step with the rapidly evolving social and national realities of the USSR? The February 1990 Central Committee meeting endorsed his proposals to drop constitutional references to the leading role of the Communist Party, to move to multi-party elections, and to establish a strong executive presidency, a position tailor-made for Gorbachev. Implementation required the further endorsement of a Party Congress and of the Congress of People's Deputies. The Party Congress was originally intended to meet in February 1991, but, as Gorbachev said, to wait that long would be impossible and 'could finish off the country'; thus he advanced the meeting date to October 1990, and then to early summer 1990. Even this was not soon enough. He felt it was necessary to put the key decision that affected the administration (that of the executive president and the organization of the elections) on the agenda of the Supreme Soviet and a hastily called special session of the Congress of People's Deputies. At that Congress Gorbachev was elected to the newly-formed and very powerful executive presidency. Even so, whether there is still sufficient time to adapt political objectives and institutions to the swiftly evolving situation remains moot. And there can be no assurance that the new position, and the way in which it will be used, will gain sufficient legitimacy to prevent an intensification of the struggle over policy and power that is now under way.

To construct a democratic government – or even something resembling one – in a country with no democratic traditions is a daunting task under the best of circumstances. To move from a centrally planned economy to something resembling a market economy is an equally Herculean task (it has been likened to unmaking an omelette). In a country ripe with nationalist conflicts and rising expectations, and with an underdeveloped and tottering economy, these tasks look impossible. Forces have been unleashed in the Soviet Union which pose awesome obstacles to the exercise of idealism; ethnic feuds and suspicions are being fed by a number of extremist groups and some charismatic personalities. It looks more and more likely that – for better or worse – this is more the hour of the clever tactician than of the democrat.

Even if Gorbachev's gamble succeeds and his reforms finally begin to work, much time will be required before the Soviet people derive any real benefits. But patience may be running out. The introduction of even partial market mechanisms will inevitably result in more, not less, hardship for some time to come. Whether the Soviet people will be willing to accept this, particularly if the distribution of wealth should become even more visibly uneven in the process, is highly uncertain, to say the least. The public's revulsion against 'acquisitive' co-operatives, and the leadership's capitulation to public pressures on this score, are not a reassuring omen. The attraction of extreme positions, offering apparently easy answers, may grow.

Perhaps most worryingly for the Kremlin, the very existence of the Soviet Union within its current borders is in question. The Caucasus is in flames; Central Asia, with all too many shared features with pre-independence Algeria, is close to boiling point; the Baltic states have already left the Union in outlook and political objectives; and nationalist feeling is escalating in the Ukraine. There are schemes to transform the USSR into a confederation of sovereign republics (with more or less abstruse legal mechanisms for the exercise of the right to secede from the confederation). These schemes, however, may not go far enough for many national minorities, while going too far for many Russians and conservatives. Although designed to defuse the danger of civil war, these plans could all too easily deepen the divisions in the country and promote what they are meant to prevent. Yet the most perplexing of all the dilemmas facing the USSR may be that all other options are less attractive.

Finally, there are clear inconsistencies in Gorbachev's programme. Although he pushes for more democracy and seems willing to compromise on everything except, possibly, the territorial integrity of the USSR, he claims that it is necessary to acquire much more personal power to achieve greater democracy. Gorbachev seems to believe that an enlightened autocratic leadership is the only near-term answer to the problems besieging the Soviet Union. He may be right; yet others, such as Boris Yeltsin and the new conservative leaders, not only question this but can be expected to agitate for their own share of power.

The present Soviet leadership has adopted some bold measures that might lead to a better future. That future, however, is not only far from assured, it looks more and more doubtful. The Soviet Union appears to be sliding towards chaos, and how long, and how much of it, will remain together are very much open questions, complicated by the role which the non-Russian republics play in the USSR's economy and defence (including, in many cases the stationing of nuclear weapons). To hold the country together, Gorbachev, or a successor, may feel it is necessary to use the president's new powers in a more restrictive and illiberal way than the world hopes. In March 1990, Moscow sent ultimatums and deployed troops to counter the declaration of independence that Lithuania had flung in its face. This suggested that the Soviet Union was still considering the use of force to maintain the boundaries of its internal empire. The use of military force in this way in the Baltic states would have profound implications for Gorbachev's political and economic reforms, and for the West, which had hoped to welcome the Soviet Union into a new, less threatening world structure.

The Falling Dominoes

By the summer of 1989 Gorbachev was taking a surprisingly relaxed approach to the question of the loss of communist power in what had until recently been the Soviet Union's external empire, Eastern Europe. The fundamental reason for the successful and peaceful course of the revolutions in the six Soviet satellites (there was significant violence only in Romania) was Gorbachev's decision that the USSR would not use military might to ensure that they remained tied to the USSR. It may have been that he felt that the cost in terms of Western reaction would be too high; any hope that the USSR might have had of Western economic and technical aid, and of a benign military and diplomatic environment, would have died. Gorbachev may not have foreseen, as he has not foreseen many of the effects of the reforms he has instituted in the USSR, that allowing the people to shove aside their rigid rulers would lead not to some species of reform communism but to a dash for political and economic freedom that would totally transform the European scene. Once the process was set in motion there was no way to stop it at a sustainable cost.

The way in which the revolutions developed was not without a certain exquisite irony, particularly with regard to the example it provided of the operation of the much vaunted, but then discredited, 'domino' theory of the Vietnam War era. It was argued then that if Vietnam were allowed to fall to communist rule it would be impossible to stop the virus spreading throughout the rest of South-east Asia, from Vietnam to Thailand to Malaya. The theory itself, it turns out, was not necessarily faulty; it was simply applied in the wrong context and within the wrong time-frame. For in Eastern Europe in 1989 borders were no barriers to the spread of the virus of freedom. Communist regimes toppled like unstable dominoes with ever increasing speed, as the ubiquitous television coverage taught the people of one country after another how to carry through an essentially peaceful revolution that would rid them of the bondage under which they chafed.

The third essential ingredient of the revolutions was a combination of the undiluted courage of the people, whose mass increased in street demonstrations day after day, and the loss of will and nerve on the part of their communist leaders. Faced with the refusal of the USSR to bail them out by the use of Soviet military forces, and with their own belief in the system they were running corroded by long years of cynicism and sycophancy, they could not cope. The rot at the core of each regime was made manifest. Even in Romania, where Ceauşescu tried to shoot down those who refused to do his bidding, the panic in which he fled from the unarmed opposition spoke with greater eloquence to the army than his orders to break the people's will with force.

After the 'Europhoria', however, both Eastern and Western Europe must come to grips with the sobriety of reality. The promise of democratic rule is beginning to be realized through elections, but, given insecure organizational structures and a multiplicity of fledgling political parties all with immature programmes, the transition is unlikely to be either easy or smooth. The hope must be that the inevitable setbacks on the road to working democracies do not alienate publics from the political process. The promise of economic liberalization will also be difficult to attain without great pain and more sacrifice. Ethnic and nationalist impulses, which have been long submerged under the communists' draconian rule, have re-emerged. The renewed bloodshed between Romanians and ethnic Hungarians in Transylvania in March 1990 seems likely to be a portent of the possibilities to come, and now that the people of many of the newly-freed countries have lost the communists as an easy target to blame for failures and difficulties, there has also been a reawakening of anti-Semitism in the search for replacement scapegoats. The recrudescence of these powerful nationalist and ethnic forces is certain to lead to an increase in internal tensions in the region, and with them will come a rise in instability.

Vaclav Havel, the oft-jailed dissident playwright who was catapulted to the Czech presidency by the revolution, best expressed one of the major problems facing East European countries when he noted that 'the people have suddenly emerged from prison to an open square; they are now free and they don't know where to go'. This was only partially true of the election in March in the GDR; without knowing quite what it would mean, the people voted decisively to go as quickly as possible into a unified German state. By making their first free general election into their last, they have further complicated the political and security conundrums that have faced the West ever since the sharp division of Europe broke down. The whole world has been present at the destruction of the old order; now, as they struggle with the need to build a new order, the statesmen of the West are challenged to be as wise as those who were present at the creation some 40 years ago.

A Testing Time

When 1989 began, the 12 nations of the European Community (EC) seemed reasonably on course for further economic integration in the Single Market of 'Europe 1992', and for a move to a European Monetary Union. There would, of course, have been hitches along the way.

Some, notably France, were championing more speed and more integration than suited others, most notably the UK. The ideal might have
been watered down a bit and the Single Market might have come into
being a little later than the magic '1992'. But prospects looked bright.

Some of the vision has been blurred by the collapse of communist rule
throughout Eastern Europe, now more accurately thought of as Central
and South-east Europe. The bunching of the Soviet satellites into one
unified category had only made some sense when they were forced by
the adherence of their communist governments to a common Marxist
view to think and vote as a bloc. Now that they are individually moving
to free-market economies at differing speeds and from different economic bases, yet all desiring to take their place within a common European structure, the situation has become vastly more complicated.
And the imminent absorption of East Germany into West Germany or,
as the Germans prefer to express it, the unification of the two parts of
Germany into one country, threatens to bring a poor, highly polluted
industrial nation into the EC through the back door.

Chancellor Kohl's address to the EC soon after the East German elections in which he insisted that Germany wanted to see a deepening and
quickening of the Monetary Union, and a tightening of European ties so
that a new Germany would not be left to play a role independent of Europe was thus a very welcome one. It has helped assuage a reawakened
fear that European nations would be left once again to deal with a politically and economically very strong Germany loose in the centre of the
continent. If the expression of this German desire is followed by
significant deeds it should be easier for the European political and economic intergovernmental councils to make the necessary adjustments
to the changed circumstances. As Western Europe faces the task of helping Eastern Europe to dig its way out of the pit into which communist
rule has pushed it, it would do well to recognize that this task is fully
consistent with its own efforts to weave West European integration into
a coherent and cohesive whole. A healthy pan-European order will
require both a solid foundation in the West and economic support for
the East.

The political and economic restructuring of Europe is a daunting
task, yet it rests on the strong pillars of the work that has already been
done. Adjusting to the changing security picture in Europe will be an
even more difficult task. The first step is to recognize that the strategic
and military factors that gave meaning to the two opposing military
alliances are disappearing: the Cold War has been officially declared at
an end by such experts as Presidents Bush and Gorbachev; the division
of Europe was erased when the Berlin Wall was breached. As a consequence, the political and military requirements of the East–West confrontation have ceased to be the basic structuring factors of the European order. To most people, therefore, the stationing of large numbers
of foreign troops within both parts of Europe, the emplacement of mass-

ive concentrations of armaments, and the continuation of onerous outlays for defence will increasingly seem anachronistic.

The existing security arrangements have been very successful in Europe in ensuring peace and stability for the past 40 years. The astonishing changes of 1989 have enhanced the prospects for peace, but have
reduced those for strategic stability. Yet, within a fluid situation, having
various institutions competing for pride of place might not be a bad
thing, so long as they can do so in a peaceful environment. Some
institutions will clearly not be flexible or adaptable enough to produce a
new overriding structure for European order. Both the Warsaw Pact
and CMEA appear to be moribund organizations, and without a clear
threat to oppose, NATO's role will alter: instead of being the strategic
umbrella without which other Western institutions such as the EC could
not have been established and flourished, a continuing Atlantic Alliance
will figure less prominently. Its role is likely to be more like that of an
insurance policy, no doubt useful, indeed indispensable, but not the factor around which the European 'household' will organize its life.

Other organizations, such as the CSCE, may prove of great value in
helping to manage political and security relations from 'San Francisco
to Vladivostok', but the CSCE's constitutional rule of unanimity will
prevent it from ensuring collective security between its members; nor is
there a clear and generally acceptable foundation for a different
decision-making mechanism, such as majority voting or the establishment of a select group of nations endowed with privileged powers.
Other concepts, like the so-called 'Common European House' seem too
vague and driven by an individual country's effort to gain a particular
goal or advantage to develop into the new order. As for the EC and/or
the Western European Union, these bodies may in time play an effective security role, in the framework of a deeply modified European–
American compact, but such a prospect remains at this stage a vision
rather than a practical proposition. For some time therefore, Western
Europe may be characterized by an incomplete and disjointed security
system, with a lower-profile Atlantic Alliance, a more prominent CSCE,
and a politically more active set of Western European institutions
(notably the EC), rather than the rigorous and stable order born of the
East–West confrontation.

The political and eventual military withdrawal of the USSR from the
states of Eastern Europe is likely to mean a profound change in the geopolitical situation of these states. For 40 years what happened (or did
not happen) in Eastern Europe was of vital importance because of the
role these states played in the East–West balance and thus in the bipolar
system which dominated world politics. While it is true that the West
will have an interest in promoting democratic and liberalizing forces in
Eastern Europe through economic aid and advice, Western leaders may
well begin to question whether in the rush to create new architectures of
European security they would wish to give explicit or implied security
guarantees to these countries. How Western states marry their desire to

see progress in Eastern Europe with an equally potent concern not to get entangled in the messy aftermath of Soviet decolonization in Europe will be one of the principal dilemmas of the 1990s. Sentiment will argue in favour of a pan-European security 'system', the shape of which is a mystery at the moment, yet prudence may argue in favour of a slower intermingling of the fates of Europe's two halves. The fact remains that the nations of the Atlantic Alliance will have to think hard about the most appropriate manner to fold the emergence of a strategically non-aligned Eastern Europe into their defence doctrines.

While it is difficult to judge exactly how new security arrangements will be made because changes within Eastern Europe, the Soviet Union and Western Europe continue to come thick and fast, any arrangements must include the US and the USSR within their purview. Security arrangements that do not provide sufficient safeguards to uphold legit-imate superpower interests, to involve them in the functioning of a European system, and to alleviate their justifiable concerns cannot be expected to last.

The Last Superpower
The Bush Administration has been faulted for being slow to respond to world changes and for ignoring the need for highly imaginative new visions for the bright future. Yet there is much to be said for not rushing forward with grandiose plans before the situation to which they are to apply is clear. At certain key points during the past year the Adminis-tration has provided useful and timely concepts to help bridge growing cracks; President Bush's May 1989 proposals to NATO and Secretary Baker's December speech in Berlin addressing EC concerns were both essential in pointing the right direction.

The Administration has properly insisted that European political, economic and security co-ordination are matters in which Europeans should, and must, take the lead. At the last juncture in European history when comparable decisions were being made it was inevitable and essential that the US, as the only Western power not devastated by the war, provided the impetus. Now its more proper role is a co-operative and supportive one, consulting with its allies for mutual benefit. Both the arms-control measures that have already been negotiated and the logic of present developments mean that the enormous force that the US has stationed in Europe for the past 40 years will be reduced, per-haps sharply. While the US recognizes this, and even welcomes it, it is essential that the US remains intertwined, even enmeshed, in a Euro-pean security structure in a significant way.

The US faces domestic economic and social pressures that add weight to the arguments that now that peace appears to have settled on the world, and the Soviet Union has lost its 'superpower' status, great benefits can be derived which should be wholly devoted to improving life at home. It is a siren song that should be resisted. Isolationism failed dismally before the First World War and again before the Second; the world's politics and economics are now so much more interdependent that it is certain to be no more successful if tried again.

A massive debt, imploding inner cities, an eroding infrastructure, and adverse trade balances have convinced many Americans that their country has settled into a decline from which it will not be able to recover. But, serious though these illnesses are, none of them, nor all of them together, need be terminal. The US economy is still the largest and most broadly based in the world. Despite the almost paranoid fear of an economic 'attack' from Japan (Americans now rate Japan as the greatest danger they face, with the Soviet Union dropping to the bottom of the charts), this fear is hardly justified. If President Bush could bring himself to call on his present support (as high as 80% of the electorate in some polls) to create new revenues with which to tackle the outstanding problems, they could begin to be put into proper perspective.

Some Dark Spots

Throughout much of the world the insistent determination of ordinary people to live under freer political and economic conditions was triumphant in 1989. In addition to the six Warsaw Pact European countries, Mongolia turned from totalitarian communist rule towards multi-party elections and the beginnings of free market economics; Nicaragua voted out the Marxist *Sandinista* regime; the US forced Panama's tyrannical despot Noriega from power; South Africa has begun to move with surprising and encouraging boldness away from its insistence on an apartheid structure and helped bring independence to Namibia; and Vietnam has begun to institute freer economic, if not yet political, measures. There is scarcely an area of the globe where people did not gain new hope and freedom for themselves and, in most cases, surprisingly peacefully. At the same time, there were all too many regions in which progress remained far too slow, or even non-existent. In the Middle East and the larger portion of Africa, for example, things may not have become worse, but are no better.

Only in China did the pendulum actually swing the other way. Here non-violent demonstrations for further relaxation of tight political and economic controls were brutally crushed. Since the ruthless army action in early June 1989 in Beijing, the elderly Chinese leaders have regressed to tighter political and economic controls. The result is certain to be a country once again isolated from the mainstream of world events, with investment from abroad dropping, a sullen and less productive working force, and thus vastly poorer economic prospects. As the ideological certainty of the leadership is diluted through death in the years to come, these factors can be expected to bring the Chinese back to the realization that the only way forward is one closer to that being attempted by other former communist governments.

As old bipolar antagonisms have faded, an opportunity has been created to deal with growing transnational problems. The unequal distribution of wealth is no longer just a North–South question; it has expanded to an East–West dimension. The natural desire of the wealthier nations of the West to help those who are just emerging from bondage in the East threatens to affect the efforts that had been started to ease the burden of debt of the economies of the world's underdeveloped countries. While security and stability may no longer be threatened by communist ambitions and power, they continue to be affected by implacable environmental pressures, by the scourge of narcotics, and by the increasing demands of political refugees and economic migrants around the world. None of these problems is amenable to easy or quick answers, but they can only be expected to become more difficult if a beginning is not made soon by those nations which have seen their defence burdens decline.

Boldness, But With Caution, Please

Before he embarked on his extraordinary voyage in 1985 Gorbachev would have done well to have pondered Machiavelli's wise words: 'There is nothing more difficult to take in hand, more perilous to conduct, or more uncertain in its success, than to take the lead in the introduction of a new order of things'. As he struggles now with the Soviet Union's multiple problems and finds that each solution he uncovers for one leads straight on to another, Gorbachev might well think that his early optimism was somewhat misplaced. For, while it is difficult to be sure of many things in these speeded-up times, it is certain that the Soviet Union will not end up where Gorbachev was originally heading.

There is perhaps a lesson in this for Western statesmen. Faced with the necessity of bringing into being a newer order of things it would be sensible for them to mix their boldness with considerable caution. They have a tremendous advantage over Gorbachev; the system that he set out to change was failing miserably and required almost total overhaul. The one that they will be adjusting is one that has worked superbly to achieve the ends for which it was established. The challenge for Western statesmen, however, is to recognize that they cannot stand pat, for the fundamental changes the world has undergone have produced an environment which will require changes in the existing structures and which presents new challenges. On the one hand, they should not overestimate the need for complete changes. The present security arrangements have proved their worth; what is probably best done is to adapt them with care to the new circumstances, for there are certain to be yet newer circumstances in the not-too-distant future. On the other hand, it is not a time to relax, for the new challenges are likely to require just as much imagination, dedication and resolute investment as went into the build-up of those security structures which served the world so well for 40 years, and which played midwife to the birth of this bright, new world.

The Superpowers

THE SOVIET UNION: A DISSOLVING EMPIRE

When Mikhail Gorbachev became General Secretary of the Communist Party of the Soviet Union (CPSU) five years ago, he called for a 'revolution without bullets'. A revolution is what he got; but it is no longer without bullets and it is probably more far-reaching and dangerous than the Soviet leadership had either anticipated or desired. In the past year the Soviet position in Eastern Europe has collapsed. More ominously, crises, chaos and change on an unprecedented scale have enveloped the Soviet Union itself.

The situation in the country today is inherently unstable. Neither politically nor economically can the Soviet Union remain as it is; it must either take several steps forward in its drive for reform, or several steps backward. Gorbachev seems willing to risk further change, recognizing that any step backward, any return towards Brezhnevism (or even Stalinism) would lead straight to disaster. What remains far less clear, however, is whether he has any genuine answers to the ever growing, ever more dramatic problems in the USSR, whether those answers are relevant, and whether they will be formulated and put into practice in time. For the dizzying speed of developments in the Soviet Union, as in the former communist states of Eastern Europe, has placed an unmistakable stamp of immediacy on the need for change.

For a number of years, there have been alarming signs of developing crises in many areas. By early 1990, however, the problems had not only intensified, they had become ineluctably interlinked. In summer 1989, the volatile mix exploded when large-scale strikes rapidly evolved into a political challenge which has shaken the leadership. Since then, there has been an acceleration of the crisis. In addition to the events in Eastern Europe, it is a combination of three factors which has been responsible: the deteriorating economic situation and the accompanying collapse in the supply of essential consumer goods to the Soviet population; the increasing virulence of the nationalities problem; and the deepening political crisis in the country.

Truly Dismal Economics

The continuing failure of the Gorbachevian reforms to improve Soviet economic life is a fundamental cause of the present difficulties. Without a degree of economic success, the population's rising expectations fuelled by *glasnost* simply cannot be met.

The Soviet economy had not done well in 1988; in 1989 it deteriorated even further. According to official (and probably over optimistic) statistics, national income grew by just 2.4% in 1989 (1988: 4.4%) and thus badly missed the planned target of 5.7%. Gross national product

went up by 3.0% (1988: 5.5%) and not the planned 7.0%. Industrial production grew by only 1.7% (with a target of 3.4% and an increase in
1988 of 3.6%). Dismal though these figures may be, what is of even
greater concern is that what growth there was occurred early in the year
and then plummeted. Industrial output, for example, increased in the
first two quarters of 1989 by 2.7%, declined to 1% in the third quarter,
and became negative in the final quarter.

Specific production figures only confirm this gloomy overall trend.
While the grain harvest was a fairly decent 209 million tons in 1989
(1988: 195 mt, 1989 plan: 236 mt), total agricultural production failed
to reach its planned targets. Oil production declined from 624 mt in
1988 to 608 mt in 1989, and production problems in the Caucasus will
make it difficult to achieve even this reduced output in the future (50%
of all Soviet oil rigs are produced in Baku and production there is at a
standstill). The declining trend in oil production will seriously affect
future Soviet hard currency earning potential. Net foreign indebted-
ness, indeed, followed the sharp rise upwards that it had taken in 1988,
although at $32.8bn, it remained tolerable.

Coal production declined. The foreign trade position of the USSR
worsened, with exports rising by only 1.7% while imports went up by
7.9%. The USSR actually ran its first trade deficit (of some 2bn roubles)
in living memory. Labour productivity grew by a mere 2.2% (1988:
4.8%, 1989 plan: 4.5%) and fell steadily throughout the year. Inflation,
on the other hand, rose by an official 7.5%, but if the black market
(whose importance to the economy continues to grow) is taken into
account, the true rate is somewhere between 11% to 15%.

Since wages increased 5.4 times faster than production, the demand for
goods continued to outpace their supply. Excess demand in 1989
amounted to at least 70bn roubles, a figure that must be seen in the context
of earlier accumulated savings of over 300bn roubles. The budget deficit
increased to 130bn roubles and continues its upward trend. The investment programme came nowhere near its targets: of the 157 main investment projects scheduled for completion in 1989, only 108 were actually
finished. While investment funds increased by 3%, and thus corresponded
roughly to the planned target, the value of finished investment projects
decreased by 3%. Half-finished investment projects correspondingly grew
to a staggering 204.1bn roubles in value. In short, by the end of 1989 the
Soviet economy was practically in a state of free-fall.

Five years after the drive for *perestroika* and economic reform began,
these are shocking results. Even Brezhnev had done better in his final
years. Thus far, the only significance of the economic reform in the Soviet Union has been to make it clear that the old economic system no
longer functions, but that there is, as yet, nothing to replace it. In fact,
the piecemeal reforms which have been offered to date are actually
worsening, rather than improving, the situation.

Nowhere was this as clear as in the consumer goods market. Today
the supply of essential consumer goods is on the point of collapse.

According to Soviet figures, in autumn 1989 no less than 243 of the 273 main consumer items were no longer, or not regularly, available on the shelves. Since November meat, flour, most vegetables, fruits, rice and soap have been virtually unobtainable, even in Moscow's state shops. The situation in the rest of the country can be imagined. Nearly 73 years after the October Revolution, a genuine threat of famine has arisen in the USSR. Academician Aganbegyan, one of Gorbachev's key economic advisers, has said that without swift change (i.e., far-reaching and comprehensive economic reforms) some regions would have faced the first signs of famine in the winter of 1989–90, and he predicted that by the next winter there would be large-scale famine of the type that was seen during the early 1920s. The situation has become particularly desperate for old-age pensioners and the unemployed (now officially admitted to be some six million). The frustration and anger of the entire population have grown markedly. This anger is now being directed against the government, including Gorbachev himself, whose personal popularity and credibility have declined markedly over the year.

The Acute Nationalities Problem

The growing social and economic hardships suffered by the people, the lack of any credible means of improving matters quickly, and the new right to express opinions more openly, have proved to be a highly dangerous mixture in a country that remains essentially an undivided colonial empire. There has always been unrest among the many nationalities of the Soviet Union, but in the past it had been ruthlessly suppressed. Matters changed in the mid-1980s when national protests became more visible – and went visibly unpunished.

The increased possibility of speaking out, along with the obvious decline in the standard of living, created the necessary preconditions for the outbursts of national sentiment during 1989 and the early months of 1990. Ethnic ties became the natural rallying point for opposition and for demands for fundamental change. The nationalist unrest was most acute in five regions: the Caucasus, the Baltic Republics, the Soviet Western Republics, Central Asia, and in Russia itself. In each it took a different form, and in each it posed a different challenge to the central government.

The Crumbling Caucasus

The most violent turn of events took place in the Caucasus, fuelled by the age-old tensions between Christians and Muslims in the region. The problem presented by the predominantly Armenian enclave of Nagorno-Karabakh had already led to bloodshed (see *Strategic Survey 1988–1989*, p. 74), but when the enclave was placed under the direct administration of Moscow, and security forces of the Ministry of the Interior were reinforced, matters calmed down on the surface. But it was only an uneasy calm that prevailed, and when Moscow, perplexed by the problem and unable to formulate a coherent nationalities policy, restored Nagorno-Karabakh to Azerbaijan towards the end of 1989, the

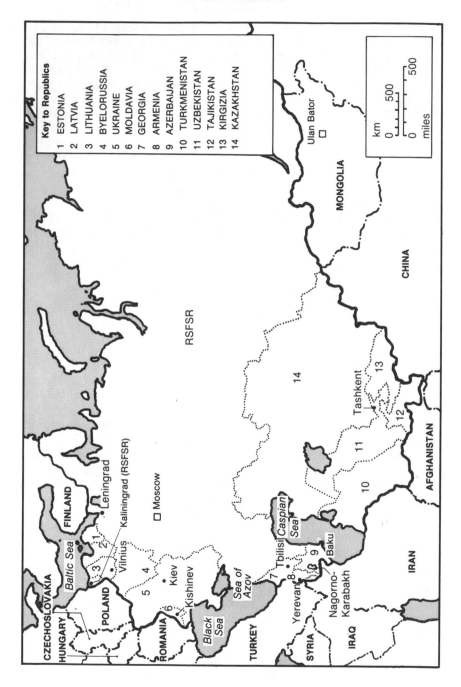

The Soviet Socialist Republics

whole region erupted with a savage fury that left hundreds dead and forced tens of thousands to flee their homes.

The civil war between Armenians and Azerbaijanis, which had already begun to resemble, on a smaller scale, the situation in Afghanistan (with vital goods reaching Armenia, if at all, only under heavy military escort), escalated. In effect, national fronts in both republics replaced existing local and communist power structures. Both sides were heavily armed (including guns, armoured vehicles and even helicopters). More than 25,000 firearms had been stolen from army depots in the first nine months of the year alone. To stop the worst fighting and to regain at least a semblance of control over the region, the Red Army had to deploy over 55,000 troops to the area and literally storm Baku, the capital of Azerbaijan, causing heavy casualties. The fighting has slowed, but the brutal reality remains that central government has virtually collapsed in the Caucasus and the region has turned into a war zone, or, perhaps more accurately, an occupied territory.

Other Violence

Bloody unrest was by no means restricted to Armenia and Azerbaijan. Turmoil has also engulfed neighbouring Georgia, where a national front is striving for independence. Violence is a constant possibility. Undoubtedly the most frightening incident occurred in April 1989 when the army used poison gas to crush a peaceful demonstration in Tbilisi; dozens of people died and hundreds were injured. If anything was needed to fan the flames of national unrest in Georgia higher, the Tbilisi action certainly did it. Further ethnic strife broke out between the Georgians and other minorities in the Abkhazian and Northern Ossetian regions.

Shots were also fired in Moldavia. Unrest had been mounting gradually throughout the year, with calls for reunification with Romania becoming more frequent. When demonstrators prevented the October Revolution parade from taking place, and an angry crowd stormed Party headquarters in Kishinev, the militia opened fire. They left well over 200 dead and wounded.

Severe rioting also began in many parts of Soviet Central Asia, particularly in Uzbekistan, Tajikistan and Kazakhstan. Tajikistan was placed under emergency law in February 1990 after the bloodiest ethnic riots in Central Asia thus far – that they were caused by rumours that Armenian refugees would be given preferential housing treatment illustrates how problems in one area breed those in another. The danger that unrest would soon engulf the entire southern rim of the USSR grew steadily throughout the year.

The Baltics

An entirely different sort of problem was created by the Baltic states. Occupied by Stalin under the terms of his pact with Hitler and forcefully annexed, Latvia, Estonia and Lithuania have never felt part of the USSR. National feelings and a desire for independence have remained powerful; they have been strengthened by the central government's attempts at Russification and by the environmental risks imposed on them by Moscow. With *glasnost*, the Balts felt the time had come to declare illegal the forceful annexation of 1940.

They did not resort to violence, however, but used clever political and legal tactics instead. Informal 'People's Fronts' were established, which the central government first had to tolerate, and finally to accept. Local Party authorities soon recognized that their only chance for political survival was to wrap themselves in the same nationalist flag as their opponents. New leaders of the Communist Party organizations like Algirdas Brazaukas, who became First Secretary of the Lithuanian Communist Party in October 1988, supported many of the demands of the nationalist forces. Some of these nationalist movements, such as the Lithuanian 'Movement for Restructuring' (*Sajudis*), quickly turned into independent parties in all but name. The monopoly of power of the CPSU collapsed, creating an important political precedent whose significance went well beyond the Baltic states themselves.

Concrete steps towards secession (a right granted, in theory, to all republics under Article 74 of the Soviet Constitution) followed. In November 1988 Estonia declared itself a sovereign state within the USSR and claimed a right of veto over all legislation adopted by the Supreme Soviet of the USSR. National flags and emblems were first displayed, and then officially accepted; new national passports were issued; the right to establish relations with foreign countries was claimed; and a multi-party system was introduced. *Sajudis* publicly defined its objective to be an independent and neutral Lithuania.

Helplessly, the Soviet central government watched these steps towards *de facto* independence, particularly in Lithuania which is ethnically the most homogeneous, non-Russian area (some 80% of the population is Lithuanian). When it eventually appeared to be on the point of taking a firm stand (after the Lithuanian Communist Party in December declared its formal independence from the CPSU), its attention was soon diverted to an even more serious issue – the threatening civil war in the Caucasus. In the end, the CPSU merely exhorted the Lithuanian communists to reverse their decision and promised that everything could be discussed more calmly at the forthcoming Party Congress. Yet, by all measures, it had been a tense moment – tenser perhaps than many realized. The picture of Gorbachev, during his trip to Vilnius, alternately pleading and quarrelling with Lithuanians, was a dramatic one. His opening remark that he had come 'without the Army' and that events in the Baltic states had created a serious threat to *perestroika* contained an ominous note, particularly against the background of rumours (and some evidence) that conservative forces had asked for a military intervention in the Baltic Republics.

The February/March 1990 elections in Lithuania realized Moscow's deepest fears. The pro-independence movement swept to an overwhelming victory: *Sajudis*-backed candidates won more than three-quarters of the seats. The run-off elections in the 45 races that had not been decided on 25 February, because no candidate had won more than half the votes, were brought forward to 10 March so that the Lithuanian Parliament would be in a position to declare independence before the Supreme Soviet in Moscow could vote Gorbachev sweeping new powers. And on 11 March the newly-elected members voted formally for secession from the USSR. This action has faced Gorbachev with a serious challenge: it has brought the integrity of the Union very much into question (Estonia, Latvia and Georgia are poised to follow the Lithuanian lead), and it breaches the borders fixed in 1945. An independent Lithuania will leave that part of Prussia annexed by the USSR in 1945, and which incorporates a major naval base at Kaliningrad, physically cut off from the Soviet Union. Yet Gorbachev has few means of stopping the Lithuanian action short of the massive use of force. Having already forsworn military action, he has fallen back on threats of exacting an economic price so astronomically high that he hopes Lithuania will agree to accept a long time-table for association within some undefined variety of confederation instead of full independence. It seems a forlorn hope.

A More Serious Challenge
Nationalist sentiment has also been growing in the Ukraine and to a lesser extent in Byelorussia. A Ukrainian National Front has been established, and mass rallies have been held, most particularly in the western Ukraine, where national sentiment has been fuelled by the religious aspirations of a population which, to a large extent, looks to Rome, not Moscow, for spiritual guidance. If the pace has been slower here, the challenge to the future of the USSR is potentially even more serious. The Ukraine and Byelorussia are part of the industrial heartland of the Soviet Union – without them the USSR cannot survive as a superpower. The tense realities of the underlying situation in the Ukraine were revealed by the swiftness with which the coal-miners' strike that broke out in the Siberian coalfields in summer 1989 spread to the Ukraine, and escalated from economic to political demands.

Common to all the unrest is a combination of national fervour and dissatisfaction with the economy. The non-Russian republics feel increasingly exploited by Russia and are now asking for economic autonomy and fair prices for their products. This is not only very often the first crucial step on the way to claiming independence, but a trend which inevitably must cause havoc to central economic planning, already severely shaken by the collapse of much intra-COMECON trade. Forced time and again to accept economic demands from the republics, Gorbachev soon faced another fundamental problem: if everyone wanted a larger share of the cake, somebody's share would have to shrink and, given the sluggish economy, shrink dramatically.

Many Russians were beginning to feel that it was their slice of cake that was in most danger. Protests by Russian minorities in the non-Russian republics multiplied to the point where central government had no choice but to appease them. Above all, however, nationalism has grown more strident in Russia itself. This was not only made manifest by the increasing activities of extremist groups, such as the fascist, chauvinist and anti-Semitic *Pamyat* organization, but also in more subtle forms. Czarist flags reappeared during the year, and many Russian politicians – even Boris Yeltsin as he eyes the prize of leadership of the Russian Soviet Federative Socialist Republic (RSFSR) – began to include Russian nationalist concerns in their speeches. In the longer run, a clash between non-Russian minorities and growing Russian nationalism in the USSR may be an even more frightening prospect for the Soviet leadership than unrest in the border republics. It is no exaggeration to say that the very existence of the USSR is now at stake.

Political Crisis

The CPSU, however, has had to face what is probably its most fundamental challenge in the political realm. The 19th Party Congress, meeting in June 1988, had profoundly changed the Soviet legislature. The old Supreme Soviet, which had rubber-stamped Party decisions, was dissolved and replaced by a Congress of People's Deputies of 2,250 members (two-thirds of whom are more or less democratically elected, with the remaining third appointed by various social organizations, including the CPSU). The Congress then elected from its members a new 450-deputy Supreme Soviet; the first actual working parliament of the Soviet Union since Lenin decreed the country a dictatorship of the proletariat.

Elections to both bodies were stormy, but as far as could be observed, more or less fair. When the Congress of People's Deputies convened in May 1989, it was not necessarily the most democratic of parliaments, but definitely one of the most interesting. The formal working results were not impressive in scope. A new Supreme Soviet was elected, with some arm-twisting in the background, as evidenced by the not quite democratic correction of Boris Yeltsin's original failure to win a place through the ballot. As expected, Gorbachev was appointed Chairman of its Presidium, and hence in practice President.

What was more impressive, however, and what kept the entire Soviet population glued to their television screens (so much so that live broadcasting of parliamentary sessions had later to be abolished because labour productivity was said to have decreased by 30% during the first session of the Congress) was the new style of debate, and what that debate meant. For the first time ever the sober realities of the Soviet crisis were being discussed publicly and at length. The debate was not always orderly; in fact it was often erratic, if not chaotic. Yet all the issues were addressed. The country learned much about itself, and began to grasp how bad things really were. The frankness of the debate created a new political style, a style which quickly swept the country.

The difficulties with which many of Prime Minister Ryzhkov's ministers were confirmed by the new Supreme Soviet (whose debates mirrored those of the Congress and reinforced their impact) indicated openly that the *nomenklatura*, the Party establishment and its *apparatchiks*, were vulnerable. Some names could not even be put forward for high positions; other candidates for ministerial jobs fell by the wayside; even the once all-powerful position of Minister of Defence was reduced to human size when Dmitri Yazov's appointment was only confirmed through a very obvious manipulation of the required quorum. Most important of all, some of the deputies began publicly to measure Soviet realities against moral standards – none of them with greater authority than Andrei Sakharov, whose death in December 1989 was a serious blow to the nascent democratic forces in the USSR.

In this environment, maintaining the monopoly of power guaranteed by Article Six of the Soviet Constitution had become an impossible task. Yet the Party seemed determined to do just that. Both the Supreme Soviet and the Congress voted, by narrow margins, against proposals to abolish Article Six. Gorbachev himself shouted down Sakharov in a heated exchange over this matter in December, shortly before Sakharov's death. It was a futile attempt. The first genuine parliamentary debates seen in the Soviet Union had profoundly altered the thinking of the entire Soviet population, probably irreversibly so. Party authority collapsed, not only in the Caucasus and other border republics, but on a local level which affected even major cities such as Leningrad and Kiev. It was often a trivial incident which triggered the reaction. In the Ukrainian town of Chernigov, for example, a drunken driver caused an accident, which wrecked his car. The uproar that resulted when bystanders realized that it was a Party car full of the kind of food and drink that they could only dream of, spread rapidly through the entire population and brought down the local communist leadership within 24 hours. Then the rapid collapse of the communist regimes in Eastern Europe raised the question, ever more urgently and impatiently, of why freedom and democracy should be possible in Prague, or even East Berlin, but not in Moscow. The social and political crisis in the country began to overtake the political reforms on which an openly divided leadership could compromise. The Soviet Union was fast moving in the direction of a true revolution, this time not from the top but from a popular base.

Gorbachev's Gamble

General Secretary Gorbachev tried first to cope with this crisis in the traditional fashion. He seemed to realize that further change was necessary, as evidenced by his frank television address on 9 September, but he also knew the strength of conservative forces in the top leadership and, above all, in the lower ranks of the Party and the apparatus. He appears to have concluded that these forces had to be weakened before anything else could be done.

He had made his first effort in April 1989, when he forced a third of the Central Committee to 'offer' their resignations, resignations which were immediately, if not necessarily gracefully, accepted. To defuse the explosive situation in the country at large, and thus to reduce his own political vulnerability, Gorbachev tried to step up the supply of consumer goods. Priority was given to the consumer goods industry and output actually increased in 1989 by 5.2% (but the plan called for 6.7%, and in 1988 an increase of 5.4% had been attained). The conversion of military plants to civilian purposes was pushed; a total of 176 plants are claimed to have been involved by early 1990. Yet these conversions – which require enormous investment – brought about their own massive problems. The production of consumer goods at these converted plants turned out to cost two to ten times as much as that of civilian factories. The printing of paper money soared; it increased from 11.8bn roubles in 1988 to some 18bn roubles in 1989. In April 1989 the USSR announced that it would import some $5-bn worth of consumer goods (soap, pharmaceuticals, tights, razor blades) and in the wake of the coal-miners' strikes, another 10bn roubles were reserved for such imports. Joint ventures with the West were pushed and the relevant legislative restrictions were relaxed. By the end of 1989 there were 1,274 such joint ventures, although most of them were in the service sector and mostly in Moscow. At the same time, legislation governing the desperately needed co-operatives was tightened, not to improve their lot but because they, and their profits, had increasingly become the focus of bitter criticism by large sections of the population. And there were also clear signs that some conservatives had little interest in any improvement in the situation that would lead to a strengthening of Gorbachev's position. Accusations of quiet sabotage, designed to wreck *perestroika*, became more frequent.

Further change was clearly needed. It came at the plenary meeting of the Central Committee on 19–20 September. Some of the conservative members of the Politburo lost their jobs, most notably the long-serving Ukrainian Party boss Shcherbitsky (whose successor in Kiev, Ivashko, was elevated to the Politburo on 9 December), former KGB chief Chebrikov, and the former head of Gosplan, Talyzin. Loyal but incompetent Politburo members were also sacked, such as Gorbachev's one-time ally Nikonov. The new appointments to the Politburo clearly strengthened Gorbachev's hand. They included as full members the new head of the KGB, Kryuchkov, and the new head of Gosplan, Maslyukov; the head of the Party Control Commission, Pugo, and the Chairman of the new Soviet of the Union, Academician Primakov, were appointed candidate members. The Central Committee Secretariat was bolstered by the appointment of four new secretaries, all judged capable people from the provinces who had apparently come to Gorbachev's attention.

In spite of, or perhaps because of, these changes conservative resistance clearly stiffened in the last quarter of 1989. It was no longer

Ligachev, the figure-head of the conservative camp, who led the attack, but a new generation of opponents of *perestroika*, represented by figures such as the new Leningrad Party boss Gidaspov and the commander of the Kiev Military District, Gromov.

Gorbachev's dilemma, that he could continuously strengthen his position at the top while being unable to make anything move elsewhere, was apparent. Unable to force the Party on a reform course no matter how many heads he replaced, and confronted by a rapidly deteriorating political and economic situation, Gorbachev tried to muddle through. He pleaded the necessity for *perestroika* and made compromises on both the left and the right. The only result was that both the conservative and liberal wing (now organized as a formal opposition faction within the CPSU, the Democratic Platform) of the top leadership gained influence, while Gorbachev's personal following eroded. By the end of 1989 Gorbachev had essentially only three options left: he could continue to replace personnel and try to muddle through with present policies (probably ensuring his eventual downfall); he could turn conservative (and assure the failure of reform); or he could make the demands of the liberal wing his own (and thus try to regain both credibility and freedom of manoeuvre at the price of a show-down with the conservatives). He might consider becoming more authoritarian on the basis of democratic legitimacy, i.e. by direct election of a Soviet president with emergency powers, to enforce a radical programme. He would clearly have preferred to make his choice only after the Party Congress, scheduled to meet in the summer of 1990, from which he could expect a serious weakening of the conservative faction in the Central Committee. But to wait was no longer possible.

In mid-January 1990, Gorbachev seemed to have accepted this sober reality and decided to risk the gamble. A Central Committee plenary session, due to prepare the platform for the forthcoming Party Congress and to address, once more, the nationalities problem, was chosen for the scene of battle. It was postponed for one week in somewhat murky circumstances; when it did meet, on 5 February, it was as an enlarged plenary.

The plenary was clearly seen by all sides as a decisive meeting. In the days before it met the conservatives made open allusions to the disastrous situation which Gorbachev's policies had caused – his position on the German question was also openly challenged for the first time. But Gorbachev once again proved himself the superior tactician. Day after day *Pravda* carried articles highlighting the importance of the plenum, and leaking many of its details. More importantly, for the first time in the Soviet Union, *Interfax*, a news agency of Radio Moscow, revealed on the eve of the meeting the content of the proposals Gorbachev was to make. Rumours were floated that Gorbachev might resign as General Secretary if he could not get his way; his vehement denial of these rumours only gave them more currency. At just the right moment there were revelations about corruption cases in the old Party establishment, a not too subtle warning by Gorbachev's supporters in the KGB to the conservatives. Finally, on the day preceding the plenary, an officially tolerated mass rally of some 200,000 to 500,000 people (the number depended on the source) was addressed, and dominated, by Boris Yeltsin, thus indicating what the alternative to Gorbachev might be. It was the biggest demonstration in the Soviet Union since the days of the October Revolution.

These tactics boxed the conservatives in. Gorbachev could not tolerate any dilution of his platform without losing credibility. Yet the conservatives would have found it difficult to accept the blame for failure, once everyone could compare the initial outline of the Party platform and the final result. Perhaps most importantly, the conservatives could offer no genuine alternative. Far from resolving the country's problems, Gorbachev's removal – or his resignation – would exacerbate them. The conservatives had lost the battle before it was even begun.

The plenary was nevertheless a heated affair. The debates were bitter, and the meeting had to be extended by a day, but the result was preordained. While there were no personnel changes, probably because Gorbachev had wisely omitted them from his agenda at this time, there was dramatic political change. The platform which was finally adopted with only one negative vote (from Yeltsin for whom it did not go far enough) stipulated that:

- the Central Committee would propose to the Party Congress the amendment of Article 6 of the Constitution, thus giving up its monopoly of power and permitting the formation of other formal political parties;
- the Politburo of the CPSU should be abolished and be replaced by a Party Presidium, headed by a Party chairman and two deputies, with 27 members representing the 15 republics and other sectors of society;
- the new office of a (possibly popularly elected) President of the USSR, with significant but vaguely expressed extended powers should be created;
- a radical economic reform would be necessary, including drastic changes in agriculture and a mixture of private and state ownership in the means of production.

The language of the platform, which was published on 13 February 1990, remained ambiguous in many areas, but it was nevertheless a revolutionary document. One part of the platform was quickly put in place by a hastily called session of the Congress of People's Deputies which met from 12 to 15 March. After three days of vigorous debate that resulted in a few modifying changes to the original proposal, it elected Mikhail Gorbachev to a five-year term as the new President of the USSR, with vastly extended, if still poorly defined, powers. Thus, even before the Communist Party meets on 2 June to pass the other parts of the platform which will end the exclusive rule of the CPSU, the Soviet Union has taken a decisive step into a new, and very different, future. What this future will look like, however, remains a question as open as it is important.

THE UNITED STATES: FACING A BRAVE NEW WORLD

When he moved into the Oval Office in January 1989, George Bush insisted that he did not plan to preside over major changes in US foreign policy. However, the cataclysmic events that time and time again shook the world in succeeding months dictated otherwise. The disintegration of the Warsaw Pact and Germany's rush towards unification forced Western leaders to reassess NATO's *raison d'être* and the West's role in both German affairs and the reconstruction of Eastern Europe; American conventional and nuclear forces in Europe were sure to be reduced sharply as a result. The Sino-Soviet *rapprochement*, the Chinese government's vicious crackdown on student demonstrators in Tiananmen Square, and the CPSU's renunciation of its guaranteed monopoly on power put Sino-American and Soviet–American relations on a new footing. At the same time, American concerns over the trade deficit with Japan and Japanese investment in the US contributed to a deterioration in US–Japanese relations. The fall from power of Manuel Noriega and Daniel Ortega in Panama and Nicaragua, respectively, presented US–Latin American policy with both new opportunities and new challenges.

Throughout these tumultuous months, President Bush guided American foreign policy with a steady, if not always deft, hand. Many appreciated Bush's pragmatic approach to unfolding events, given that the West faced an inchoate situation. Others wondered if Bush had the political vision to formulate a grand strategy for the US as it faced the brave new world of the 1990s.

Settling In

The Bush Administration got off to a slow start. Although Bush indicated soon after the November 1988 election that he intended to nominate James Baker as Secretary of State and Brent Scowcroft as National Security Adviser, other key slots took much longer to fill. The belated selection and ultimate Senate rejection of former senator John Tower as Secretary of Defense was the most obvious case in point; Representative Dick Cheney was approved for the top job at the Pentagon only on 17 March. The Administration was also slow to nominate candidates for many sub-cabinet positions, which meant that policy in several areas drifted for months.

This problem was compounded by the fact that the President's first substantive initiative – a comprehensive review of East–West relations, US defence programmes, and arms-control negotiating positions – took until May to complete. Critics complained that the Administration's preoccupation with its internal review prevented it from pushing ahead

with nuclear and conventional arms-control negotiations or responding
in a timely way to the dramatic changes that were beginning to sweep
across Eastern Europe. The President retorted hotly on 9 April that he
and his advisers would 'react when we feel like reacting'. No significant
changes resulted from Bush's strategic review, however, and his
approach to foreign affairs remained cautious. Although Bush said in
May that he hoped to move beyond a policy of containment, 'integrating the Soviet Union into the community of nations', he warned that
'we won't be stampeded into something that might prove to be no good
for the alliance, and no good for the US'. He consequently opposed unilateral reductions in NATO forces and voiced scepticism over deep,
bilateral cuts in conventional forces. He also stressed the importance of
maintaining robust nuclear capabilities at both theatre and strategic
levels.

Superpower Relations
Relations with the Soviet Union developed slowly in 1989. As the Bush
Administration settled in and pursued its policy review, it kept Soviet–
American arms-control negotiations on hold. Public statements by
Secretary of Defense Cheney, Deputy National Security Adviser Robert
Gates, and Vice-President Quayle in April and May indicated that some
influential advisers in the Administration harboured serious doubts
about the implications of President Gorbachev's long-term goals for the
West and what his chances for survival were. They argued that the best
thing the US could do at this stage was to wait and see how events in the
Soviet Union developed. As the year progressed, however, the
Administration's attitudes towards the Soviet leader seemed to warm
considerably. The START negotiations were resumed in June, and the
Soviet Union subsequently dropped its insistence on linking a treaty on
offensive forces to an understanding on defensive systems; agreed to
handle sea-launched cruise missiles in a separate agreement; and
announced that they would destroy their controversial radar system at
Krasnoyarsk, which the Soviet leadership itself admitted was a violation of the Anti-Ballistic Missile Treaty. This led Secretary of State
Baker to conclude that the two sides had moved 'from confrontation to
dialogue and now to co-operation'. By the end of the year, Administration spokesmen were unequivocal in their support for both
perestroika and President Gorbachev.
    The summit in Malta between Bush and Gorbachev on 2 and 3
December was consequently a roaring success, at a climatic and rhetorical, if not always at a substantive level. The two leaders held an unprecedented joint press conference at the conclusion of their meeting, and
Soviet spokesmen later pronounced that the Cold War had come to an
end. However, a Soviet proposal for a 35-nation CSCE summit to discuss European security did not receive a favourable US response at the
time, although President Bush stated that Soviet policy demanded new
thinking from the US and the West. The co-operative tone of the two

leaders was reflected in some tangible agreements as well. The two sides pledged to attempt to conclude a START treaty in time for signing at the next summit, which was scheduled for 30 May 1990 in Washington. They also stated that they hoped to complete a CFE agreement in 1990. Bush agreed to support a Soviet request for observer status in the General Agreement on Tariffs and Trade meetings. In addition, he promised to grant most-favoured-nation status and export-import bank credits to the USSR, once a satisfactory emigration bill passed the Supreme Soviet, a somewhat paradoxical situation in light of the American decision to restrict Jewish emigration to the US. Soviet–American relations further improved after the CPSU relinquished its guaranteed monopoly on power in February 1990.

European Relations

While the Bush Administration was in the midst of its strategic review, NATO and Warsaw Pact negotiators opened the first round of the Conventional Forces in Europe (CFE) negotiations on 6 March. Rapid progress in the talks indicated that it might be possible to complete a conventional arms-control treaty in short order. However, CFE was soon overshadowed, for a brief but worrying period, by the eruption of a long-simmering Alliance disagreement over short-range nuclear forces (SNF).

Although the modernization of nuclear forces had always been a contentious issue for the Atlantic Alliance, it became especially problematic after the INF Treaty was signed in December 1987. Since Soviet and American ground-based missiles with ranges of 500 to 5,500 kilometres were to be eliminated when the INF Treaty was implemented, the short-range *Lance* stood out as NATO's only remaining ground-based nuclear missile in an arsenal which had declined from 7,000 warheads in 1979 to some 4,600 in 1988, as a result of unilateral NATO reductions. The strong differences of opinion within the Alliance over how to deal with the problem threatened to boil over as NATO's 40th anniversary summit approached in late May.

At this point, Bush stepped in with his most impressive foreign-policy showing of the year. In one clean action, he seized the initiative on the conventional arms-control front and defused NATO's incipient SNF crisis. Bush's proposals evoked a warm reception from Western European leaders, and the NATO summit was an unexpected triumph for both the President and the Alliance as a whole. The allies agreed that an 'appropriate mix of adequate and effective nuclear and conventional forces' would be maintained for the foreseeable future. NATO leaders also agreed that a CFE agreement would have to be signed and at least partially implemented before SNF negotiations could begin. The SNF negotiations themselves would be aimed at 'partial' reductions in American and Soviet short-range nuclear missiles, down to equal and verifiable levels. As a short-term measure, this formula satisfied not only the West Germans, who had been advocating significant reductions in

SNF deployments, but also US and UK leaders, who wished to ensure that short-range forces would not be eliminated from NATO's arsenal.

At the same time, developments in Poland and Hungary placed additional demands on the Bush Administration. Talks between Solidarity and the Polish government led to legalization of the independent union as well as fundamental constitutional reforms in April. Consequently Bush announced that an economic assistance package would be forthcoming. Events continued to unfold rapidly in Poland, as Solidarity candidates swamped their communist opponents in the June elections, the first partially free elections in Eastern Europe in over 40 years. Meanwhile, the Hungarian government began dismantling the barbed-wire fences between Hungary and Austria in early May; the Iron Curtain was beginning to come down. Round-table discussions between the Hungarian government and opposition leaders on democratic reforms began in June.

President Bush travelled to Poland and Hungary on 9–12 July to endorse these developments and to outline his plans for economic assistance to the East in more detail. In his speech to the Polish parliament (*Sejm*) in Warsaw, Bush announced that he intended to: provide $100m in direct economic aid; encourage the other G-7 countries to formulate economic assistance plans of their own; support a $325-m package of credits from the IMF; reschedule Poland's debts; and provide $15m for pollution control. The President then visited Hungary where he presented similar, but even more modest, assistance packages. Later, in Brussels, he suggested that the European Community should take the lead in providing aid for Eastern Europe. Although Bush's visit had symbolic value, most Europeans and Americans were unimpressed by the meagre amounts of money he was prepared to provide Poland and Hungary at this historic juncture. Lech Walesa, for example, had asked for $10bn in Western aid, and was unable to conceal his frustration with Bush's plan. Bush supplemented his package with $100m in emergency food aid for Poland in September. Congress went a step further in November when it approved $938m in aid for Poland and Hungary, but this package was to be disbursed over a three-year period. While conscious of the constraints imposed by the twin deficits and Bush's self-inflicted limitation on new taxes, critics were left wondering how the US could spend almost $80bn (in 1990 dollars) on Marshall Plan aid and hundreds of billions of dollars defending Western Europe from the Warsaw Pact, and only a pittance on countries that were trying to shake off the political and economic strait-jackets that had made the Soviet bloc so terrifying in the first place.

There were similar but even more dramatic changes in East Germany, and by the end of the year the collapse of the East German government placed the question of German unification high on the NATO policy agenda. In commenting on the rapidly changing situation, President Bush was careful to reassure the Soviet Union that the US would not take advantage of the tumult in Eastern Europe. But he stressed too that the German people had the right to political self-determination, within the framework of existing international borders. After Chancellor Kohl of West Germany unveiled a ten-point unification plan on 28 November without informing any of his NATO allies (and without explicitly addressing the issue of a unified Germany's borders), the US, the UK, France and the Soviet Union convened the first meeting of the Allied Control Council in Berlin since 1971. This served to remind the Germans that the interests and legal rights of the Allied Powers had to be kept in mind as Germans deliberated over their future.

Secretary of State Baker sketched out the Administration's vision of the new European order, 'a Europe whole and free', in a speech to the Berlin Press Club on 12 December. Baker argued that the question of German unification had to be answered by the German people, but he expressed hope that, if unification did come about, it would do so gradually and peacefully. He noted that the legal rights of the four occupying powers had to be respected as the unification process unfolded. Baker maintained, moreover, that a new German state would have to be a member of both NATO and an increasingly integrated EC. Expanding on this theme, he argued that transatlantic relations should be strengthened to ensure that the US would continue to be linked to an ever-more unified Europe. This 'new Atlanticism', as he put it, might be based on new institutional arrangements, possibly including a new treaty between the US and the EC. Finally, Baker called for new ties between East and West, to be built on the institutional foundations provided by NATO, the CSCE and the EC. Baker's speech incorporated a comprehensive framework for American policy towards Europe, and it was well received by governments and commentators on both sides of the Atlantic. The idea of formalizing US–EC ties through a series of biannual summits was soon receiving high-level attention.

These important developments, however, were overshadowed by the maelstrom of European events. The tidal wave of reform in Eastern Europe swamped the communist government in Czechoslovakia in late November. In December, during the violent overthrow of the Ceauşescu regime in Romania, Baker maintained that the US would not object if the Soviet Union intervened militarily in support of Romanian opposition forces. This put the Secretary of State at the cutting edge of 'new thinking', and certainly far ahead of most other NATO powers.

By the end of the year, the governments of all six of the Soviet Union's Eastern European allies had fallen. As 1990 began, the new governments in Hungary and Czechoslovakia asked the Soviet Union to withdraw its military forces from their countries, and the results of the 18 March East German elections made it clear that the GDR would seek early unification with the FRG. The Warsaw Pact was in a shambles; the President and many others in the US concluded that the Cold War was over and that it had ended in a victory for the West.

However, the endgame over German unification had yet to be played. The Bush Administration worked closely with the FRG in February to develop a framework for negotiations on German unification ('two plus four' talks, with the outcome to be blessed by the 35 CSCE states), but the price that would have to be paid to assuage the legitimate security concerns of all involved had yet to be determined. The policy agenda for 1990, therefore, would be dominated by the many issues that had to be resolved – Germany's borders, alliance relationships, stationed troops and nuclear weapons – over the course of deliberations on German unification.

Relations with China and Japan

Sino-American relations began on a positive note. President Bush had a long-standing interest in China, dating from his days as chief of the US mission in Beijing in the early 1970s, and he visited the PRC after attending the funeral of Emperor Hirohito in February. Relations between Beijing and Washington soon soured, however. The mid-May Sino-Soviet summit ended 30 years of enmity between the major communist powers and led some commentators to suggest that Sino-American ties would suffer as a result. Bush argued that Sino-American links were not threatened by the Sino-Soviet *rapprochement*, but this did not immunize Sino-American relations against the fall-out from subsequent events. The Chinese government's brutal repression of the peaceful protest movement in Tiananmen Square on 3–4 June led the US, along with most Western governments, to condemn the PRC for its actions. To satisfy the American public's demand for a firm response, Bush banned military sales to China, gave shelter to dissident astrophysicist Fang Lizhi and his wife in the US Embassy in Beijing, extended the visas of all Chinese studying in the United States, and announced the cancellation of all high-level contacts with the PRC. Domestic critics complained that the Administration had not gone far enough.

Although student demonstrators continued to be arrested and prosecuted in China throughout the summer and autumn, Bush sent National Security Adviser, Brent Scowcroft, and Deputy Secretary of State, Lawrence Eagleburger, to Beijing in mid-December. This trip – which was kept secret until Scowcroft and Eagleburger were in China – met with a storm of criticism in Washington. While defending the mission, Secretary of State Baker revealed that Scowcroft had also visited Beijing in July, only a month after the massacre. Although Bush claimed that these visits were necessary to keep open the lines of communication with the government of a great power, domestic critics pointed out that the President had contravened his own embargo on high-level contacts with the Chinese regime, which to some made him look at best inconsistent and at worst duplicitous. Particularly striking was the fact that this was a case where a brutal communist government had slaughtered peaceful demonstrators whose demands were similar to those of protesters in Eastern Europe. Bush nonetheless went on to resume export-import financing for China, and vetoed a bill that would have guaranteed residency rights for Chinese students in the United States, although he took some steps to safeguard these students' rights through administrative actions. As a result, the Administration's China policy was attacked by both liberals and conservatives.

American relations with Japan took a turn for the worse in 1989, as economic relations between the two powers remained strained and American attention focused increasingly on economic issues as the military threat posed by the Soviet Union subsided. The US trade deficit with Japan lingered in the region of $50bn per year, even though Japanese imports of American goods doubled in the late 1980s. As far as the US was concerned, this was an area in which more had to be done. The two sides consequently engaged in a series of talks designed to lower Japanese structural barriers to foreign imports even further. Little was accomplished during these sessions in early 1990, however, which aggravated protectionist sentiments in the US Congress. Relations between the two powers were also strained by American concerns that Japanese investors were buying up prize assets in the US at an alarming rate; the purchase of Columbia Pictures in California and a share of the Rockefeller Center in New York stood out in this regard.

As the Cold War seemingly came to an end, public opinion polls indicated that most Americans saw Japan's economic challenge as a greater long-term threat to the US than the Soviet Union's military might. Opinion polls also showed that the percentage of Americans with positive attitudes towards Japan was dropping sharply (from 87% in 1985 to 67% in early 1990), while the number of Americans with negative views towards Japan was correspondingly rising (from 8% in 1985 to 25% in 1990). Public attitudes, occasionally galvanized by bipartisan Japan-bashing in Washington, raised the ominous prospect of a trade war between the two powers, a prospect that President Bush and Japanese Prime Minister Kaifu endeavoured to head off during their March 1990 summit in California. However, the fact that the US had not completed an inter-agency review of US–Japanese relations at the time of the summit did not bode well for the Administration's ability to steer US policy through these troubled waters.

Central American Conundrums

Although the Administration's policy review precluded new initiatives in many areas, Secretary of State Baker moved swiftly in March and April to address one of the Administration's thorniest problems – its interest in supporting the Nicaraguan *Contras* in the face of stiff Congressional opposition to further military assistance for the US-backed rebels. Baker worked out a plan with Congressional leaders that would provide $4.5m a month in non-military aid to the *Contras* until freely-contested elections, scheduled for February 1990, were held in Nicaragua. The White House and Congress agreed that no further military assistance to the rebels would be forthcoming and that the US would accept the outcome of the Nicaraguan elections, which were to be the subject of close international scrutiny. Although Nicaraguan President Ortega suspended the 19-month cease-fire and attacked *Contra* forces on 1 November, Washington was unwilling to respond with anything beyond condemnatory rhetoric. As far as the US was concerned, the fate of the *Sandinista* regime and the *Contras* was in the hands of the Nicaraguan electorate. To virtually everyone's surprise, the *Sandinistas* were soundly defeated in the February elections by a rag-tag movement united mainly in its opposition to the government. This left the Bush Administration basking in the glow of a victory it had not expected, and reflecting on the problem of rebuilding Nicaragua's shattered economy, an economy ruined not only by *Sandinista* ideological excesses, but also by American economic sanctions and a civil war underwritten by the US. The cost of reconstruction would be high, and the new Nicaraguan government lost no time in seeking US financial assistance.

One sore spot in Soviet–American relations was El Salvador. Washington complained that the Soviet Union was supplying weapons to the leftist FMLN rebels in El Salvador through its allies in Cuba and Nicaragua. When the FMLN mounted a strong attack against the right-wing government of Alfredo Cristiani on 11 November, US criticism of Moscow intensified, especially after El Salvadorean government troops shot down an aircraft bound for rebel forces and loaded with SAM-7 anti-aircraft missiles. Although the level of violence in El Salvador occasionally reached horrific proportions, the US took no direct action except to deplore the loss of life brought about by the increasingly vicious civil war. The Bush Administration's attention was soon focused on other parts of the region.

The American campaign to topple Panamanian dictator Gen Manuel Noriega and bring him to trial in the US on drug-trafficking charges continued throughout 1989. However, economic sanctions and diplomatic pressure had little effect on Noriega, who felt no inclination to extradite himself to the US. He annulled the results of the May election, which the opposition apparently won by a three-to-one margin, and he tightened his grip on power during the rest of the summer and autumn. When rebel officers attempted a coup in October, President Bush was lambasted by critics at home for failing to provide prompt assistance to the mutineers.

Another opportunity to tackle Noriega soon presented itself, however. After numerous scuffles between US citizens and Panamanian troops, the shooting of an off-duty US officer on 16 December, and Noriega's public claim that a 'state of war' existed between Panama and the US, Bush acted swiftly. On 20 December, US-based forces and Southern Command forces stationed in Panama attacked troops loyal to Noriega in the largest American military action since the Vietnam War and hurriedly swore in a 'legitimate' Panamanian government under President Endara within the safe confines of a US base. Several

days of fighting followed, during which over 20 US soldiers and several
hundred Panamanians were killed. At the same time, Noriega escaped
capture and later took refuge in the Vatican Embassy in Panama City.
He remained there for 11 days before surrendering to US troops that
had surrounded and besieged the embassy with loudspeakers blaring
rock music. Upon his surrender, Noriega was flown to Florida where he
faced trial on several drugs charges.

Administration officials argued that the US was justified in trying to:
protect the lives of 35,000 US citizens living in Panama; protect the
Panama Canal under the terms of the Panama Canal Treaty; safeguard
democracy in Panama; and apprehend Noriega and bring him to trial.
Most Latin American and West European allies of the US were
unimpressed by the Administration's legal reasoning, but the US action
received little sustained criticism from abroad. Although some domestic critics wondered how the President, Vice-President Quayle and
Secretary of State Baker could go off on their scheduled Christmas
vacations while American soldiers were still fighting in Panama, most
Americans had few reservations about the operation and gave the President record approval ratings in the public opinion polls. In Panama
itself, the new government needed massive amounts of money to revive
the economy, which had been shattered by American economic sanctions imposed during the final months of the Noriega regime. With this
in mind, the White House proposed a $1-bn assistance package for
Panama in January 1990.

New Budgetary Realities

President Bush's initial plan to increase US defence spending by 1–2%
per year in the early 1990s was derailed by domestic fiscal constraints
and the collapse of the Warsaw Pact.

The Gramm–Rudman–Hollings Act obligated the Bush Administration and the Congress to reduce the federal budget deficit to $100bn
in FY 1990, which began in October 1989; reduce it to $64bn in FY
1991; cut it to $28bn in FY 1992; and eliminate it altogether in FY
1993. Since President Bush remained adamant about not raising taxes,
public spending had to be slashed. And since many programmes, such
as social security and veterans' pay, were untouchable, the defence
budget had to bear a disproportionate share of the cuts that were made.

In addition, three out of four Americans surveyed in a January 1990
poll expected the West's 'victory' in the Cold War to generate a big
'peace dividend'. Public pressure to reduce American overseas commitments consequently grew. This applied not only to Europe, but also to
the Far East, where Japan and South Korea were seen as increasingly
capable of contributing more to their own defence.

Some Congressmen contended that the FY 1990 defence budget,
which was based on a deal struck between the White House and Congress in the spring of 1989, was the last 'Cold War budget'. The $305-
bn budget provided funding for both the MX and *Midgetman* ICBM;

two out of the three B-2 bombers the Administration had asked for; another *Trident* submarine and $1.5-bn worth of missiles for the *Trident* programme; and $3.8-bn for SDI. Congress also reinstated funding for the Marine Corps' V-22 transport aircraft and the F-14D, both of which the Administration had tried to cancel. Even so, American defence spending dropped by about 2% in FY 1990 (after correcting for inflation), the fifth year in a row in which it had declined. As a result, US defence budget outlays had already shrunk by approximately 15% in real terms over the course of the late 1980s.

Even deeper cuts in US defence spending seemed to be in the offing for the early 1990s. By January 1990, many in Congress were pushing for annual cuts (after inflation) of around 5%. Richard Darman, the Director of the Office of Management and Budget wanted to see 4% cuts over each of the next several years. A few analysts maintained that defence spending could be halved by the end of the decade without damaging national security interests.

The Bush Administration's FY 1991 budget, which was put forward at the end of January, called for $295bn in defence spending, a cut of only 2.6% in real terms – but it nonetheless signalled a psychological turning-point insofar as it was the first negative growth defence budget an American administration had put forward since the Carter Administration in the 1970s. In addition, Bush proposed real cuts of only 2% per year until FY 1995, far short of what Congress was looking for. To the consternation of many in Congress, Bush's budget did not seem to reflect the fact that the world scene had changed in fundamental ways over the course of 1989. Bush's plans to increase spending on SDI and the B-2 bomber programme by approximately $1bn each were particularly notable in this regard. Nevertheless, even Bush's streamlined budget would force the Pentagon to overhaul its force structure and procurement plans; both had been based on the assumption that defence spending would increase in the early 1990s.

In order to reach its FY 1991 target, the Pentagon proposed the closure of 35 military bases in the US (29 in Congressional districts controlled by Democrats) and 12 overseas bases. Significantly, American cutbacks abroad were not confined to Europe. Indeed, Defense Secretary Cheney planned to withdraw approximately 10% of the US troops stationed in Japan and South Korea over a three-year period.

On the domestic front, the M-1 tank production run was curtailed. Two US-based Army divisions were to be deactivated, starting in 1992. The Air Force planned to halt *Minuteman* II modernization, retire some B-52s, and stretch F-16 procurement. It also planned to cut into its operating and support accounts. The Navy, which faced less severe cuts than the other services, planned to deactivate eight nuclear attack submarines, two nuclear cruisers and two of its four World War II battleships, only recently reactivated as part of the Reagan build-up. Once again, the Marine Corps' V-22 transport aircraft was cancelled. In addition, Cheney was reviewing four particularly expensive Air Force and Navy programmes – the B-2 bomber, the C-17 transport plane, the Advanced Tactical Fighter, and the A-12 Advanced Tactical Aircraft – to determine whether legitimate military requirements still existed for these programmes.

As a result, after spending most of 1989 exhorting its NATO allies to refrain from unilateral force reductions while the CFE negotiations were in progress, the Bush Administration spent the last few months of 1989 and the first few months of 1990 planning deep cuts in many elements of the US force structure.

Critics were concerned that the Pentagon's planning process was driven more by looming budgetary constraints than changing military requirements. Although strategic reassessments were being made by the Pentagon, the pace was slow and they were not being integrated into the planning process in a timely manner. The January 1990 *Defense Policy Guidance*, the long-range planning document issued by the civilian leadership in the Department of Defense, recommended few fundamental changes in US military strategy. The *Guidance* still assumed, for example, that it would be 'imprudent' to count on receiving more than 14 days' warning of a Soviet attack in Europe, even though the US National Intelligence Estimate stated in late 1989 that, due to changing circumstances in Eastern Europe and the Soviet Union, NATO would know of such an attack 33 to 44 days before it began. The *Guidance* also maintained that the superpowers would continue to have an intense rivalry in the Third World because the Soviet Union will continue to seek overseas bases and 'subservient regimes'. American military strategy, therefore, appeared slow to adapt to the strategic realities of the 1990s; Congress was critical of what it saw as the Pentagon's intellectual inertia.

The Pentagon's defence review in late 1989 and early 1990 consequently became a 'Brazilian rain-forest drill', a slash-and-burn exercise. As Congressman Les Aspin observed, 'Any resemblance to rational debate on defense priorities is purely accidental'. Many believed that, as a result of the changes that were taking place around the world, the US should reallocate defence resources from heavy to light forces, from forward deployment to rapid reinforcement, from active to reserve units, and from East–West to other contingencies.

In short, President Bush's first year in office was blessed by an extraordinary amount of luck – he happened to be on watch when the Iron Curtain disintegrated – and characterized by a refreshing degree of competence. Bush's advisers generally earned high marks for their professionalism, and Bush himself was deeply involved in both the formulation and execution of US foreign policy. Nevertheless, there were no grounds for complacency as the new decade began. Economic problems loomed both at home and abroad, and major political challenges were still to come in Europe and the Soviet Union. Given the pace of events around the world and the range of issues still to be addressed, it will be difficult for an Administration still trying to come to terms with 'the vision thing' to chart a steady course for American foreign policy.

Europe

Beethoven's magnificent setting of Schiller's 'Ode to Joy' would have been a fitting unofficial anthem for Europe as the 1980s ended with the collapse of communist control in most of the states of Eastern Europe. Western Europe observed the *annus mirabilis* with surprise and excitement, and with a welcome lack of triumphalism. But, as it saw the states concerned one after the other cast off the shackles of state socialism and emerge, blinking like the prisoners in *Fidelio*, to grope towards democracy, pluralism and market economies, it could not but be conscious of the possible fragility of the process. Even as new opportunities for trade and influence opened, the West had to recognize that Eastern Europe would have a desperate need for aid of all kinds.

One result of the changes of government in the region was to reduce the Warsaw Pact to a hollow shell. The numbers of Soviet forces stationed outside Soviet borders were set to reduce rapidly and significantly, in part through unilateral action, in part at host nation request, and in part through negotiated arms control. Welcome as this process was, it also deeply affected the rationale for much of NATO's force structure and called into question the basis for NATO's strategy, if not for the Alliance itself. The real prospect of an end to the division of Europe confronted everyone once more with the German question, which had been dormant since 1945. As a result, an immediate problem re-emerged: how to provide adequate assurance and insurance to other European states, including the USSR, that a united Germany would never again pose economic, political or, even less, military threats, while at the same time not 'singularizing' Germany with constraints which current or future generations would resent as punitive. Thus, both Western and Eastern Europe entered the 1990s in a mood of elation tempered with trepidation; the history of this region warned that without careful management dangers could lie ahead.

THE TRANSFORMATION OF EASTERN EUROPE

The changes that took place in Eastern Europe in 1989 were breathtaking. The rapidity with which the communist systems that had been imposed on the region after 1945 capitulated to pressure for change illustrated their inability to gain any legitimacy in the eyes of their subject populations. While the process of change in 1989 was comparatively orderly and gradual in Poland and Hungary, in the other Warsaw Pact states the communist-run governments fell to pressures from their publics in a matter of weeks. By the beginning of 1990, all the states in the region were moving towards some form of free elections, and it was clear that their communist parties would suffer further and decisive setbacks.

The changes were in part wrought by, and in part induced the appearance of new forces on the political stage. For the first time in 40 years, there is now a real prospect of substantial political pluralism in most Eastern European states. In some, opposition groups developed almost spontaneously out of disillusionment with the existing system; in others, tiny groups which had protested against government controls formed a nucleus around which other dissent could expand. The exception is Solidarity in Poland; it had endured as a *de facto* opposition organization for the last ten years. In several instances, religious institutions played an important role over the last decade by nurturing opposition views. The efforts of the Catholic Church in Poland and the Lutheran Church in the GDR to foster political change were fundamental factors in the ensuing developments in 1989.

Another critical factor enabling the East European revolutions to proceed as they did was the startling change in the Soviet Union's attitude towards the region. While Moscow remained cautious in its acceptance of the steps Poland and Hungary had taken early in 1989 towards more pluralistic systems, by late summer it appeared to have deliberately withdrawn its support from non-reforming governments in the Eastern bloc, opening the floodgates to the upheavals in the GDR, Czechoslovakia, Bulgaria and eventually Romania. The Warsaw Pact's official denunciation of the Brezhnev Doctrine, by which Moscow had justified the invasion of Czechoslovakia in 1968, formalized the USSR's acquiescence in the removal of communist control in Eastern Europe.

Hungary

The appointment of Karoly Grosz as General Secretary of the Hungarian Socialist Worker's Party (HSWP) on 22 May 1988 signalled the beginning of serious political and economic changes in Hungary. From that point the Party and government took dramatic steps to change the structure of the Hungarian state: in January 1989 the basis for a multi-party system was legalized by the Hungarian parliament and at a Party conference in February, the HSWP gave up its constitutional right to play the 'leading role' in Hungarian politics. Opposition groups began to use the new laws almost immediately to establish themselves, and the HSWP quickly found itself on the defensive.

In an even more drastic step, reformist Politburo member Imre Pozsgay announced that a special commission of the Central Committee, set up to re-evaluate the state's history, had concluded that the 1956 revolution was a 'popular uprising against an oligarchic rule that had debased the nation'. Subsequently, Imre Nagy (prime minister at the time of the 1956 Soviet invasion and executed in its wake), was rehabilitated and reburied, the 1968 Soviet-led invasion of Czechoslovakia was re-evaluated, Kadar's leadership criticized, and the state renamed, in non-ideological terms, the 'Republic of Hungary'.

Pozsgay's comments brought to light disagreements within the Party leadership over the direction of reforms. While even conservatives accepted the desperate need for reform in light of the deteriorating economic conditions, they nonetheless favoured the continuation of a socialist system led by the HSWP. The reformers prevailed, and in June began discussions with the Opposition Round Table (a loose coalition of opposition parties), and with representatives of social organizations, on questions concerning the future structure of the government and the creation of a new constitution. These talks ended in September 1989 with a new constitution and a decision of hold presidential and parliamentary elections the following spring.

Concurrent with its efforts to reshape the government, the HSWP restructured itself in an attempt to maintain a role in running the country. The existing party was dissolved in October, and a 'renewed' Hungarian Socialist Party (HSP) established. Some of the more conservative elements of the old party refused to join it; at least one group formed a new 'communist' party which they renamed the HSWP, in order to uphold Marxist-Leninist values.

Meanwhile, the new opposition movements were organizing themselves and gaining strength. By early 1990, some 27 opposition parties had been formed, the most substantial being the Hungarian Democratic Forum (HDF) and the Alliance of Free Democrats. Several parties had also formed using the names of pre-war parties, such as the Smallholder's Party, and claiming to carry on their traditions. Yet no single party succeeded in attracting a broad membership; the majority of the Hungarian population appeared to have rejected formal party affiliation. The potential strength of the opposition parties was confirmed in October when they compelled the government to hold a referendum on the timing of presidential and parliamentary elections, arguing that the president should be chosen by parliament after the spring elections, rather than directly by the people. This would clearly favour the opposition over the HSP, whose candidate, Imre Poszgay, was then thought likely to win in a direct vote. The opposition party's position prevailed in the referendum – a good omen for the likelihood of fair elections, and a bad one for the Communist Party's standing. Yet this decision was reversed by parliament on 1 March 1990, in favour of a direct presidential vote. On the eve of the March elections, a resurgence of strife in Transylvania between ethnic Hungarians and Romanians affected the political climate, strengthening the position of the conservative HDF.

Along with the domestic political reforms enacted during 1988–9, the leadership quietly began changing important aspects of Hungary's foreign policy. It agreed on a special trade relationship with the EC in July 1988, and was the first Warsaw Pact state to apply for membership of the Council of Europe. The HSWP also participated in talks on regional co-operation in November 1989 with representatives from Italy, Yugoslavia and Austria.

The reorganization of the Hungarian armed forces, begun in 1987, continued in 1989 and was accompanied by independent security initiatives. In spring the fences Hungary had maintained on its frontier with Austria were dismantled, and on 9 September, in a dramatic affirmation of its support for human rights, that border was opened to East German citizens wishing to go to the West. The government also proposed a new confidence-strengthening zone on its frontiers with Austria and Yugoslavia, in which frontier guards would be the only military forces allowed. By the end of the year, defence budget cuts of 25% had been announced, and in January 1990, the government (still run by the HSP) followed Czechoslovakia's lead and asked the USSR to withdraw its forces from Hungary, which it agreed to do by June 1991.

As it enters the 1990s, Hungary thus appears likely to be governed by an uncertain coalition of new centrist and right-wing parties whose policies generally are unclear and whose capabilities are unproven. It remains to be seen whether the political landscape will lend itself to the establishment of a stable government after the elections of 25 March–2 April, and whether the state's plans for gradual change from a command to a market economy can work. In its favour are the early start the country made on reform and the depth of Western support and goodwill; against it are the extent of its economic troubles, and the worrisome growth of nationalism.

Poland

The reawakening of Solidarity as a political force during a new round of wage strikes in May 1988 radically changed Poland's political climate. Yet it was not until January 1989 that the Polish government agreed to open round-table discussions with Solidarity to find some way to address the country's political and economic problems. These discussions began in February, and culminated in an announcement in early March of a series of fundamental political reforms. The Party and the union agreed to create a freely-elected upper chamber in the *Sejm*, the country's parliament; a six-year presidency, which the Communist Party insisted on controlling for the first term; and a power-sharing formula for the existing house of the *Sejm*, where 65% of the seats would be allotted to the ruling party and its supporters, the United Peasants' Party, and the Democratic Party, the remaining 35% being chosen in free elections. As a result, the Party accepted the existence of a legal opposition, and Solidarity's status was legalized.

Solidarity candidates won an overwhelming victory in the June 1989 election, garnering 99% of the seats they contested. In humiliating contrast, only two of the Party's slate of 33 unopposed candidates, and five candidates for the 299 communist-controlled seats, received enough votes to gain a seat in the *Sejm*, since even unopposed candidates had to receive 50% of the votes cast in order to win a seat.

This led to a debate over the organization of the government, which continued throughout the summer. As part of an intricate compromise,

Jaruzelski was elected president by the *Sejm* in July. His election was
based partly on his promise to resign his position as party leader (this
post went to Mieczyslaw Rakowski). When Jaruzelski's attempts to convince Solidarity to join a communist-led coalition government or to
accept his nominee for prime minister failed, Tadeusz Mazowiecki, a
staunch Catholic and Solidarity member, became prime minister in
August 1989. The coalition Polish government was the first non-
communist-led government in the Eastern bloc in 40 years.

As a result of the dramatic changes that took place in 1989 the communist party faced a severe crisis. At its Congress in January 1990, it
formed itself into the Social Democratic Party of the Polish Republic
(SDRP) in a forlorn attempt to gain more national support. The opposition was far from united on the policies it ought to adopt, or even on
its participation in the government. Solidarity faced the prospect that it
would now be held at least partially responsible for Poland's continuing
economic problems. Moreover, it remained at least nominally a trade
union, not a political party, and the changes that would be necessary if
the Polish economy were to be revived would inevitably be difficult for
any trade union to accept, involving – as they were bound to – the
removal of subsidies on foodstuffs, closures of loss-making enterprises
and massive unemployment.

Yet all of the factions in Solidarity and the Party agreed that the
government's top priority had to be to resolve Poland's massive economic crisis. After consulting with a team of American economists, the
government decided to create a market economy by simultaneously cur-
tailing the money supply, eliminating subsidies, relaxing foreign-trade
regulations, and creating a nominally convertible zloty. In so doing it
would create the conditions for an agreement with the International
Monetary Fund (IMF), which was crucial for Poland to receive substantial Western financial assistance. Although this would undoubtedly
create great hardship and some chaos in the short term, it held out the
prospect of economic improvement within a year or so, which no other
proposal could do. The government's plan went into effect at the beginning of January 1990 and immediately led to a rise in inflation (petrol
prices doubled on the first day), but it appeared to meet with support, if
not enthusiasm from the Polish people.

The new leaders also found themselves in agreement with the Soviet
Union over the issue of German unification. Faced with West German
Chancellor Kohl's evasion of the question of Poland's border with the
GDR, Prime Minister Mazowiecki insisted that Poland deserved a say
in Germany's future security arrangements. He noted that there would
be no discussion of changes in Poland's military ties with the USSR
(including the future of Soviet forces stationed in Poland) until the
future of the two Germanies was clearly decided.

Poland's near-term future rests on the success of its dramatic leap to a
market economy, and on the extent of public tolerance of the unavoid-
able pain involved in the process. The rationale for the economic rev-

olution is that 'you cannot cross a chasm in two jumps', but it is equally true that one jump will not succeed if the chasm is too wide. Much will depend on the solidarity of Solidarity, which is becoming doubtful. Divisions, and further elections – probably on a new constitution which would eliminate the Party's gerrymandered position – seem all too likely. But then so does a Western safety net against all but the worst turns of fate.

The German Democratic Republic

The East German government under Erich Honecker had made clear that it did not want to follow the Soviet example and restructure its economic and political system. Indeed, by 1989, East German Politburo members had become increasingly open in expressing their concern over the direction of reforms in the bloc, and emphasizing the key place of Marxist-Leninist ideology as the cornerstone of a separate East German state. Yet the situation in the GDR changed dramatically in autumn 1989. For the first time in almost 40 years, large demonstrations calling for reform began to take place in East German cities, primarily Leipzig.

This was the result of a series of developments, the first being the opening up of an escape route for East Germans through Hungary to the West. By August, the number of East Germans in Hungary trying to move West was estimated to be near 60,000. The government of the GDR did nothing about these refugees until the Hungarian frontier was opened in September. Though it then sharply criticized this move, and restricted travel to Hungary, the emigration problem did not abate. The number of East Germans seeking refuge in West German embassies in Prague and Warsaw soared, and the East German leadership was compelled to allow these citizens to travel to the FRG only days before the GDR's 40th anniversary celebrations in October.

The opening of the Hungarian border led ultimately to Soviet involvement in the growing crisis. Gorbachev showed his support for the GDR by attending the 40th anniversary celebrations in East Berlin. However, he made his support for reform equally clear, championing *perestroika* in his speeches and in his discussions with the East German leadership, with no appreciable effect on Honecker. The anniversary celebrations in East Berlin took place under tight police control while demonstrations throughout the country increased in size and frequency, more than 10,000 people marching in Leipzig on 2 October in a demonstration organized by New Forum. Government spokesmen began comparing the situation in the GDR to that in China earlier in the year, a warning that the demonstrators could face a brutal crackdown.

The first sign of change came on 11 October, when the Politburo acknowledged the need for dialogue with the population. Within a week Honecker resigned. Although his successor, Egon Krenz, promised to hold discussions with the opposition, the demonstrations continued to gain momentum, with a crowd of 500,000 marching in East Berlin on 4

November. The wave of refugees continued to swell as the government allowed free travel through Czechoslovakia to the West, evidence of pervasive public scepticism about the promises of the communist party. In quick succession, first the government, then the Politburo resigned. On 9 November, the government lifted all travel restrictions to the West and, in a heart-wrenching moment of drama, the Berlin Wall was opened.

Clearly, this was an attempt by the Party to prove its sincerity in undertaking political and economic reforms. Yet it was clearly disintegrating as internal differences, the weight of popular disapproval and allegations of high-level corruption damaged its standing. And in early 1990, East Germans were deserting to the West at the rate of 2,000 per day. By the end of the year, Krenz and the entire leadership had resigned. Gregor Gysi was elected leader of the renamed SED-PDS and he agreed to set up free and open elections for May 1990. Hans Modrow, a reform-minded communist, remained prime minister of what was by this point clearly a caretaker government.

The inchoate character of the opposition remained a major obstacle to political reform in the GDR in early 1990. New Forum, which had gained widespread support as a rallying point during the demonstrations, refused to become a political party for several months because it rejected the existing political system. None of the opposition parties had an explicit programme for a future East German state. Only in early January 1990 did the opposition groups agree to work together through negotiations with the government (in a round-table discussion modelled on that in Poland). This group reluctantly agreed to join a non-affiliated coalition government with the SED-PDS on 28 January 1990, and the elections were moved forward to 18 March 1990. By this point, feasible challengers to the SED-PDS had emerged. The two most prominent were the Social Democratic Party, formed in early October 1989, with links to the West German SPD, and the 'Alliance for Germany', a three-party coalition with ties to the West German CDU and CSU. West German political figures of both right and left dominated (and to a considerable extent financed) the election campaign in the GDR, and in the end, the 'Alliance for Germany' won 48.9% of the vote, reflecting a strong East German desire to share in West Germany's affluence through rapid reunification. The SED-PDS, with 16% of the vote, did unexpectedly well, whereas the SDP garnered only 22%, belying pre-election opinion polls forecasting its victory.

The future of the GDR appears the most assured of all East European states; it will marry West Germany and hopes to live happily ever after. The speed of the process has yet to be established, however, and it may well be less rapid and immediately significant than many in the GDR currently imagine. And the security bargain which emerges from the 'two plus four' process may leave the territory of the former GDR in a unique security situation.

Czechoslovakia

Czechoslovakia's hard-line communist leaders, led in 1988 by Milos Jakes, totally opposed political and economic reforms. The brutal repression by government forces of a demonstration organized by dissidents and human-rights supporters in January 1989 to commemorate the self-immolation of Jan Palach 20 years earlier, confirmed its continued opposition to liberalization. Such repression, however, did not stop the opposition movements, though still small and unstructured, from spreading.

Nonetheless, it was not until November 1989 that these scattered groups and the people's general sense of discontent metamorphosed into wave after wave of mass demonstrations, galvanized by widespread outrage at police brutality during a demonstration in Prague on 17 November and fed by the images of the opening of the Berlin Wall. Two days after these protests, opposition leaders came together to form Civic Forum.

Within a week, continuing pressure and internal divisions had led the Party leadership to resign *en masse*. A relative newcomer, Karel Urbanek, was appointed to head the Party, and the new Central Committee pledged to begin a dialogue with citizens. Yet it proposed only minor adjustments to the constitution, which would leave the Communist Party firmly in control of the political system. This did not satisfy the growing opposition movement, which on 28 November called for a nationwide strike and received strong support. Within days, the government yielded and Prime Minister Ladislav Adamec endorsed far-reaching reforms, including the acceptance of non-communist participation in a new government, effective immediately. In mid-December, a new cabinet was announced; although the premier, Marian Calfa, was a communist, 13 of the 20 ministers named were not. Jiri Dienstbier, a founding member of Charter 77, was named foreign minister. Gustav Husak resigned as president, Alexander Dubcek was elected head of the National Assembly, and the country's most famous dissident, Vaclav Havel, was elected president of the Czechoslovak republic.

Although the protests had begun spontaneously, the ability of the fragmented groups of protesters to organize quickly gave them a singular advantage in their negotiations with the Communist Party. Within days, Civic Forum had presented a list of demands to the government, made clear its intent to work for fundamental constitutional changes, and had begun discussions with Prime Minister Adamec. The movement in Czechoslovakia also had prominent figures like Havel and Dubcek willing and able to lead it, in sharp contrast to the GDR, where well-known opposition figures had been exiled or were wary of participating in government-led discussions.

At least in foreign policy, the new leadership moved startlingly quickly to find a new identity for itself in Europe. Within a month, the new government had questioned the viability of the CMEA, raised the possibility of improved relations with Israel, and requested the USSR to remove its troops from Czechoslovak territory. Moscow agreed to do so by July 1991. Equally notable was the effort by Vaclav Havel to create a new Central European consensus. He chose to make his first foreign visit to the two Germanies, a reflection of Germany's changing role in Europe, and he made it clear that he expected that Czechoslovak relations with any German state would be positive in nature. Havel followed this with a proposal for a Central European confederation of Poland, Hungary and Czechoslovakia, arguing that these states ought to work together to find their place in Europe, rather than competing for Western attention and aid. He also suggested that Poland and Czechoslovakia join Hungary, Yugoslovia, Italy and Austria in an expanded version of the quadrilateral talks held in November 1989, to discuss their future role in Europe. These moves highlighted an effort to avoid the earlier nationalist and ethnic conflicts which had divided this region for centuries.

Despite being a late-comer to reforms Czechoslovakia looks well able to weather the changes better than some others. Above all, it has a relatively sound economy, a solid industrial and entrepreneurial tradition, and the legacy of the inter-war period of democracy. It also has the guiding influence, for now, of a philosopher-president with a broad world view and the wisdom to forgive and forget the bitter past. There is reason, therefore, to hope for a relatively painless transition to a pluralist and economically sound future.

Bulgaria

Despite Todor Zhivkov's insistence that he and Gorbachev agreed about the importance of reform, *perestroika* in Bulgaria had been primarily a paper exercise. The government had passed a law in January 1989 which abolished central management channels and created self-financing industries, but few changes were incorporated in practice.

In contradiction to any glimmer of reform, the Zhivkov government renewed its persecution of the ethnic Turkish minority in the spring of 1989. This might have been intended to raise popular support among ethnic Bulgarians by appealing to nationalistic sentiments. In November 1988 Turkish leaders in Bulgaria had established the Democratic League for the Defence of Human Rights, which aimed to work for a multi-party system as well as defending the Turkish minority's interests. The group organized mass demonstrations in eastern Bulgaria in the spring, which the Bulgarian government quashed. The repression led over 300,000 ethnic Turks to flee Bulgaria by August 1989, with the government vehemently claiming that these exiles were not leaving the country but merely 'vacationing' abroad. It blamed the recent ethnic tension on external forces and organized rallies against Turkish interference, supporting the impression that Zhivkov was trying to mobilize support among the Bulgarian population.

The Bulgarian Communist Party's lukewarm attitude towards reform gave way abruptly in late 1989. Zhivkov 'resigned' on 10 November, and his successor, former foreign minister Petar Mladenov, promised to implement a far-reaching reform programme, including greater separation of state and party, and greater freedom of expression. To some degree, this was simply a palace coup. Zhivkov appeared intent on suppressing what little dissent remained in Bulgaria, and those in the Politburo who opposed him, such as Mladenov. This, and the stirring events in the GDR may have led members of the Bulgarian leadership to conclude that changing their system was inevitable. Zhivkov's 'resignation' was therefore forced by more reform-minded opponents in the party leadership.

Following his departure, the Bulgarian Communist Party (BCP) introduced steps that could lead to a radically different political system. At the same time, it called for a reorganization of the Party, to strengthen its domestic position. Bulgaria was initially unwilling to go as far as others in the bloc, however. Party spokesmen stressed that it would follow the Soviet model of restructuring, while maintaining a one-party socialist system. Similarly, though the BCP agreed to hold elections in May the interim provisional government it created included only BCP members.

Although the disparate aims of smaller independent groups in the country could handicap opposition unity, an umbrella organization, the Union of Democratic Forces, staged demonstrations in mid-December demanding political changes similar to those sweeping Eastern Europe. Though it continued to insist that the BCP would play a substantial role in state affairs, the Party agreed to open round-table discussions on a multi-party system and free elections with several opposition parties in early January. Yet it tried again in early January 1990 to inflame ethnic Bulgarian sentiment against the Turks – and by implication, against the opposition movements who supported their human rights – arguably as a way to avoid addressing the issue of creating a truly democratic system in the country.

Of all the East European states, Bulgaria has always been most akin to the Soviet Union. As a result, its reform process could follow the Soviet pattern more closely than the other reforming states.

Romania

In the wake of the wave of reforms that swept Eastern Europe in 1989, Romania became increasingly isolated as the only anti-reform state in the bloc. In December 1989, however, the government's efforts to exile an ethnic Hungarian Protestant pastor in Timisoara catalysed a protest which quickly took on an anti-government tone. Despite repression by the army and the *Securitate*, Ceauşescu's secret police, the riots and demonstrations which this incident spawned spread to other cities.

On 21 December, Ceauşescu's address to an organized, pro-government rally in Bucharest was interrupted by protests; within hours the *Securitate* had begun firing on demonstrators, and revolt against Ceauşescu's rule erupted. Ceauşescu and his wife Elena fled the next day as fighting spread throughout the capital, and an organization calling itself the National Salvation Front (NSF) declared itself the new government of Romania. The army went over to the side of this new government when it was announced that the defence minister, Vasile Milea allegedly committed suicide after refusing to order troops to open fire on the population. The Ceauşescus were subsequently captured by army troops, and on 25 December, they were summarily tried and executed by army representatives of the NSF.

The NSF was initially billed as a loose coalition between many of the disaffected groups in the country, including the few prominent dissidents who remained in Romania, and former members of the Romanian Communist Party. It established itself as an interim government prior to the creation of a multi-party system in Romania, abolished the leading role of the Communist Party, and announced that free elections would be held in April 1990. Additionally, it reiterated Romania's commitment to the Warsaw Pact, in ironic contrast to Ceauşescu's hostility towards affiliation with this organization. Yet its integrity quickly came into question as former dissidents accused former communists who were members of the NSF of trying to perpetuate communist rule under a new name, and several prominent figures left the Front. Indeed, after vacillating for the first few weeks of its existence, and in spite of popular anger against some of its peremptory methods, the leaders of the NSF opted to create a separate political organization to compete in the elections. A Provisional National Council of Unity was formed in conjunction with opposition groups to govern in the interim, and the elections were postponed to give opposition groups more time to organize.

The situation in Romania remains confused, and in some respects, deeply disturbing: renewed clashes between Romanians and the ethnic Hungarian minority have undermined hopes of a smooth passage to democratic waters and respect for human rights. Having destroyed its tyrants, Romania has entered a period rife with continuing dangers of internal strife – both ethnic and political, with strong forces still apparently backing some form of communism without Ceauşescu. This does not bode well for Romania's near-term future.

Albania

In early 1990, hints of reform emerged even in Albania. President Ramiz Alia announced to the Central Committee in January that the government intended to introduce democratizing measures, albeit with the intent of preserving 'socialism' in Albania. These would include decentralization, contested elections for some posts, and changes in the pricing structure. At the same time, the government quietly began to relax its isolation from the outside world, raising the possibility that the last ideological wall in Europe might soon be breached.

Albania has been in self-imposed isolation for so long, and its political pulse is so difficult to feel, that it is nearly impossible to take stock of its current situation. There seems little sign of public demand for change – indeed, popular pressure for action against Serbia's repression of ethnic Albanians in Kosovo is striking in its absence – and the tentative openings to the wider world probably represent a gradual and limited government/party perception of the opportunities foregone by isolation rather than pre-emptive moves to head off public discontent.

Yugoslavia

Two trends, nationalism and separatism, dominated the Yugoslav political landscape in 1989. The two are related, since both the go- it-alone attitude of those republics aiming for economic reforms and a multi-party system of government, and Serbian demands for control over Kosovo, changed the internal balance of power built into the federal framework created by Marshal Tito. Both trends threaten the fragile unity of the state; the background for both is provided by continuing economic chaos throughout the country.

In February and March 1989, the tension between ethnic Albanians and Serbs over control of the autonomous province of Kosovo erupted with a series of strikes by Albanian miners to protest Serbia's demands that it be given direct control of the province. Serbia eventually prevailed at the end of March, though not without bloodshed and the imposition of curfews in Kosovo.

At the same time, Slovenia and Croatia were implementing steps intended to make multi-party governments possible in these two republics, and independent political parties were legalized and established there in January and February. Slovenia (joined to a lesser degree by Croatia) condemned Serbian dominance in the east and its repression of the ethnic Albanians in Kosovo, and threatened that its Communist Party might boycott the all-Yugoslav Communist Party (YCP) Congress scheduled for late 1989. The Serbian government, under the populist Slobodan Milosevic who had been elected President on 6 April, implemented a policy of 'differentiation' in job recruitment in Kosovo to favour Serbs; offered incentives to encourage Serbians to move to Kosovo; forced ethnic Albanian party officials to resign and arrested nationalist leaders for fomenting the wave of strikes; and held an enormous Serbian demonstration in Kosovo to commemorate the 600th anniversary of the battle of Kosovo, Serbia's most famous defeat by the Ottoman Turks.

In the meantime, the Yugoslav economy continued to deteriorate. A new government was sworn in in March, after the previous leadership resigned at the end of 1989 because it could not deal with the country's economic problems. The new government declared its intent to set the country on a path towards a market economy, and stressed the need for drastic measures to stop inflation. Nonetheless, by September, inflation had spiralled to such a point that currency exchanges were being reported in cubic metres of dinar, and railway workers went on strike, demanding that their salaries be set in pounds sterling.

In July, the Slovenian Communist Party drafted a new constitution which included provisions for holding free elections in spring 1990, and the right to secede from the Yugoslav federation. This constitution was approved in September despite attacks from most of the other republics, and in particular from Serbia, which claimed that Slovenia was 'destabilizing' the Yugoslav federation, and could not unilaterally change its constitution. (Milosevic, however, had done just that with Serbia's constitution in June, in order to take fuller control of Kosovo and Vojvodina.) Serbian activists planned a protest in the capital of Slovenia and, when Slovenian officials refused to allow this demonstration to take place, Serbia 'invited' all of its institutions, and ordered its enterprises, to cut off ties with Slovenia, in effect starting an economic blockade of the republic. The Yugoslav state had now essentially split into three parts: Slovenia, the Serbia-dominated east, with the remaining republics uncomfortably sandwiched in between.

The federal government was largely ineffective in the face of these political conflicts. It denounced the blockade as a violation of the constitution, but could do little to stop it. However, the government did announce a radical package of economic reforms in December, including a plan to introduce a new dinar and to link its exchange rate with the Deutsche Mark, which in effect would make it the first convertible currency in Eastern Europe. This package was rejected by Serbia, on the grounds that it would 'trigger social upheavals'. Serbia appeared to be a minority, however, in its insistence on maintaining single party rule, as the YCP voted in December to give up its constitutional monopoly of power, and Croatia advocated adopting a multi-party system throughout Yugoslavia. The army, however, sided with Serbia by voicing concern about the prospect of a multi-party system.

In January 1990, the breach in the YCP was formalized when the Slovenian CP walked out of a hastily called Extraordinary Party Congress. A month later, the Slovenian communists formally seceded from the Yugoslav League of Communists, and renamed their party the Democratic Renewal Party. In Slovenia and Croatia free elections were scheduled for April 1990. Serbian leader Milosevic apparently lost support at the January Congress, when he declared that Slovenia's absence was unimportant and tried to continue the meeting with one republic missing. Understandably, no other republic supported this stand. In addition, a renewed round of strikes broke out in Kosovo to protest Serbian control. The country was left in much the same mess that it had been in a year earlier, but at higher levels of tension and recrimination.

Many Problems Remain

Despite the auspicious political changes under way throughout Eastern Europe, the economic situation in much of the region remains grim. For the political reforms to succeed in the long run, the new governments must address the problems caused by 40 years of inefficient central planning, outdated plant, appalling environmental destruction, and massive foreign debt. This is a daunting task. Fledgling governments will have to take responsibility for painful economic reforms or continued stagnation, neither of which will endear them to voters who expect democracy to solve these problems quickly.

Each faces the problem of evolving a democratic polity from inchoate new political forces, largely without clearly identifiable programmes, and from the residue of the old and discredited communist parties whose failure has tended to tarnish all forms of socialism by association. New parties will probably govern initially through coalitions, whose community of interests is likely to diminish as parties become more individual. They will have to work through, or may be impeded by, bureaucracies established under the former regimes; in some cases still loyal to the ideology they served, in others having held their party cards only as an essential piece of political expediency. And each country faces the risk that the earthquake of revolution will be followed by aftershocks of unpredictable force and nature, before political equilibrium can be established.

Though the future shape of Eastern Europe cannot yet be predicted with any certainty, some features were discernible in early 1990. First, the two Germanies are headed for early economic and political unification and the security arrangements under which this occurs will influence security arrangements in the rest of the region. Second, all the states of Eastern Europe want to expand their ties with the West, particularly with the EC. All advocate a massive influx of Western aid to help the economic problems they face. And third, the historic diversity of the region will undoubtedly re-emerge. Several states are adopting increasingly independent foreign and security policies, notably reducing their defence budgets, requesting the removal of Soviet troops, and developing new notions of their role in Europe. There is no way to return to the previous state of affairs in Eastern Europe; indeed, 'Eastern Europe' will no longer exist as an unit. But how the individual states will fit into the strategic structures which will emerge in Europe is one of the many unknowns of the new decade.

WESTERN EUROPE: ADJUSTING TO THE CHANGE

Western Europe entered 1989 very conscious that it faced the challenges of adjusting to a changing and less confrontational international environment. At the start of the year it seemed that this adjustment might be achieved in a measured way by a combination of: '*status quo* plus' adjustments to security policy, modifying but not radically revising the already existing political road-map; conventional arms control at its own, probably slow, pace; further consolidation of Western European integration, predominantly through the 1992 process of the European Community (EC) and steps towards other somewhat vague integrative goals enunciated in the 1985 Single European Act; and cau-

tious selective aid and encouragement to the reforming states of Eastern
Europe. By the beginning of 1990 everything had been overtaken by the
revolutionary turn of events in the East. Within a six-month period it
had become clear that, instead of cautious adjustments, new or substantially revised political, economic and security arrangements would be
needed.

EC Integration and Eastern Europe

The emergence of the East European states from their chains, all
seriously in need of assistance to make the unprecedented transition
from centralized to market economies, and the majority requiring aid,
credits, debt relief, know-how and enhanced trade opportunities, presented the EC with challenges and opportunities not altogether easy to
reconcile with its planned course towards the Single Market of 1992 and
its less agreed course towards integration and monetary union. The pre-
sumptive unification of Germany presented particular problems. It
would divert the attention, and potentially a significant part of the
resources, of the Community's most powerful economic actor. More
threateningly, absorption of the former GDR would add to the EC roll
of less-developed or declining industrial areas, and would introduce the
problems of the GDR's subsidized and grossly polluting industries and
general failure to match Community standards in a way which its former 'back-door' access by trading through the FRG had obscured.

The fear of a 'Fortress Europe' which had affected relations with the
US in 1988 largely abated – or at least declined to watchful caution –
with the reference of some trade disputes to GATT for resolution, and
US agreement in May to exclude the EC from accusations of 'unfair
trading practices' under Section 301 of the new US trade act. Indeed, as
Eastern Europe and the Council for Mutual Economic Assistance
(CMEA) fell apart, the US Administration came to look with increasing
favour on the Community. Under the circumstances, a politically
united Western Europe was seen as a strength rather than a threat
(although US Administration and Congressional tolerance for such a
politically united Europe taking an adverse view on, for example, a
Middle East issue has yet to be tested).

Deputy Secretary of State Eagleburger told the Senate in June that the
Single Market was 'emphatically in our interest', while President Bush
saw a unified Western Europe as a 'magnet' to guide Eastern Europe to
pluralism and free enterprise. And the Group of Seven (G-7), meeting in
Paris in June, tasked the Community with the co-ordination of Western
aid to Poland and Hungary, a remit which led eventually to an agreement by the EC in December 1989 to establish a European Reconstruction Development Bank. Nevertheless, from an Eastern European standpoint, acknowledgment of the EC's magnetism and
example, and its functions in aid disbursement, remain tempered by
some continuing fears of a 'Fortress West Europe', fenced off by structural barriers and a protective agricultural policy.

The need to extend a helping hand to the emergent and increasingly democratic East European regimes placed the Community in something of a dilemma. It now had to find the optimum blend of policies between the on-going process of *completing* the Single Market by the end of 1992, *deepening* the Community by means of a three-phase transition to European Monetary Union (EMU) starting in 1990, and *widening* it to embrace, in a so-called European Economic Space and at various degrees of association, the European Free Trade Association (EFTA) states and other potential applicants, whether East European or other. The EMU concept was based on the Delors Plan, first announced on 17 April 1989, which would eventually involve an unprecedented transfer of national power, and about which the UK government has strong reservations. Negotiations with the EFTA states had already begun in 1989, and there were outstanding applicants for membership (Turkey had applied in April 1987, followed by Austria in July 1989).

French President Mitterrand strongly favours an accelerated deepening of the Community and the implicit move towards federalism, primarily as a means of binding the FRG (or a united Germany) more firmly into the West and militating against the *Drang nach Osten*. It would, however, almost certainly preclude full membership by any additional neutral states unless security policy, and hence key aspects of foreign policy, were to be excluded from the ambit of federal political co-operation.

Widening of the Community would bring problems of accommodating states with insufficiently robust economies, finding means of opening the EC to their agricultural products, and risking an influx of migrant workers. It would also divert Community resources from its existing less-developed regions, principally in the South, and from favourable trade arrangements with the countries of North Africa, with possible deleterious effects on security in the Mediterranean region. On the other hand, it would help Eastern Europe and impede federalism, and hence gets Prime Minister Thatcher's vote.

Having been torn in two directions by its special relationships with both France and the GDR, the FRG initially appeared to vacillate on the issue of monetary union, but at the EC's December Strasbourg Summit it confirmed its support for the Delors Plan, and in March 1990 appeared to accept that German monetary union should not impede the preparation of the Inter-governmental Conference which is to deliberate on EMU. Despite the distraction of German unification, there was no apparent sign that German attitudes in Brussels would lead to a slowing of the EC's integrative process. The outcome is thus likely to be a Europe of concentric circles: an inner federalist EC, eventually enjoying monetary and, increasingly, political union (with or without the UK), and secondary and tertiary rings of associated states with varying degrees of Community support and access.

However, the East European dimension has already resulted in one casualty to the policies of EC development, which could prove a harbinger of other difficulties yet to materialize. The FRG, France and the

Benelux countries had agréed at Schengen in June 1985 to a trial run of some aspects of the Single Market by abolishing checks at all road frontiers among them by 1 January 1990. The detailed agreement was due to have been signed on 15 December, but at the last minute Bonn felt unable to accede to it because of the possible implications for, and of, the German unification then in prospect.

Notwithstanding this setback, some internal frictions and dissension over the direction and rate of progress, and uncertainties over how best to help the evolution of Eastern Europe, a significant testimony to the burgeoning power and influence of the Community came from the United States. First, in an address to the Berlin Press Club on 12 December, Secretary of State James Baker explicitly sought for the US 'institutional and consultative links' with Brussels. Then, at a meeting in Washington in early March, President Bush and Irish Prime Minister Charles Haughey, president of the day of the EC, agreed that there should be regular yearly meetings between US and Community presidents, and biannual meetings between the US secretary of state and Community foreign ministers. An increasingly integrated Community may thus develop the key North American political linkage that only NATO among Western European institutions has hitherto enjoyed. However, Germany's partners will probably not agree to the abandonment of sovereignty entailed in further European integration if they are not confident that a united Germany will remain within the Western security system. In this sense, there is a correlation between Germany's attitude towards the Atlantic Alliance and the future of the EC.

The Re-emergence of the German Question

While the other broad problems posed to Western European leaders and policy-makers by developments in 1989 were relatively benign, the emergence of the German question as one now requiring a definitive solution presents very substantial difficulties. Since German unification will re-unite in one nation the two states which have been at the frontline of the East–West divide and which are central to their respective military and economic alliances, it will not only crown the collapse of the post-war European order but will also set in place the key central element of the new. Given the burden of history, the manner in which this is achieved in the short term is likely to govern European security and stability over the long term.

The emergence of a German question in 1989 should have been no surprise to NATO. The FRG had long been the Alliance's key front-line state, making its most sizable dedicated military contribution, and bearing the heaviest day-to-day burden of militarization and troop presence, but without its voice being given proportional weight in Alliance counsels. The harsh pressure exerted on Chancellor Kohl during INF Treaty negotiations in 1987 over the *Pershing*-IA based in the FRG, and Mrs Thatcher's sudden abandonment of support for his position in the run-up to the UK general election of that year, may well have constituted 'last straws'. FRG insistence in 1988 on NATO's development of a *Gesamtkonzept* linking its conventional, nuclear and arms-control strategy signalled a new level of German assertiveness. The tough fight to postpone decisions on a follow-on to the *Lance* missile and to keep SNF negotiation options open was another sign.

German self-perceptions were strengthened by President Bush's explicit recognition, during his visit to the FRG after the May NATO Summit, of a 'leadership partnership' between the two countries. Hierarchical adjustments in the Alliance 'pecking order' were, however, never likely to be achieved without pain. This became the more obvious in the latter half of the year as domestic FRG electoral considerations combined with intra-German opportunities to produce political moves which alarmed non-Germans, East and West, and some Germans as well.

With German federal elections scheduled for December 1990, Chancellor Kohl's CDU/FDP coalition entered 1989 looking decidedly shaky, behind in the polls and shortly to be rocked by defeats in municipal elections in West Berlin and Frankfurt. In both cities 'Red-Green' (SPD/Green) coalitions took power. The far-right made an unexpected mark in both elections and began to appear as a significant threat, most notably in Bavaria where the death of Franz-Joseph Strauss had left the CSU, the CDU's Bavarian partner, without ballast against extremist pressures. Electoral considerations – the need to accommodate public nuclear *Angst* – accounted in large measure for Bonn's stand on nuclear modernization and SNF negotiations. The welcome extended to Gorbachev on his visit to the FRG in early June, a high point of Western 'Gorbymania', further confirmed public support for the active pursuit of arms reductions and accommodation with the East, as did mid-1989 polls that showed only 24% of the population perceived the USSR as a threat.

The surge of immigrants from the GDR, first through Hungary then through Czechoslovakia and even via Warsaw, which rose as high as 10,000 in some weeks after September, and even to 10,000 on some days just before the Berlin Wall was breached on 9 November, exacerbated existing housing shortages and raised fears that jobs would be lost in the FRG. The opening of the border and the subsequent rapid collapse of the East German communist regime briefly stanched the flow and raised the possibility that a sufficiently democratic and competent government would emerge in East Berlin to persuade Easterners to stay put. But the flood picked up again (reaching some 2,500 per day by February 1990) and, as the demonstrators in the GDR began to wave banners and shout slogans in support of unification, a straightforward end to the long-enforced division of the country seemed the only solution.

The situation demanded an early statement of position from Bonn. On 28 November, after little or no consultation with his allies or the Four Powers with residual post-war responsibilities for Berlin and for Germany at large, Kohl responded with an announcement of a ten-

point programme for a three-phase process through 'confederal structures' to a single federal state. As near-anarchy developed in the GDR,
and elections originally scheduled for May 1990 were brought forward
to 18 March, Kohl increasingly stressed the imminence of an economic
collapse in the GDR, mooted the possibility of a more rapid path to
unity by voluntary post-election adhesion of the five reconstituted East
German *Länder* to the FRG under the terms of Article 23 of the 1949
West German Basic Law, and plunged actively into the GDR's election
campaign in support of the East German CDU and its right-wing
'Alliance for Germany'. In similar fashion the FRG's principal key
opposition party, the Social Democrat SPD, disclaimed their earlier
negotiations with the GDR's ruling communists and weighed in, with
Willy Brandt in the van, in support of the newly-formed East German
SPD, both favouring a slower route to unification, via a new jointly-
created constitution. The outcome of the 18 March elections was a
handsome, if unexpected, victory for the 'Alliance for Germany',
impetus for early unification, and a substantial boost for Kohl.

German unification, however, carries implications stretching well
beyond German borders. The four principal wartime Allies maintain
residual powers, and a number of adjacent states have interests and
fears. Unification requires resolution of the conundrum posed by the
current place of the two Germanies in their respective alliances, including their respective hosting of foreign stationed troops in substantial
numbers; the future security status of a unified Germany; and assurance
of the legitimate security interests of all other states concerned. This last
consideration was given added weight by Kohl's prolonged refusal to
accept firmly the present border between Poland and the GDR in spite
of the express concern of the Poles and of his Western allies.

Although the FRG has on occasion been somewhat more ambivalent
than its allies, NATO has firmly insisted that a unified Germany remain
in the Alliance. To meet expected Soviet objections West German
Foreign Minister Hans Dietrich Genscher devised a plan in February
that would extend the present NATO boundaries to the Polish border,
but no foreign or integrated NATO troops would be allowed east of the
current inner-German border. Soviet troops could remain for an indeterminate transition period before a negotiated complete removal.
Although Gorbachev accepted the inevitability of German unity in January 1990, the Soviet Union has thus far stood out firmly against a solution ranging Germany in NATO, and in favour of a neutral status with
a level of forces significantly reduced from current *Bundeswehr* strength.

At the 'Open Skies' conference in Ottawa in February the foreign
ministers of the six nations concerned evolved a 'two plus four' formula
whereby the intra-German modalities of unification would be agreed
between the two German states, and the security structure, status and
obligations of a united Germany agreed between them and the Four
Powers. The finished package would then be reported to a 35-nation
CSCE Summit (Helsinki II) later in the year. Smaller nations objected

to their exclusion, and the Polish government is to be involved in those discussions affecting its borders, but the mechanism otherwise stands, and meetings of both the two and the six began shortly before the GDR elections.

The difficulty and delicacy of the problems that the negotiators face cannot be overstated. They must devise a formula which provides adequate safeguards for the legitimate security concerns of Germany's neighbours, particularly in the East, and which does so without producing festering resentments in Germans at unique constraints on their sovereign rights, or in East Europeans or Soviets who feel that a potentially threatening security environment has been forced upon them because current political circumstances gave them a weak negotiating hand.

To most observers, a united Germany bound firmly into the Atlantic Alliance and the EC seems unarguably the best, and arguably the only, practicable solution. But the vigor of Soviet objections to an outcome which ties an enlarged Germany to a traditionally anti-Soviet alliance should not be underestimated. Nor would a NATO connection designed to 'keep the Germans down' be tolerable to Germany itself. Some adjustment to NATO's posture, perhaps preserving the North Atlantic Treaty and applying it to Germany as a whole while downplaying the military components of its Organization may prove to be a necessary price to pay to establish a durable security outcome acceptable to all.

One thing is certain, however. The time for negotiation is short and could be further shortened if dissatisfaction develops within Germany over the rate of progress; the risks are particularly great in East Germany where hopes of early economic benefits are high. The past 12 months has been a period of increasing German assertiveness, with some insensitivity about the interests and concerns of non-Germans but acute sensitivity to any criticism from such quarters. The next 12 months are likely to require a return to moderation, sober caution and sensitivity to outside interests on the part of all Germans, if the German question is to be solved for good – and not for recurring ill.

The Security Dimension

The INF Treaty and Gorbachev's historic UN speech of December 1988 announcing significant unilateral force reductions for completion by 1991 (rapidly followed by all other Warsaw Pact countries except Romania) meant that 1989 opened in a more than usually benign European security climate. Ready Eastern agreement to a mandate for the Vienna negotiations on Conventional Forces in Europe (CFE), the early establishment of much common ground on the CFE objectives, and progressive convergence between the negotiating positions of the two sides have fostered high hopes for a treaty in 1990, and have further diminished threat perceptions. At the same time, the political developments in the non-Soviet Warsaw Pact countries and the planned rapid reshaping (and/or decay) of their armed forces to little more than territorial defence capabilities and roles, coupled with Soviet agreement to quit Hungary and Czechoslovakia by July 1991, have eliminated the long-remote threat of a co-ordinated Warsaw Pact onslaught on the West.

A surprise conventional attack no longer seems possible. A late 1989 US National Intelligence Estimate reportedly postulated some 33–44 days' warning of a Soviet offensive in Europe; the completion of currently-planned Soviet unilateral reductions and withdrawals will increase the warning of attack and even further reduce its likelihood. Implementation of the likely CFE bargain will further diminish any residual Soviet capability for attack but may take longer to effect, since the Soviet Union already faces the social and economic problems of assimilating large numbers of demobilized officers, and equipment destruction will also take time. But, depending on the security arrangements governing German unification, the West can now look forward to a time when the Soviet Union will at most have only a force of 195,000 (but probably far fewer) troops deployed in the eastern part of Germany and in Poland, and might well have withdrawn wholly from Eastern Europe. Nevertheless, the USSR, although much less militarized, would remain the strongest single military power in Europe.

Faced with these developments, many of which were not foreseeable at the beginning of the year, NATO's security concepts have developed only slowly, fitfully and at times fractiously. NATO passed its 40th anniversary on 4 April with European nations still uncertain what policy initiatives to expect from the Bush Administration, and forced to wait until May before the lengthy US policy review was completed. The CFE process has produced its own strains: between France and the US over co-ordinating a NATO line with the avoidance of explicit bloc-to-bloc negotiation; between Turkey and Greece over the geographical definition of the zone; between the flank countries and those of the Central Region over the key targets for reductions and over zonal schemes which might increase threats to Norway and Turkey; between the major European countries and the US over constraints on armaments production; and general differences over acceptable provisions for verification and data exchange. Even the significant impetus injected into the CFE process by Bush at the May NATO Summit, while widely welcomed as securing the negotiating initiative and the 'high ground' in terms of public perceptions, emerged with minimal consultation.

A more serious, because more strategically fundamental, dissension arose in the early part of the year over short-range nuclear force (SNF) modernization, most particularly concerning the follow-on to *Lance*. The substantial Warsaw Pact advantage in land-based SNF and even more the FRG's position as both as a key front-line state and the locus for the overwhelming majority of NATO's SNF deployment, caused Foreign Minister Genscher to seek early negotiation with the East on reduction to parity. He was also clearly opposed to the implementation of the modernization policy agreed by NATO at Montebello in 1983.

Chancellor Kohl, while prepared to accept modernization, saw it as a highly undesirable political hot potato and sought to postpone any commitment until after the December 1990 FRG elections. The US sought an early commitment to deployment in order to persuade Congress to agree funding for the new *Lance*; the UK strongly opposed any abandonment of the Montebello position, and in particular any agreement to early SNF negotiation, as a dangerous step on a potentially slippery slope to denuclearization. France, for its part, also saw such a trend as a threat to its own planned *Hadès* weapon.

A serious rift at the key May NATO Summit was averted only at the last moment by a Solomon-like compromise advanced by President Bush, which postponed a decision on deployment of the *Lance* follow-on until 1992, but which also put off any negotiation on SNF reduction until a CFE bargain had been agreed and its implementation was under way. The bargain, also embodied in the new comprehensive concept adopted at the meeting, effectively papered over the cracks of a deep difference between the FRG and its allies over the needs of Flexible Response and the relative risks borne by Alliance partners. Whether it would have stood the test of time is doubtful; for all practical purposes, however, the SNF issue has been overtaken by the developments in East Europe which now make the targeting of Eastern European states by NATO nuclear weapons virtually unthinkable. The question now is not whether there will be an improved *Lance*, but whether the existing *Lance* will see out its life and how long nuclear artillery capabilities will be maintained in Europe.

While the burden-sharing dispute which had bedevilled European–American relations in 1988 was much abated, uncoordinated moves towards force reductions and 'structural disarmament' continued in response to resource pressures, public perceptions of reduced threat, and electoral considerations. Few defence budgets showed increases in real terms; the majority stood still or declined. The FRG, facing a demographic trough, announced its 'Bundeswehr 2000' concept which involves 'hollowing out' its active forces by embodying a larger reserve component, postponed until 1992 an earlier decision to extend conscript service from 15 to 18 months, and expressed its intention to cut its armed forces by 20% by the mid-1990s. The US, introducing a manpower element into the CFE negotiations as a response to Soviet demands, first proposed superpower ceilings for stationed manpower (deployed outside national territory) in the ATTU zone of 275,000 – a reduction of some 45,000 from current US levels – and later reduced this to 195,000 in the Central Region, with an additional 30,000 US soldiers and airmen to be permitted elsewhere in the CFE area. It is far from clear that there was much Alliance consultation about either figure, and little likelihood, despite protestations, that 195,000/225,000 will prove to be a durable floor.

Fears of a possible diminution of the US commitment to Europe, and of the FRG's *Drang nach Osten*, drove France and the UK to some enhanced measures of defence co-operation – and most significantly to revive a feasibility study of a joint air-launched stand-off nuclear-capable missile – but neither increased their defence budget. Indeed, the planned French budget increase was cut back and programmes prolonged or cut, while the UK budget was reduced in real terms for the fourth year. The Netherlands and Belgium both expressed eagerness to draw down troops from Germany. Throughout the Alliance, declarations of intent to do nothing to anticipate the CFE outcome and its to-be-agreed burden-shedding share-out faced keen public anticipation of a 'peace dividend', the appetite for which can only be expected to sharpen with continuing Soviet retrenchment and East European liberalization.

The result has been a rapidly developing mismatch between NATO's force structure and strategy, and its realistic security requirements and objectives. The CFE process, while remaining important by embedding force levels and verification arrangements in an enforceable treaty, has largely been overtaken by the collapse of the Warsaw Pact as a meaningful military instrument, and the very considerable reduction in the immediacy of any conceivable conventional Soviet threat. The liberalization and promised democratization of the states of Eastern Europe, and the impending unification of Germany, affect key elements of long-standing NATO strategy. The future of stationed forces in Germany – indeed the future of Germany in the NATO alliance – will depend on the outcome of the 'two plus four' negotiations on the unification process and related security guarantees.

At an extreme, these could call into question the continued viability of NATO; the complete denuclearization of German soil, a total and statutory removal of foreign-stationed forces from German territory, or German defection from the Alliance (however unlikely) or even from its integrated military structure, could all deal the Alliance a death-blow, and all could be sought by Moscow as the price for agreement to unification. But even short of such an apocalyptic outcome, few scenarios offer much of a convincing rationale for maintaining the current forward defence strategy for forces based in the territory of the current FRG. Under the changed circumstances defence would conceivably no longer require active stationed forces of significant size. The continuing requirements could perhaps largely be met by reserves and/or a rapid force reconstitution capability. One thing that is certain is that substantial active stationed forces with no demonstrably relevant role would soon prove unsustainable, both for the supplying countries, for Germany, and for the forces themselves. A role of restraining a potentially resurgent Germany could hardly remain covert and would be no more sustainable.

As for Flexible Response, while a theatre component of nuclear deterrence is still likely to be viewed as a requirement for the West, the need is likely to be for an arsenal of minimum quantity but high quality – one which could reach if necessary, beyond the new and *de facto* non-aligned democracies of Eastern Europe to Soviet territory itself. Given the INF

Treaty, this must be an air- (or possibly sea-) launched weapon. The means of fulfilling this element of NATO's MC 14/3 strategy will therefore need early revision.

While little beyond prudent contingency analysis and planning can be achieved until the nature of the security aspects of German unification are clear, NATO assuredly faces a pressing requirement to redefine its role and goals. Rhetoric notwithstanding, it is difficult to see NATO becoming more political, although it could readily become less military – notably in terms of permanent organization, superstructure and forces-in-being. It may be that such a change will be required to reassure Gorbachev that German unification within NATO does not threaten legitimate Soviet security concerns. The Alliance must also consider its arms-control role and what if anything are its conventional arms-control objectives after conclusion of a first-phase CFE agreement.

If the evolution of Europe's security architecture includes a greater role for CSCE, as many currently suggest it should, NATO may have a significant role to play in co-ordinating a Western caucus within the 35-nation group. It is probable, however, that NATO will cease to be a structuring element of the new system in the way that it has been for the past 40 years. The military requirements of the East–West confrontation determined the European order, with NATO creating both the conditions under which the EC could emerge and mature and an environment within which a meaningful CSCE could develop. In the future, other institutions and forces will shape the European system, and the Atlantic Alliance, it is to be hoped, will continue to play the indispensable role of a good insurance policy.

In early 1989, with the 40th anniversary of the Alliance looming, the key question had been 'Whither NATO?'. A year later that question remains valid and is no easier to answer; but a second question, 'Whether NATO?', lies not far below the surface.

Africa

Some African countries had begun taking important steps towards democratic reform in the late 1980s, but many of those which had not, by early 1990 found themselves dealing with the political and economic effects in their own countries of the spectacular East European revolutions of 1989. As reform in Eastern Europe accelerated, African leaders, in common with others in the developing world of the South, began to lament a prospective loss of attention and aid from the West which they saw as predisposed to assist the process of reform in the East at the expense of their failing partners in the South.

In December 1989, the 68 African, Caribbean and Pacific (ACP) countries and the EC signed the fourth Lomé Convention which promised 12bn ECU (about $14bn) of assistance over five years. (Namibia on independence will, in all likelihood, become the 69th state.) This represented a 25% increase in real terms over the Lomé III accord and was therefore a figure which, having been negotiated just as the momentous events in Europe were taking shape, represented the highest the Lomé states could reasonably have expected. However, having promised this level of aid in difficult circumstances, it is likely that bilateral assistance to Africa from European countries will suffer a decline. The need for African states, in any case, to take severe austerity measures resulted in strikes and riots in many capitals, which this year, more than before, were accompanied by calls for more pluralistic political processes. African leaders were therefore compelled, as the decade opened, to grope for new ways to demonstrate their political legitimacy to their populations, and their economic needs to traditional donors from outside the continent. Dealing with the challenges of democratic pluralism and possible Western aid fatigue will no doubt prove to be the two main management tasks in Africa for the next few years, alongside the traditional and unabating challenges of underdevelopment.

At least in theory, the countries of North Africa appeared better prepared than most to cope with such changes in the international scene. Algeria and Tunisia had already begun to institute important political reforms in 1988, and while such changes were less evident in Morocco, Libya and Mauritania (the other three states of the Arab Maghreb Union (AMU) established in February 1989), the very existence of this organization seemed to promise positive changes. As so much political capital has been spent promoting the virtues of the AMU, it will have to be seen to be delivering promptly on the hopes it has engendered, before the people of the Maghreb begin making more pressing demands on their leaders, as they did so dramatically in Algeria in 1988. Already the AMU has shown that it cannot finesse the main regional conflict between Morocco and the Polisario rebels of the Western Sahara, and until that conflict is settled the process of regional unification is bound to remain slow and uncertain. One of the main stated reasons for the AMU's creation had been the perceived need to co-ordinate economic policy amongst the member states in such a way as to be in a position to deal with the consequences of a single European market.

The countries of sub-Saharan Africa, however, have generally been slower to anticipate the need for political and economic change. As a group, they were examined in an impressive long-term study published by the World Bank in November 1989. The report highlighted the many known features of sub-Saharan Africa's deepening crisis: weak agricultural growth; a decline in industrial output; climbing debt; and ecological degradation. It also emphasized the importance of social indicators for sustainable development and notably drew attention to that great unspoken African need of good government, arguing that 'because countervailing power has been lacking, state officials in many countries have served their own interests without fear of being called into account'. Solving this crisis of governance, the report argued, 'requires a systematic effort to build a pluralistic institutional structure, a determination to respect the rule of law, and vigorous protection of the freedom of the press and human rights'. Movement along this more enlightened path in 1989 and early 1990 was hampered, however, not only by the traditional concern of African leaders that more pluralistic political institutions would entail dangerous divisions along ethnic lines, but by the persistence of local and regional conflict which drew political energies away from institution-building.

The Francophone states of Africa, normally considered the most stable on the continent, were particularly besieged during 1989 and early 1990. Now that both the West African and Central African banks that manage the CFA franc are showing overdrafts, the viability of the CFA franc (which is automatically convertible to the French franc) is being called into question. Leaders in the states closest to France (Senegal, Côte d'Ivoire, Gabon and others) were put under pressure following public demonstrations to allow for greater democracy. Francophone Africa felt most strongly the dual pressures of the events of 1989: a fear that in hard times bilateral aid to them would be 'diverted' to Eastern Europe; and a challenge to the style of personal rule which may have made dealings with France easier, but was now seen by domestic opinion as unjust.

Throughout much of sub-Saharan Africa, the fear of coups and the distrust of neighbours occupied the attentions of heads of state. The President of Chad, Hissène Habré, survived a coup attempt in April 1989, and, despite his deep suspicions of Libya's Col Gaddafi, encouraged his foreign minister to negotiate an end to the territorial dispute over the Aouzou Strip which has been one of the principal causes of conflict between the two countries during the last 16 years. In August the foreign ministers of Chad and Libya agreed in Algiers to submit the border dispute to arbitration by the International Court of Justice if they were unable to agree within a year. The chances of this happening seemed slim at the end of 1989 as Habré continued to accuse Gaddafi of using a Libyan military presence in Sudan's Darfur Province to destabilize his regime. In this context, Habré ensured his re-election for seven years with 99.03% of the vote in December.

In April a minor grazing rights dispute between Senegal and Mauritania escalated, leading to riots in Dakar where unemployed Senegalese looted the premises of Mauritanian shopkeepers. By the end of the month, Senegalese were returning from Nouakchott complaining of racial attacks by Mauritanians, but, more significantly, over 15,000 black Mauritanians were effectively expelled from the largely Arab country on the pretext of a 'repatriation agreement' with Senegal. In the next few months many thousands more were shunted across the border in both directions. By July, and despite the diplomatic efforts of France and a number of North African states as well as a visit from the UN Secretary-General to the region in June, the dispute continued with each president accusing the other of fomenting dissent. In January 1990 there were reports of artillery exchanges across the border. Senegal also had problems during the year with its confederal partner Gambia, whose leader, Sir Dawda Jawara, has been growing anxious about his country's junior status in the Senegambian confederation. He grew even more nervous when in August Senegal withdrew its 1,400 soldiers stationed in Gambia to help protect Jawara's regime.

In Nigeria, which is preparing for the return to civilian rule by 1992, Gen Babangida decided in October 1989 that none of the 13 political parties which had sought government recognition met the government's criteria, since all appeared to have ties with 'old power structures'. Nigeria's military leader therefore resolved to create two parties himself, one left-of-centre – the Social Democrat Party – and the other right-of-centre, the National Republican Convention, in the hope that suitable members could be found for both from across the tribal spectrum. This did not prevent Babangida from being widely accused in January 1990 of garnering more personal power, having dissolved in 1989 the Armed Forces Ruling Council which since 1985 had had collective responsibility for Nigeria's governance. In the north, Christians who rioted in Kaduna, Jos, Yola and Bauchi in early 1990 were more particularly concerned by the fact that the most important ministerial portfolios were going to Muslims and that their own status in Nigerian society was in decline.

Liberia's President Samuel Doe brutally repressed the National Patriotic Forces rebel movement which on 24 December launched attacks in Nimba Province. Thousands of refugees poured into neighbouring Côte d'Ivoire over the New Year. In late January Doe announced that funds earmarked for the registration of voters prior to elections scheduled for 1991 would have to be used to finance the army's campaign against the rebels. Reports of summary executions and the killing of hundreds of unarmed civilians in Nimba Province will probably entail a decline in US economic assistance to Liberia.

The first West African country openly to respond to the changes taking place in the USSR was Benin, which in September announced economic reforms including the privatization of banks, reductions in the size of the civil service and openings for foreign investment. In early December Marxist-Leninist ideology was officially rejected, yet despite this thousands of people took to the streets in the capital Porto Novo calling for the resignation of President Mathieu Kerekou. While France will no doubt play a role in encouraging liberalizing moves in Benin, officials were concerned by the challenges to other Francophone regimes traditionally closer to France. Gabon's President Omar Bongo, who on 23 February 1990 announced the dissolution of the Gabonese Democratic Party and the creation of an allegedly more broadly based social democrat grouping, was besieged by strikes the following week by people calling for more genuine moves away from the one-party state. In both Niger and Côte d'Ivoire, soldiers were called out in February to put down demonstrations by students calling for multi-party democracy, while in Senegal, one of the few African countries with a true multi-party system, eight opposition groups demanded the resignation of the president and the holding of genuinely free elections.

In January 1990 President Joachim Chissano of Mozambique presented a liberal draft constitution which proposed direct elections for the presidency and the People's Assembly, as well as the right to strike and to own property. This proposed liberalization helped to accelerate the prospects for formal negotiations with Afonso Dhlakama, leader of the rebel group RENAMO. For much of 1989, Mozambican church leaders and the presidents of Kenya and Zimbabwe had sought to bring the rebels and the government together for peace talks. These various attempts failed precisely because of Chissano's insistence that the rebels formally recognize the government of Mozambique, which they refused to do. Even though the proposed constitutional reforms do not go as far as the rebels would like, the atmosphere has been improved.

These developments have meant that in early 1990 Mozambique was about as far down the road towards serious negotiations in its civil war as Angola, where the divisions between President dos Santos and UNITA leader Jonas Savimbi remained acute. Neighbouring Namibia surprised most observers in 1989 as its Constitutional Assembly successfully drafted a constitution following free and fair elections which were arguably the most liberal on the continent. The transfer of full independence on 21 March 1990 thus appeared to have been achieved under more propitious auspices than could have been expected at the beginning of the process. The Republic of South Africa, which in February 1990 released the world's most famous political prisoner, Nelson Mandela, seemed committed to accelerating a process of reform, mindful, but no longer fearful, of the risks of a backlash. Yet in the Horn of Africa, the many problems for which Africa has become tragically notorious – civil war, autocratic rule, clan politics, economic mismanagement and natural disasters increased in intensity.

REAL HOPE IN SOUTH AFRICA

The winds of change which toppled the *anciens régimes* in Eastern Europe began to swirl through South African politics in 1989. By early 1990 they had reached hurricane strength, sweeping away most of the old assumptions about the stubborn longevity of the apartheid state. On 2 February 1990 President F.W. de Klerk announced that the African National Congress (ANC) and the South African Communist Party (SACP) would be released from their bans, the death penalty would be suspended and reviewed, the State of Emergency would be lifted, and Nelson Mandela would be released after 27 years in prison. South Africans of all colours and persuasions faced a dramatically altered political landscape, including the prospect of a negotiated end to more than 300 years of white domination at the southern tip of Africa.

The change was the result of a unique confluence of events in South Africa and abroad, and the boldness of two men – President de Klerk, emerging from the right wing of the ruling National Party, and Nelson Mandela, regarded throughout the world as the icon of the black liberation struggle. Despite their disparate backgrounds, both appeared willing to break out of the vicious cycle of conflict, repression and isolation in which South Africa had long been trapped and to explore the path of peaceful negotiation. It is a high-risk venture for both sides, threatened equally by white right-wing extremists who regard de Klerk as a traitor to the white cause and black radicals who scorn compromise in the belief that 'people power' and the politics of mass protest will secure the transfer of power to black majority rule without the need for negotiation.

The picture is complicated by the fact that the far-right is over-represented in the South African Police which, long charged with implementing apartheid and state repression, is having acute difficulty adjusting to its new role in a more tolerant climate. Renewed township unrest and police violence could thus feed off each other, narrow the negotiating space and imperil the delicate climate of confidence which both men are trying to maintain before the negotiating process starts in earnest. Should the process collapse, de Klerk could be swept from power and South Africa might resort once again to the full panoply of state repression, thus condemning itself to even greater isolation by an outraged world.

The risks for the ANC in abandoning the mantle of a liberation movement and adjusting to the role of a political party after 30 years in exile are equally high. If it makes too many compromises it risks losing support to more extreme black movements such as the Pan Africanist Congress, and it courts conflict both with ambitious internal political and trade union leaders unwilling to accept a junior role in the negotiations and with the more extreme elements in its own not wholly united ranks. An unwillingness to compromise, however, could cost it much international support – especially from Western leaders who have said that once negotiations begin, both sides will be subject to the same tests of good faith. Knowing the risks, within three weeks of de Klerk's speech the ANC had nevertheless agreed to meet the South African government to discuss the willingness of the latter to meet the ANC's remaining preconditions for negotiation.

Although it is expected that the 'talks-about-talks' phase could last months, there was nevertheless hope that the real constitutional negotiations leading to a non-racial South African democracy could be under way before the end of 1990. There was also widespread acceptance that the new constitution will have to be in place in five years – when the life of the present parliament runs out, thus obviating the need for another white election and thwarting the right-wing Conservative Party's drive to win power and turn back the clock.

Getting from There to Here

One key factor which helped to transform the South African political landscape in 1989 was the forced resignation of the previous president, P.W. Botha, and the subsequent loss of power by the dominant security establishment. Another was the decision by the Soviet Union, preoccupied with Eastern Europe and its own domestic troubles, to withdraw from regional conflicts and to wind down its support of Third World liberation movements. Following the Angolan–Namibian accord, it stepped up contacts with Pretoria and pressed the ANC to seek a political settlement in South Africa. The ANC's subsequent loss of its Angolan bases and of Soviet and Eastern bloc arms supplies compelled it to examine negotiation as a serious option.

Other forces were also at work. The changes in Eastern Europe and the resultant marginalization of Africa, deprived of its role as a surrogate zone for East–West conflict and as a recipient of aid and investment, meant that a number of Front-line and Francophone states began to urge a way out of the South African impasse that would increase their access to the only fully industrialized economy in Africa. Dr Kenneth Kaunda of Zambia led the way in orchestrating contacts between the ANC and representatives of the South African white establishment and in subjecting the ANC to subtle pressure – including the scaling down of its Lusaka-based operations and the removal of its Zambian-based military cadres to Tanzania.

Nevertheless, 1989 began unpromisingly, with South Africa in the frozen grip of President Botha. Having exhausted his earlier capacity for meaningful reform, he had retreated behind the barricades of his all-powerful office. Deaf to the rumblings of discontent in his own ruling National Party, increasingly contemptuous of parliament, he appeared willing to listen only to the advice of those in the security establishment – the so-called securocrats – who had come to dominate all major policy-making institutions by the end of his 11-year rule.

The result was a baleful combination of domestic repression, increasing international isolation and economic recession. In January 1989, President Botha suffered a mild stroke which appeared to open up the possibility of his resignation. Instead, he resigned as National Party leader but insisted on retaining the presidency, thus plunging the country and his party into a major constitutional crisis. The 1984 tricameral constitution had created the preponderant office of State President, but had failed to separate the executive and legislative branches of government, or to build in the checks and balances normally characteristic of democratic systems. Nor was the president elected by popular vote, but owed his office in effect to the parliamentary caucus of the majority party in the white House of Assembly.

On 4 February 1989 when President Botha severed the connection between himself and his party, he left F.W. de Klerk, his successor as NP leader, with responsibility, but no power. At the same time it became imperative for the government, faced with a threat from the far-right Conservative Party which could only strengthen as the months passed, to call an early general election before its mandate ended in early 1990.

On his return to office in March, Botha faced down a revolt by his cabinet and the NP's provincial leaders, but finally called a general election for 6 September, indicating however that he intended to remain as president until the following year. But he was skilfully outmanoeuvred by de Klerk who first united the cabinet and caucus, then capitalized on Botha's increasingly irrational behaviour to force a showdown. Botha was driven ignominiously from office three weeks before the general election. Behind the bizarre constitutional crisis, however, de Klerk – who had won the leadership of the NP with a bare nine-vote majority over his nearest rival, Finance Minister Barend du Plessis – was beginning to fuel a tentative optimism with openly reformist speeches which called for 'drastic and speedy change' and contrasted oddly with his hitherto cautious and conservative views.

Sceptics, however, remained unconvinced and their doubts were reinforced by de Klerk's insistence on 'racially defined groups' – long interpreted as code for a prettified form of apartheid and the maintenance of a white veto – as the basis for any power-sharing formula with black South Africans. Their doubts were not assuaged by the mid-year publication of the National Party's Five Year Plan for constitutional change. For the first time the NP embraced the concept of sharing power with black South Africans, but while the written plan was long on rhetoric, it was conspicuously short on specifics.

Nonetheless it formed the basis of the government's election campaign, which abandoned the security scare tactics of previous elections for an openly reformist platform. De Klerk had taken a clear decision not to try to win back Afrikaner hardliners who were defecting in growing numbers to the far-right Conservative Party. With some liberal Afrikaners and many English-speaking South Africans voting for the newly formed Democratic Party – an amalgam of the Progressive Federal Party, the Independent Party and the National Democratic Movement – the government lost heavily in the September election to both the left and the right, sacrificing 29 seats and reducing its overall majority to 26.

The Conservative Party, its hopes fuelled by widespread disaffection with the government's economic mismanagement, by endemic inflation and by disclosures of government corruption, did less well than it expected and its performance, under ideal conditions, suggested that there was a ceiling to its support. Despite the NP's losses, de Klerk was not frightened away from his reformist track. Instead, by adding the left-of-centre DP's vote to his own, he insisted that 68% of white voters had provided him with a clear mandate for change. He had also won valuable endorsement on the eve of the election from President Kaunda, following a meeting between the two leaders in Livingstone.

Creating a New Climate

De Klerk, who had also impressed Prime Minister Thatcher and Chancellor Kohl during mid-summer visits to the UK and the FRG (a proposed visit to Washington was called off when a significant number of US Congressmen objected) lost little time in making good his promise to create a new climate in South Africa. A parliamentarian with little love for the security establishment, he made no secret of his determination to re-introduce the principle of parliamentary accountability into South African politics. One of his first acts was to dismantle the National Security Management System, a nationwide control structure devised by and operating under the State Security Council (SSC). The Council, on which the military and police chiefs were heavily represented, had been elevated by Botha into a super-cabinet. Its first defeat came during Botha's illness when the cabinet overruled the SSC and ordered the release of 700 detainees who had gone on hunger strike.

By the end of 1989, the SSC had been stripped of most of its policy-making powers, which were shifted back to the cabinet. In a symbolic move, de Klerk also stripped the presidential office of most of the military pomp introduced by Botha. By November the arch-hawk in the Defence Ministry, Gen Magnus Malan, had been persuaded to announce the end of South Africa's destabilization policies: the South African Defence Force (SADF), he said, would no longer engage in cross-border raids and saw no reason to support anti-government groups in neighbouring countries. This assurance was subsequently accepted by Mozambique's President Joaquim Chissano during a meeting with de Klerk. South Africa, he stated, was no longer supporting the anti-Frelimo insurgents, RENAMO.

In January the SADF revealed that more than 2,000 military personnel were to be dropped as part of a wide-ranging series of moves to trim the defence budget. Other cuts included the closing of bases and the withdrawal from service in several types of aircraft. Finally, de Klerk announced a reduction of the period of compulsory military service for white males from two years to one. It is significant that much of the money thus saved was allocated, in the 1990 budget, to a massive increase in government spending on black education, health, housing and welfare. In addition, Finance Minister du Plessis announced the establishment of a R2-bn fund to be administered by community leaders and the private sector for blacks.

De Klerk may have clipped the wings of his military hawks but one invention of the Botha years – the misnamed Civil Cooperation Bureau (CCB) – emerged to haunt the first months of his presidency. Rumours of the existence of a South African 'death squad' had been circulating since the killing of a civil-rights activist, David Webster in May, and the murder in Windhoek of a white SWAPO lawyer, Anton Lubowski in September. When a former member of the 'death squad' disclosed its activities to the press before quitting the country, de Klerk was forced to act. He appointed a Provincial Attorney General, Tim McNally, to investigate the claims, but then bowed to pressure and appointed a judicial commission of inquiry. Evidence before the commission revealed that the CCB, although staffed by policemen, had been a lavishly funded secret SADF operation. Although Gen Malan denied ordering the killings, the disclosures appeared to signal the end of a political career more in tune with another era in South African politics.

De Klerk's most important challenge to his security chiefs came within days of the National Party's return to power. The Mass Democratic Movement (MDM) – an alliance of extra-parliamentary political organizations and trade unions formed after the banning of the United Democratic Front the previous year – had launched a mass defiance campaign, echoing the campaigns of the 1950s which had led to the banning of the ANC in 1960. Aimed at the desegregation of hospitals, beaches and transport facilities, the protests had initially been treated by the authorities with a degree of restraint. On election night, however, scores of protesters in the Cape Peninsula were victims of police violence.

In an unprecedented move which reversed more than 20 years of government policy, de Klerk ignored the advice of the 'securocrats', announced that the government would no longer object to peaceful and orderly protests and gave permission for a march in Cape Town – in which some 35,000 people took part – to protest against the police action on election night. Later, at a secret, but widely reported meeting, he told 500 police chiefs that the government would no longer burden the police with the enforcement of apartheid laws, and that the police should henceforth dedicate themselves to combating crime. Protest marches, at which the still formally banned ANC flag was openly displayed, took place without incident in Johannesburg and Pretoria, the apartheid heart of South Africa, and soon became a part of everyday political life in most of the major urban centres.

De Klerk also announced the desegregation of South Africa's beaches and the abolition of the Separate Amenities Act which Conservative town councils had used to maintain 'petty apartheid' in municipal parks, libraries and other facilities. But it was his tolerance of mass protest and the release of eight long-serving, high-profile political prisoners, including ANC leader Walter Sisulu, that set the scene for South Africa's sudden transformation. By making it clear that he would not use the police to suppress peaceful dissent, de Klerk had effectively unbanned the ANC. Within days of Sisulu's release, a mass rally was held under the banners of both the ANC and the hammer and sickle of the SACP, and attracted a crowd estimated at 70,000. If de Klerk was living up to his promise to create a climate conducive to negotiations, Sisulu, whose release had been designed to test the waters in advance of the freeing of Nelson Mandela, met his side of the bargain. This and subsequent ANC rallies did not spill over into urban violence.

Moving to Negotiations

It also became increasingly evident that de Klerk and his government were not acting unilaterally. The strategy had been orchestrated in consultation with Nelson Mandela. Members of the cabinet, led by Justice Minister Kobie Coetsee, had been holding talks with Mandela for some three years. Initially these had revolved around Mandela's refusal to accept a conditional release. Later, however, they developed into exploratory negotiations. Transferred from Pollsmoor Prison to a warder's bungalow at the Viktor Verster Prison, Mandela held court with a widening circle of political leaders, and remained in touch both with the Pretoria government and the ANC in exile.

The basis of the consultations appears to have been Pretoria's need to get off the hook on which it had impaled itself – its insistence that the ANC publicly renounce 'the armed struggle' before it could enter into negotiations. A major breakthrough came in the last days of President Botha's rule when Mandela, still a prisoner, sought and was granted an interview with the President. In his account of the meeting, Mandela said: 'I would like to contribute to a climate which would promote peace in South Africa'. This phrase was echoed by de Klerk when he called on all those who had, 'for historical or other reasons excluded themselves from peaceful processes' to take part in negotiations. All that was required, he said, was a commitment to peaceful solutions. The government was thus no longer seeking the formal renunciation of the 'armed struggle' which the ANC's military wing, isolated in its camps in northern Tanzania, was finding increasingly difficult to maintain.

There were, however, strong indications that the government's willingness to negotiate and Mandela's strategy had caught the ANC leadership in exile – already weakened by the stroke which had incapacitated its president, Oliver Tambo – off guard. Only a few months earlier senior spokesmen of the ANC and the MDM had said that there was nothing to negotiate about – and were demanding the simple transfer of power to the majority.

They certainly did not believe that the government would meet the ANC's preconditions which were later endorsed in the Harare declaration by the Organisation of African Unity, by the Non-Aligned Movement and still later, in a form modified through UK and US efforts, by the UN General Assembly. The declaration, which was an attempt by the ANC to regain some of the diplomatic high ground, called for the release of all political detainees, the unbanning of all organizations, the lifting of the State of Emergency, the withdrawal of troops from the townships and free political activity.

Mandela, after discussions with cabinet ministers and some MDM leaders, successfully re-shaped the strategy, accepting that the call for a straight transfer of power was unrealistic. Certain MDM leaders, including trade union leader Cyril Ramaphosa, responded by trying to de-mythologize him, but the revolt was short-lived. Sisulu and the other six former ANC prisoners who had consulted with Mandela before their release, travelled to Lusaka in January. At a National Executive Committee meeting there, the Secretary-General and Acting President of the ANC Alfred Nzo admitted that President de Klerk was pushing ahead with reform at a speed designed to outmanoeuvre those fighting against apartheid. He also admitted that the ANC was no longer able to conduct the armed struggle in any meaningful way. The Executive subsequently confirmed its commitment to negotiations and said it would agree to a mutual suspension of hostilities once the preconditions of the Harare declaration had been met.

The culmination of this *rapprochement* came in de Klerk's speech at the opening of parliament when the President, who had had talks with Mandela in December, met most of the conditions. The two exceptions were his refusal to release prisoners jailed for acts of violence and his agreement to only a partial lifting of the State of Emergency.

Both of these points will be bargaining counters in the talks about talks. De Klerk, who remains concerned about the endemic internecine violence in Natal between UDF and *Inkatha* supporters which has claimed some 2,000 lives, is thought likely to lift the State of Emergency in exchange for promises of an end to urban violence. There is also a strong indication that the government is prepared to amend the Internal Security Act under which several returning exiled ANC leaders could be indicted and to contemplate a general amnesty. The ANC has already made it clear that it will not demand the removal of the remaining pillars of apartheid – the Group Areas Act and the Population Registration Act, which colour-codes each South African at birth – as a precondition for talks and that these issues could be put on the negotiating agenda.

De Klerk, once the arch-exponent of 'group rights', has already said that he is not ideologically obsessed with the concept, and the cabinet's chief constitutional negotiator, Dr Gerrit Viljoen, has subtly changed the language from 'group rights' to minority protection. Meanwhile, as the pace of change accelerates, major cities such as Johannesburg and Cape Town have desegregated their facilities, and the Group Areas Act has been effectively abandoned as they apply to be declared 'free settlement areas'. Viljoen has also announced key changes which could take much of the apartheid sting out of the Population Registration Act.

In his 2 February speech, de Klerk insisted that he sought a universal franchise and the end of white domination, and that he would enter the negotiations with an open agenda. Mandela, who since his release has been exquisitely careful not to depart from the ANC line on the need to maintain both sanctions and the principle of armed struggle (perceived to be the organization's only remaining weapons in its diplomatic armoury), has nevertheless stressed the need to calm the fears of the white minority.

The stage has thus been elaborately and carefully set by both sides. Key questions, however, remain about the nature of the drama that is about to unfold. Few are more important than the negotiating mechanism itself. The ANC favours a constituent assembly elected through nationwide elections. The government claims that this will undermine the sovereignty of parliament, which must continue to govern until the new constitution is in place. It also believes that a constituent assembly elected by a universal franchise would guarantee the ANC victory before negotiation. The government favours negotiations between the major actors – itself and the ANC – who together will decide to invite representatives of other constituencies, such as Chief Mangosuthu Buthelezi, the President of *Inkatha*. The resulting constitution could then be tested by a national referendum.

Although it remains silent on its 'bottom line', observers believe that the government's plan encompasses a lower house elected on a 'one man, one vote' basis, with an upper house made up of different interests and groups to safeguard minority rights. Both sides are agreed on the need for a bill of rights. The ANC is said to favour a Namibia-type of constitution, a concept designed to elicit international support.

Other questions involve the role of the SACP which enjoys a great deal of symbolic support among black South Africans, and the threat to the ANC by the Pan Africanist Congress which, with its slogan of 'one settler, one bullet', has rejected negotiations out of hand. Although it has been weak in exile, its rejectionist stance could appeal to the radical youth. It could benefit from defections from the ANC should the negotiations break down.

Equally important is the economic debate which has been unleashed following Mandela's adherence to the old ANC line of the nationalization of the commanding heights of the economy. ANC opinion is divided on the issue, but the leadership of black trade unions and their economic advisers include dedicated Marxists who openly reject the recent lessons of Eastern Europe. However, after a prolonged and heated debate with Moscow, SACP Secretary-General Joe Slovo in February 1990 finally revised his previously Stalinist line, enthusiastically embraced the Gorbachev reforms and accepted the need for a multi-party democracy. This will not necessarily allay fears in the South African and international investment community that a black majority government will feel compelled to introduce a command economy which will cut off investment and stifle growth – with potentially dire effects for the whole of southern Africa.

A More Hopeful Future

Central to the success or failure of all future negotiations remains the character of the two men who are destined to face each other across the negotiating table. Nelson Mandela was elected Deputy President of the African National Congress in Lusaka in March 1990 and, given Tambo's ailing health, will probably be elected President at the organization's national congress planned for 16 December in South Africa. De Klerk, on the other hand, has admitted that he does not expect to still be President of South Africa in five years' time. Whether or not he will succeed in negotiating himself out of office, depends crucially on his motives. Mandela, Kaunda and other leaders who have met him accept his integrity. Equally important, however, is whether or not he is simply a skilful crisis manager, or a victim of the momentum which he has created. Evidence is accumulating, however, that de Klerk, who lays great stress on the need for logical consistency, knows precisely what he is doing.

When he took office, he was brought to the conclusion that South Africa faced a critical choice. The government could continue to deploy the full panoply of military and police power to suppress black dissent. White South Africa could thus maintain its hold on power, but at the cost of increasing unrest, isolation and economic impoverishment. He would have been willing to accept that price if it offered a long-term solution to the country's problems. Persuading his cabinet and party caucus that further repression would not produce solutions, he seized on the fact that the white electorate had, through its endorsement of the National Party's vague Five Year Plan, accepted the principle of real power sharing with black South Africans. Moving carefully and deliberately out of the cul-de-sac into which 42 years of Nationalist policy have led South Africa, F.W. de Klerk has unceremoniously and publicly dumped the apartheid ideology. Instead, describing a 180 degree ideological turn, he now pursues the ideal of a common nationhood shared by all South Africans in what he terms 'the new South Africa'.

His immediate rewards have been the *de facto* relaxation of international sanctions pressure. But observers are convinced that he is playing for higher stakes: a continuing role for white South Africans in a non-racial democracy. It is a high-risk venture which could easily be derailed by radical elements in both white and black ranks. Those risks will increase with time. The pressure is therefore on both sides to make sufficient compromises to reach agreement as quickly as possible. Although there can be no certainty that the compromises will be successful, what is certain is that the process begun by Mr de Klerk is irreversible.

NAMIBIA: THE ROAD TO INDEPENDENCE

Namibia's 16-month transition to independence began with uncertainty, and moved through a period of growing suspicions and armed violence, before culminating in an astonishing move towards national reconciliation. Former enemies were eventually able to find common ground as Namibians to write a constitution and create democratic institutions apparently congenial to the territory's unique political and ethnic realities.

The process was set in motion by the December 1988 peace accords, under which South Africa agreed to implement UNSC Resolution 435 in exchange for the withdrawal of Cuban troops from Angola. Resolution 435 called for a cease-fire between South African forces and the South West Africa People's Organization (SWAPO), the nationalist movement that had waged a low-level guerrilla war for two decades against South African rule in Namibia. The accords also called for free elections under UN supervision to a Constituent Assembly, followed by South African troop withdrawal and national independence. An Administrator-General (A-G) appointed by South Africa would administer the territory during the transition period. The UN Secretary-General's Special Representative, Martti Ahtisaari, arrived in Windhoek with a small staff on 31 March to oversee the process.

Suspicions and Violence

The cease-fire was to begin on 1 April 1989. By then South African forces were to be restricted to their bases, SWAPO guerrillas confined in their camps north of the 16th Parallel in Angola, and a UN force of 7,500 troops deployed along the Namibia–Angola border to monitor the cease-fire. In mid-January, however, the first hitch occurred when the UN Security Council decided to cut the UN military force from 7,500 to 4,650 as an economy measure. African and other Third World states vigorously opposed the cut, fearing it would open the door to South African manipulation of the elections. Dissension over this issue, including a threat to withhold funding of the entire peace-keeping operation, was finally resolved in mid-February by a face-saving agreement to carry 7,500 troops on the books while deploying only 4,650 in Namibia, but the dispute had delayed the dispatch of the UN team, known collectively as the United Nations Transition Assistance Group (UNTAG). By the 1 April cease-fire date only 1,000 UN troops had arrived, and none had been deployed to their monitoring-posts.

The three months prior to the cease-fire had been remarkably calm, with virtually no military action along the border. During the night of 31 March and the early hours of 1 April, however, it exploded in the bloodiest fighting of the 23-year bush war as some 1,200 to 1,500 heavily-armed SWAPO guerrillas, who were trying to slip into Namibia before the cease-fire came into effect, clashed with Namibian mechanized police units. As the fighting spread along a 200-mile front, resulting in hundreds of dead and wounded, South Africa threatened to repudiate the settlement and unleash its troops from their bases.

The crisis deepened during the next week as South Africa rejected a suggestion by UN Secretary-General Pérez de Cuéllar that SWAPO infiltrators be disarmed and allowed to remain inside Namibia, and SWAPO rejected an amnesty offer. On 8–9 April, senior officials from Angola, South Africa and Cuba held an emergency meeting at Mt Etjo Safari Lodge in Namibia to defuse the crisis and revive the collapsing settlement. With US and Soviet observers present, a joint statement – the Mt Etjo Declaration – was agreed which proposed safe passage for SWAPO infiltrators to UN-manned assembly points, with the UN then escorting them back to their Angolan bases. SWAPO President Sam Nujoma, under pressure from Angola, immediately agreed. But a few days later, fearing that South African forces would attack his men as they approached the assembly points, Nujoma ordered them to bypass UNTAG and return directly to Angola.

Several deadlines for SWAPO's return north of the 16th Parallel passed and were extended before South Africa accepted, on 19 May, that peace had been restored and that the run-up to independence should resume. The crisis had lasted seven weeks. But its successful resolution confirmed, as earlier events had not, that all three signatories to the peace accords – Angola, South Africa and Cuba – were committed to carrying out its terms, and that, if only under pressure, SWAPO would now acquiesce in them.

The April incursion failed to achieve SWAPO's aim of establishing a permanent guerrilla presence inside Namibia prior to the elections. By intensifying mistrust of SWAPO's intentions and raising the level of mutual hostility between SWAPO supporters and opponents, its costs were considerable. It also led to local criticism, largely unrealistic, that UNTAG had failed to prevent the incursion, or to prevent police reprisals, including the killing of many SWAPO guerrillas.

By June there was growing violence and intimidation in northern Namibia, home of the majority Ovambo people who are the principal source of SWAPO's support. With the South African Army confined to its bases, the A-G relied on a police unit known as *Koevoet* (crowbar) to conduct counter-insurgency operations aimed at searching out SWAPO guerrillas and arms caches left over from the April incursion. *Koevoet's* brutality towards the civilian population brought about widespread protest strikes and boycotts in Ovamboland. In this atmosphere the UN's programme for repatriating 42,000 Namibian refugees from Angola and Zambia ran into problems when pro-SWAPO returnees refused to leave reception centres for their home villages for fear of *Koevoet* reprisals. Although the A-G, Louis Pienaar, was reluctant to disband *Koevoet's* 3,000 men, he bowed to a virtual ultimatum in late September from Ahtisaari, demobilizing *Koevoet* and dismantling its command structure under UN monitors. In the meantime, as UNTAG military and police units deployed in greater numbers in the north, the violence diminished and the refugees returned home.

Another hitch occurred in June, when SWAPO released 204 ex-supporters from its detention camps in Angola, where they had been held on suspicion of being South African spies. They accused SWAPO of torturing detainees and keeping them in underground cells, and alleged that another 1,000 remained in detention. A special team of UN officials sent to Angola in October to investigate these claims was unable to substantiate the charges, but was nevertheless unable to find any trace of 315 of the alleged 1,000 detainees. This unresolved issue remains a bone of contention between SWAPO and the ex-detainees.

On 21 July the A-G issued a draft electoral law which Ahtisaari found seriously flawed. Its proposals for verifying and counting ballots were exceedingly complex, and appeared to be an open invitation to intimidation and fraud. Among several shortcomings, each voter's registration number would appear on his ballot, and ballot boxes would be opened three times before counting took place. Later in July the A-G issued draft procedural rules for the Constituent Assembly which also were unacceptable to Ahtisaari, since they gave the A-G authority to veto any of its actions, to adjourn the Assembly, and to assume other functions that Resolution 435 had vested exclusively in the Assembly itself.

Ahtisaari, who had no authority to nullify acts of the A-G, used his only weapons: the spotlight of publicity, and his ultimate authority to declare South Africa in violation of the peace accords and to suspend the settlement process. Pienaar appeared to be under pressure from Pretoria to exercise as much authority as he could over the transition process. But in mid-October, following a detailed denunciation of the draft electoral law by Pérez de Cuéllar and a prestigious group of US observers, the A-G issued a final decree which met all of the Secretary-General's criticisms. Similarly the A-G's final proclamation on the Constituent Assembly published two weeks later restored that body's authority to set its own rules, draft and adopt a constitution, fix a date for independence, and establish a government.

Serious problems also affected the massive programme of voter registration, which was carried out by the A-G's office and monitored by UNTAG. UN monitors reported widespread irregularities in professional and administrative conduct by local registrars, particularly in heavily pro-SWAPO Ovamboland, where they appeared to be making deliberate errors. The A-G responded to UNTAG complaints by authorizing UN personnel to re-register those with faulty forms and by extending the registration period. By the end of the period, 701,000 Namibians out of an estimated total population of 1.3 million were registered; an astonishing achievement in a far-flung, mostly rural territory three times the size of the United Kingdom.

During the run-up to the November elections distrust between opposing political groups bred fears that the elections would be rigged. Such fears were fed by dark rumours of political plots and by pre-election manoeuvring. Anti-SWAPO groups in Namibia and South Africa, for example, took advantage of a loophole in the election law to launch 'Operation Namibia', in which South African citizens who met the minimum residence requirements in Namibia were bussed in from South Africa to register as voters. Despite rumours that this was a massive campaign to place 100,000 South African whites on the rolls, only 4,300 actually registered. During this period South African military officials in Namibia spawned a succession of rumours that SWAPO forces were about to invade the territory again. A few days before the election, South Africa's Foreign Minister announced that an intercepted UN radio message reported that hundreds of SWAPO guerrillas were infiltrating Namibia to disrupt the elections. When UN officials were able to prove that the 'intercept' was a deception, an embarrassed South African President was forced to backtrack.

Sporadic incidents of violence continued during the pre-election period. In August a local UNTAG office was attacked with rockets, and on 12 September Anton Lubowski, a prominent lawyer and SWAPO member, was gunned down by right-wing extremists. In October the UN Secretary-General increased UNTAG's police contingent from 1,000 to 1,500. By early November calm was restored to the turbulent north, and almost no incidents of violence were being reported.

Encouraging Signs

Between 7 and 11 November 670,000 Namibians – 96% of those eligible to vote – cast ballots to elect a Constituent Assembly. SWAPO won 57% of the vote: enough to give it 41 of the Assembly's 72 seats, but well short of the two-thirds needed to adopt a constitution constructed to its own specifications. The Democratic Turnhalle Alliance (DTA), a multi-ethnic coalition backed by South Africa, won 29% giving it 21 seats, while two smaller coalitions – the United Democratic Front and the right-wing white party Action Christian National, won four and three seats each. Single seats were won by each of three minor parties. Not surprisingly, given Namibia's history of officially-encouraged ethnic separateness, ethnicity was a major factor in voting patterns. Thus SWAPO, a party dominated by the Ovambo, won 80% of the vote in Ovamboland but carried no other district.

By and large the election results were neither surprising nor disappointing. SWAPO won a majority as most observers had predicted; the DTA was pleased that its widespread image as a creature of the South African government did not prevent it making a respectable second-place showing; and SWAPO's opponents were relieved that SWAPO fell short of the two-thirds majority that would have enabled it to dictate a constitution.

When the 72 delegates to the Constituent Assembly gathered for the first time on 21 November, there was serious concern that enmity and distrust among the parties might block agreement on a constitution. Those concerns evaporated, however, as the delegates went to work.

SWAPO made the first, and unexpected, conciliatory move by proposing that the Assembly adopt as a 'frame of reference' a set of constitutional principles negotiated by the UN and South Africa in 1982. Essentially they incorporated a bill of individual rights, stipulations that Namibia would be a unitary, democratic state with three branches of government, an independent judiciary, election by universal suffrage, and a constitution as the supreme law of the land. The motion was unanimously adopted, along with a motion that individual articles of the constitution would be decided by a simple majority, with a two-thirds vote needed to adopt the constitution as a whole. There had been fears that SWAPO would reject a bill of rights.

The major issues still in dispute were electoral representation, with SWAPO favouring single-member constituencies and the others proportional representation; the role of the president – whether it should be executive, as sought by SWAPO, or ceremonial as most other delegates wished; and the legislature, which SWAPO proposed be unicameral and the others bicameral. Agreement was reached on all these issues by late January. Future electoral representation will be by proportional representation, there will be an executive president, but his powers will be limited. The legislature will be bicameral, but the second chamber – the House of Review – will only be established within the next few years, after local and regional elections have been held. The Constituent Assembly also agreed that the constitution can be amended only by a two-thirds vote by both chambers.

The work of the Constituent Assembly showed that the promise and responsibilities of independence which lay at the end of their deliberations were sufficient incentives for the delegates to put aside petty politics and personal animus and to act together as Namibians with a collective stake in the outcome. Nujoma, who was once described by a South African prime minister as 'conceived in Communist sin in Moscow', showed a surprising pragmatism as SWAPO approached the governing of the country. He urged white civil servants to stay on, gave encouraging signs to Namibia's private businessmen and farmers, and voiced the need for private foreign investment. Former SWAPO guerrillas and Namibians who served in the South African armed forces will be merged into a new national army, to be trained by British officers. On 21 March, in the presence of leaders from around the world, the South African flag was lowered in Windhoek and Sam Nujoma was sworn in as the first president of an independent Namibia.

ANGOLA: PEACE EFFORTS FAIL

The 1988 peace accords did not address Angola's internal conflict, in which UNITA (*União Nacional para a Independência Total de Angola*), a national movement backed by the US and South Africa, has been waging a punishing guerrilla campaign against the Marxist MPLA

(*Movimento Popular de Libertação de Angola*) government for more than a decade. Yet the accords set in motion a series of events which directly affected the course of that conflict in 1989–90.

Most immediate was the termination of South African aid and intervention in support of UNITA. That, together with the withdrawal of all South African forces from Namibia by late November 1989, meant that UNITA could no longer call on South African forces to help defend its guerrilla 'capital' at Jamba against assault by government troops, nor to fill its fuel and weapons requirements. But the accords held new risks for the Angolan government as well. Under the settlement terms 31,000 of Cuba's 53,000 combat troops left Angola during 1989, thereby reducing the defensive shield which they had provided for Angola's cities and major installations. The remaining 22,000 Cubans are to leave in stages by 1 July 1991.

In the early weeks of 1989 Jonas Savimbi, UNITA's astute and charismatic leader, showed acute concern that the peace accords would leave him militarily vulnerable and diplomatically isolated. President Bush took the unusual step of writing to the guerrilla leader in early January to reassure him of continuing US military and diplomatic support. The US also announced that it would withhold recognition of the MPLA government until it entered into direct talks with UNITA. In late January, however, US officials disclosed that they had opened talks with the government about establishing low-level diplomatic representation in Luanda. By then 30 Western aid donors had agreed to extend $95m in development aid to the government, and Angola's President dos Santos had called for a cease-fire and a political solution in which Savimbi would have no role and his guerrillas would lay down their arms in exchange for a promise of reintegration into the society without prosecution.

Savimbi rejected the offer in early February, and vowed to launch a general offensive against the MPLA regime. He then went to Washington seeking weapons, fuel and other supplies to replace the $80m in annual military assistance which South Africa had previously provided.

During February and March Savimbi also made a number of conciliatory gestures. He 'acceded' to a request from President Houphouët-Boigny of Côte d'Ivoire not to launch a general offensive earlier than July so as to give African leaders time to arrange peace talks. Since it is doubtful that UNITA would have been ready to launch such an offensive any earlier, this was not much of a concession. Savimbi also offered to talk with the leaders of Zaire, Zambia and Zimbabwe and officials from Belgium about reopening the Benguela Railway. The Benguela, a Belgian-owned line that crosses the waist of Angola to connect the economically vital copper mines of Zaire and Zambia with the Atlantic Ocean, has been effectively closed by UNITA guerrilla operations for most of the past decade. A meeting with African heads of state would of course have enhanced Savimbi's status as a legitimate African leader with important bargaining clout, but his offer had no takers.

In March Savimbi suffered a public relations setback when a former British supporter, Fred Bridgeland, who had earlier written a book praising Savimbi's leadership, charged him with torturing dissidents and burning suspected witches. These allegations, which remain unproven, did not diminish support from the US, which agreed to supply UNITA with $30m in military and related aid in 1989.

Meanwhile the US was actively pressing African leaders, particularly Zaire's President Mobutu, to make a concerted effort to bring UNITA and the government to the negotiating table. Dos Santos attempted to pre-empt these efforts in mid-May, when he hosted a meeting of African leaders from Zaire, Zambia, Zimbabwe, Mozambique, Congo, Gabon and São Tomé and Principe to rally support for his plan to grant amnesty to UNITA members. The participants named themselves the Committee on Reconciliation. At that meeting dos Santos agreed for the first time to negotiate a settlement: a major gesture that the US and USSR had been pressing him to make for more than a year.

Mobutu quickly seized the opportunity to bring dos Santos and Savimbi together. Fifteen African heads of state, plus representatives from two others, met in Gbadolite, Zaire on 22 June 1989 to try to mediate the Angolan conflict. No face-to-face negotiations took place between dos Santos and Savimbi. But after a day of indirect talks Mobutu announced that the two Angolans had agreed to a cease-fire starting the next day and to continue negotiations over such issues as the integration of UNITA members into the government and armed forces.

Within 24 hours, however, the accord, of which no written record was made, began to unravel as participants expressed sharply differing views over its terms. Zambian President Kaunda announced that Savimbi had agreed to go into exile, but an aide to Mobutu said Savimbi would enter a coalition government. Mobutu repudiated both statements the next day, saying 'there is nothing about exile', and asserting that Savimbi would not join the government. UNITA denied that Savimbi had agreed to go into exile, but also rejected Mobutu's assertion that he had agreed to UNITA's integration into the government.

Talks between government and UNITA representatives began at the end of June, as agreed at Gbadolite. Angola broke off the discussions almost immediately, however, charging UNITA with violating the 24 June cease-fire. Little fighting had occurred in the first half of 1989, as both sides waited to see what the African-led peace initiative might bring. In July–August the cease-fire collapsed completely in the face of renewed hostilities on a large scale by both sides. Angola claimed that 200 soldiers and 300 civilians had been killed in UNITA attacks during those months. By then the government had launched a major offensive in the south-east.

African leaders made several attempts in the second half of 1989 to restore the cease-fire and to arrange talks between the government and UNITA. President Kaunda convened a second meeting of the Committee on Reconciliation's eight heads of state on 22 August, but

Savimbi declined to attend. The participants reiterated their understanding that the Gbadolite accord provided for Savimbi's agreement
to voluntary retirement, which Savimbi quickly denied. South Africa's
President de Klerk, who was particularly concerned that the renewed
fighting might lead Cuba to suspend the withdrawal of its forces from
Angola, undertook a diplomatic *démarche* of his own in late August. He
met Mobutu in Zaire, and held a confidential two-and-a-half hour discussion with Savimbi in Pretoria, followed by a meeting with Kaunda
at Victoria Falls. No communiques were issued following these talks,
although Savimbi's defensive remarks to the press after his meeting
with de Klerk indicated that he was under pressure to agree to
negotiations.

Despite pressure from African leaders and the US, however, Savimbi
refused to attend a summit meeting of the Committee on Reconciliation convened by Mobutu on 18 September. In a gesture of contempt
for Mobutu and the Committee, he sent his press aide instead. A few
weeks later, Savimbi visited the US to lobby for more aid and to urge
the US to mediate the conflict in place of Mobutu, demanding the
latter's removal from the process. By then it was clear that the Mobutu
initiative had collapsed. The antipathy between Savimbi and Mobutu
had reached the point where Mobutu was obstructing the flow of US
arms to UNITA through Zaire, and was calling for an end to US support
for Savimbi. The Bush Administration none the less reaffirmed its support for Mobutu's mediation and made clear its intention to take no
direct part in peace initiatives.

Savimbi meanwhile put forward a five-point peace plan, calling for a
cease-fire, direct talks, release of political prisoners, free elections monitored by the UN, and UNITA's participation in an interim government to draft a new constitution. The US, however, called only for a
cease-fire and face-to-face talks between the two sides without
preconditions. The government continued to reject direct negotiations,
nor was it prepared to enter again into a cease-fire.

A flurry of diplomatic activity in October involved senior diplomats
from the US and South Africa in separate meetings with Angolan and
UNITA representatives in Paris. No announcement followed the three-
day talks, but UNITA spokesmen later confirmed that no breakthrough had occurred. The only hints of any loosening in the deadlock
were a UNITA statement in early November that Savimbi would
remain in Jamba and not take part in an interim government, followed
by an equally ambiguous statement by the government that it had never
insisted on Savimbi's exile, but only on his withdrawal. In late November the government's intransigence was publicly challenged by
Angola's Catholic bishops, who called for peace and free elections.

President dos Santos called a third summit meeting of the eight-
nation Committee on Reconciliation for 27 December, saying it
should 'clarify and redefine' Mobutu's role as mediator. The meeting
was postponed at the last minute, however, without explanation, and

rescheduled for 12 January 1990. That, too, was postponed to the end of January after Mobutu announced that he was too busy to attend. When January ended without a meeting, the African peace initiative appeared dead.

The failure of this third meeting to bring dos Santos and Savimbi together, however, was less attributable to inept diplomacy, though that played a significant role, than to the intransigence of the two sides, particularly the government. In 1989–90 Angola's economic, diplomatic and military prospects appeared brighter than at any time in the past decade. In September it was accepted as a member of the IMF and World Bank, and its $6.3-bn debts to the USSR and the West were rescheduled for long periods. In December the government announced the receipt of a $110-m credit from Brazil and the signing of three new oil exploration contracts by Sonangol, the state-owned oil company.

There were also grounds for the dos Santos regime to feel more optimistic about its chances of dealing a crippling military blow to UNITA and thus to be in a better position to set terms for any future negotiations. The closure of South Africa's Namibian bases and the departure of its remaining troops from Namibia in late November removed the threat of South African military intervention in support of UNITA. Meanwhile, the remaining Cuban combat forces of more than 23,000 continued to provide Angola's major towns and cities with a defensive shield against UNITA attack, thus freeing government troops for offensive operations. Further, while both superpowers were urging reconciliation, neither the US nor the USSR could be seen to cut off the flow of weapons to their respective clients.

Thus by late December the dos Santos government was pressing the war against UNITA in the south-east, where some 15,000 to 20,000 Angolan and UNITA troops on each side were engaged in mechanized combat across a broad and fluctuating front. In late January 1990 Angolan forces claimed to be in control of Mavinga – an important position from which air attacks could be launched against Savimbi's capital and main base at Jamba, 150–200 miles to the south-east. According to US officials, however, UNITA had largely blunted the initial assault and the fighting around Mavinga was continuing.

The most alarming development occurred in late January, when five Cuban soldiers were killed and four wounded in a UNITA attack in central Angola. Cuba announced a temporary suspension of its troop withdrawal pending a satisfactory explanation. Up to that time UN monitors of the withdrawal reported that the process was ahead of schedule.

Thus in the early weeks of 1990 the situation in Angola was, as a senior South African diplomat ruefully observed, back to square one, with each side prepared to continue the fighting in hopes of eventually dealing the other a sufficiently heavy blow to extract favourable terms for a settlement. But neither side seemed able to continue the war indefinitely on the scale and intensity of the December–January fighting: the government's supply lines to the south-east are long and vulnerable, while Savimbi lacks heavy armour and artillery. When the fighting once again subsides, it seems likely that outside mediation by European states, perhaps Portugal, may be the next step in attempting to bridge the deep gulf between the MPLA government and UNITA. Should the latest government offensive fail, it is possible that elements in the MPLA leadership will press the government to explore seriously the terms on which a settlement might be reached.

CONFLICT IN THE HORN OF AFRICA

For many years, the political landscape in the Horn of Africa has been as shifting and unpredictable as the desert sands. In addition to ever-changing interstate alignments, the region has been plagued by serious and long-running civil wars, drought, famine, refugees and economic mismanagement. All these problems afflicted the region in 1989, and political instability and uncertainty intensified. By early 1990, however, there were signs that some of the warring parties in the region were belatedly exploring peaceful means of settling their disputes. Former US president Jimmy Carter was at centre-stage, chairing negotiations.

From the mid-1970s the Horn had been a cockpit of superpower confrontation. Until 1977, the United States had provided military and economic aid to Ethiopia, in large part to counter Soviet aid and influence in neighbouring Somalia. The Ethiopian government, however, came under the thumb of the Marxist leader Lt Col Mengistu Haile Mariam and had begun to turn to the USSR for military aid. Moscow, whose influence in Ethiopia soared as a result, tried to maintain its position in Somalia as well; Washington, however, withdrew its support from Ethiopia and tilted towards Somalia, even though that country had invaded Ethiopia. The switch in superpower realignments was completed in 1980 when the US agreed to give Somalia military and economic aid in return for access to its facilities by US military forces.

That the region is of little intrinsic strategic value has been demonstrated by the loss of interest in the area by Washington and Moscow, following the recent improvement in US–Soviet relations. The US, in protest against human-rights violations, has cut aid to Somalia, while the USSR has also reduced its presence in Ethiopia. The extraordinary changes in Eastern Europe have also affected the situation in Ethiopia, for it is now very unlikely that East Germany, which has in the past sent advisers to that country, will continue to do so.

As the superpowers have become less of a factor in the equation, the recent increase in involvement by some Middle Eastern countries is likely to provide a new source of uncertainty in the region. Libya, which had supported Ethiopia's leader Mengistu a few years ago, has recently begun to send arms to the Somali regime. Sudan, which until a few years ago enjoyed good relations with Egypt and the US, has now improved relations with Libya and Iraq, and is seeking aid from them.

The most significant development in the area in recent months, how-ever, has undoubtedly been Israel's re-establishment of diplomatic relations with Ethiopia. Israel appears interested mainly in securing the emigration of an estimated 17,000 Falashas (Ethiopian Jews) to Israel, but it is also concerned that the possible secession of Eritrea (which occasionally receives Arab aid) could turn the Red Sea into an Arab 'lake'. Whatever its actual motives, Israel is likely to serve as a source of support for Mengistu in the months, or perhaps years, to come.

The rapidly changing and complex political developments in Somalia, Ethiopia and Sudan make predictions of the prospects for stability difficult. In 1989, each of the three countries faced deep-rooted political and security problems, with a significant challenge being mounted to each regime. In addition to these difficulties, all three countries had severe economic problems. Somalia and Sudan were overwhelmed by unprecedented shortages of food and other essential goods. The wars in Ethiopia hampered what little economic progress the country had made and brought industry to a virtual standstill. In addition, the three countries' debts were mounting rapidly, and Ethiopia faced the grim prospect of another famine in 1990.

Somalia

Somalia's relative stability in the past two decades has depended on President Mohammed Siad Barre's skilful manipulation of both dom-estic and external politics. He had maintained power by balancing and playing on clan interests and rivalries; by 1989, however, it had became increasingly obvious that he no longer had either the ability to balance those interests or the vision to lead the country quickly out of its politi-cal quagmire. There appeared to be three major threats to Siad Barre: the clan and family; opposition groups, especially the Somali National Movement; and the economy.

For many years President Barre's power base has been the military and his Marehan clan; in 1989 both pillars of power appeared shaky. The military – which until recently was dominated by the Ogadeni Somalis – has been plagued with many defections and several mutinies, especially in garrisons around Kismayu in southern Somalia. The exist-ing disquiet in the army was exacerbated by a cabinet reshuffle on 31 January 1989, when the then Defence Minister, Maj Gen Adan Abdullahi Noor, himself an Ogadeni, was demoted and given the Social Affairs portfolio. Noor's successor was former Attorney General, Hussein Abdurahman Matan, also an Ogadeni, the first civilian to head the Defence Ministry since Barre seized power in October 1969. In April, Noor was subsequently dropped from the cabinet in another reshuffle, and following disturbances in the capital, Mogadishu, in July, he was placed under house arrest.

Noor's tribulations added to the unrest that had appeared in the armed forces when Barre agreed to the Somali–Ethiopian Accord of April 1988. The agreement, which called for the demilitarization of the

Somalia: Ethnic Groups

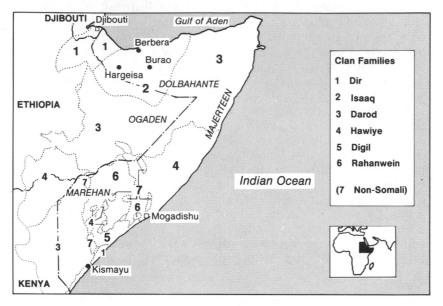

border and effectively amounted to Somalia's renunciation of its claims
to the Ogaden region of Ethiopia, was resented by Ogadenis in the
Somali Army. They felt their homeland had been abandoned and
directed their anger towards Barre. Thus, although the President's son,
Maj Gen Maslah Mohammed Siad, is Chief of Staff, Barre apparently
can no longer count on the loyalty of the military.

The President might have expected to count on his clan, the
Marehan, for support, but in 1989 some of its prominent members
openly criticized Barre for concentrating power in his family. Apart
from Maslah, members of the family in senior positions include three
sons-in-law: Gen Ahmed Suleiman Abdallah, the Deputy Secretary-
General and a member of the five-man Politburo of the Somali Socialist Revolutionary Party; Gen Mohammed Said Morgan, Minister for
Public Works; and the Chief of Police, Abdirahman Abdi Hussein. The
President's half-brother, Abdulrahman Jama Barre, was the Foreign
Minister until the cabinet reshuffle of January 1990. Even though there
are political differences within this tight family circle, other senior
members of the government from the Marehan clan have felt that the
President's family has isolated him from the rest of the community and
they have asked him to step down. At the same time, other clans –
especially the numerically powerful Isaaqs, Ogadenis, Hawiye and
Majerteenis – each linked to an opposition group – seek more of the political plums and have called for democratic reforms.

The Isaaq-dominated Somali National Movement (SNM), formed in
1981 and nurtured by the Ethiopian government, has been waging civil

war in northern Somalia since mid-1988, when, as a result of the Accord of April 1988, it was forced to leave its Ethiopian bases. It managed to take several towns, including Burao and the provincial capital, Hargeisa, but by early 1989 government troops had recaptured the major towns. The movement's fighting force increased substantially in mid-1989 when it was joined by a number of defecting Somali troops.

The Barre government's other internal challenges came from the Hawiye-based United Somali Congress and the Ogadeni-based Somali Patriotic Movement (SPM). The SPM, which surfaced publicly only in 1989, occupies the countryside near Kismayu. In November, the SPM and the SNM announced their intention to co-ordinate their policies and carry out joint military operations, but there has not as yet been any sign of joint actions. The ideological orientations of these opposition forces are similar to Barre's, and their political objectives – other than the overthrow of Barre – are vague.

The internal fighting resulted in further flights of refugees into Djibouti, Kenya and Ethiopia in 1989, and appeared to strain Somalia's relations with Kenya, Djibouti and the office of the United Nations High Commissioner for Refugees (UNHCR). One issue that particularly concerned the UNHCR was the arming of some refugees in the camps, which it claimed was a violation of the basic principles governing refugee status. There was also disagreement over the Somali government's inflation of the number of refugees in the country, in hopes of obtaining more support from the international community. A third bone of contention concerned the route through which relief supplies for the refugees could be brought into Somalia. The UNHCR sought to bring food supplies to refugees in northern Somalia overland from Djibouti, while the Barre government insisted that all consignments destined for refugees were to come by sea through Berbera, although the war made this impossible. These disagreements culminated in Somalia's expulsion of the UNHCR representative in March. Although that action might have assuaged Barre's wounded *amour propre*, it did nothing to improve the situation for refugees; UNHCR food supplies ended in late November 1989 and had not been resumed by early 1990.

Somalia's poor human-rights record in 1989, especially the activities of its security forces in northern Somalia and in Mogadishu in July, seriously affected its relations with outside powers. On several occasions, the armed forces went on the rampage, burning villages, bombing civilian targets, planting land-mines, poisoning wells and sometimes deliberately destroying livestock. A recent report by Africa Watch estimated the number of civilian deaths, from May 1988 to December 1989, at between 50,000 and 60,000, most of them from the Isaaq clan. The US government, which until recently was Mogadishu's main supporter, decided in mid-1989 to discontinue military assistance to Somalia until human rights were genuinely observed. Other Western donors, except Italy, also cut back aid.

The reduction in aid was a devastating blow to an economy already crippled by corruption, mismanagement and an external debt of more than $2bn. The Somali shilling, devalued several times in the past few years, has very little value even in comparison with the currencies of neighbouring Ethiopia, Djibouti and Kenya. Despite the fact that by early 1990 the state of the economy had become one of Siad Barre's major problems, he appeared to be doing very little to try to improve it.

President Barre tried to mollify his critics in 1989 and 1990 in various ways. He offered to talk to the rebel leaders anywhere, but none was either ready or willing to accept the offer; the SNM position is that it cannot negotiate while Barre is still in power. Barre also made some concessions in August: he promised to establish a multi-party system and to hold free elections by the end of 1990. In November, he established a six-member constitutional committee. On 9 January 1990, Barre dissolved his cabinet, accusing it of failure to address the country's problems effectively, but the new cabinet that was announced on 15 February was like a game of musical chairs; some of the players merely swapped places. The major casualty was the President's half-brother, Abdulrahman Barre, a former foreign minister with obvious presidential ambitions, who was dropped. Neither this measure nor the others which had gone before it mollified Barre's critics, who argued that he was offering too little, too late.

Ethiopia

The Ethiopian government, facing tremendous pressure from both within and without, had a dreadful year in 1989. The internal challenge came from the Eritrean People's Liberation Front (EPLF) and Tigrayan People's Liberation Front (TPLF); both made such extensive military gains that the government was forced to begin peace negotiations. In addition, an attempted coup in May by senior military officers who opposed President Mengistu's war policies and wanted the government to turn its attention instead to the country's appalling economic conditions, suggested that Mengistu's grip was weakening. Externally, the Soviet Union, which has provided Ethiopia with about $5-bn worth of arms since 1977, has begun to pressure the regime to reach a political accommodation with domestic political forces.

Mengistu's power base has always been the military, and the coup, although easily countered, was a warning that his support in the armed forces was no longer fully secure. The coup began in the Ground Forces headquarters near Addis Ababa and spread to the Air Force headquarters at Debre Zeit, the Second Army at Asmara in Eritrea, and the Eastern Sector headquarters at Harar. But the plotters apparently assumed that their action would automatically be supported by other sections of the armed forces and did not even attempt to take the radio and television stations or to close the airport and control other communication facilities in the capital. Indeed, they were completely unprepared for the stiff opposition they encountered from pro-Mengistu officers, especially the well-equipped palace guards.

By all accounts, the coup was poorly staged and managed, and most of the officers involved were either executed or held in custody pending trials which started in early 1990. Yet the attempt signalled not only that Mengistu's pillar of power in the armed forces had been weakened, but that the Ethiopian military was seriously divided over the handling of the wars in Eritrea and Tigray. That Mengistu – who was on a visit to East Germany – managed to rally loyalist forces suggested that some sections of the military preferred his leadership to that of untested military officers. Some accounts have suggested that the EPLF, by immediately giving encouragement to the plotters, aroused suspicions among some officers that the plotters might be in collusion with the separatists. This would have harmed the attempt, for although most Ethiopians do not appear to like Mengistu, they are strongly opposed to Eritrean secession and to the TPLF-led fighting in Tigray Province.

In the wake of the coup, the Ethiopian parliament (*Shengo*) voted unanimously on 5 June 1989 to start talks with the EPLF; the only precondition Mengistu advanced was that the Ethiopian government would not discuss the possibility of Eritrean independence. The EPLF, which was formed in 1971 and which operates from bases in Sudan and in some parts of Eritrea, has been waging a relentless struggle for independence. With the prospect of meaningful talks dangled before it, however, the movement has become more flexible in expressing its aims. On 29 June its Secretary-General, Issaias Afewerki, said in London that he was ready to open unconditional talks.

Preliminary negotiations between the Ethiopian government and the EPLF started in September 1989 in Atlanta, Georgia, under the aegis of former US president Carter. Although Carter was acting in his private capacity, he had the full support of the Bush Administration. The Atlanta talks were followed by further discussions in November in Nairobi, Kenya. Both sets of talks were on procedural matters, most of which were resolved in Nairobi where former Tanzanian president, Julius Nyerere, was chosen as co-chairman of the negotiations; but one of the observers suggested by the EPLF, the United Nations, declined to be involved on the grounds that the Eritrean problem was an internal Ethiopian affair and not a cross-border dispute between member states.

When the negotiations began the EPLF was in a strong military position; it controlled western Eritrea and held several small towns in eastern Eritrea. Having acquired control over such a large area, the EPLF decided to negotiate to avoid becoming overstretched or occupying areas it could not defend.

One incentive for the Ethiopian government in these talks was that a resolution of the conflict might put the country back on the path of economic progress. Already one of the poorest countries in the world, Ethiopia has been forced by the war to devote about 50% of the budget to military expenditure, thus seriously retarding industrial and economic development. The end of the Eritrean war might also lead to an improvement in relations between Ethiopia and Sudan, since Eritrean guerrillas would no longer be operating from bases in Sudan.

It has become clear that the Soviet Union has been pressing President Mengistu to seek peaceful solutions to his country's internal conflicts. The USSR has reportedly given Ethiopia notice that it might not continue to supply it with as many arms after their current agreement expires in 1991. Moscow's dissatisfaction with Mengistu stems partly from his failure to take Soviet advice to negotiate an end to the war, and partly from a perception that most Ethiopian troops were so poorly trained that they could not make effective use of Soviet arms; Eritrean guerrillas who captured Soviet arms made better use of them. The Soviet Union has apparently concluded that these wars are very expensive and unwinnable. As part of its effort to promote negotiations, the Soviet Deputy Foreign Affairs Minister in charge of African affairs, Yuri Yukalov, met with the EPLF's Afewerki in London in early July.

Just as the Ethiopian government was negotiating with the EPLF, the TPLF, which is effectively controlled by the pro-Albanian Marxist-Leninist League of Tigray, mounted a serious attack against Ethiopian forces. The TPLF had been formed in the late 1970s and operated almost entirely in Tigray Province; in 1981 it played a leading role in the formation of the Amhara-dominated Ethiopian People's Democratic Movement and in 1989 merged with it to form the Ethiopian People's Democratic Revolutionary Front (EPDRF). This manoeuvre was an obvious attempt by the TPLF to change its image of a purely provincial ethnic organization and to gain some support from the Amhara, the leading tribal grouping in Ethiopia. There has never been any doubt, however, that the TPLF, by virtue of its superior military force, has been the senior partner in the alliance and has controlled the EPDRF agenda.

The TPLF, which for much of the year co-ordinated activities with, and received assistance from, the EPLF, scored a number of military victories against the Ethiopian forces in Tigray Province in 1989. Intense guerrilla fighting forced the Ethiopian troops to withdraw from Tigray in February, thereby enabling the TPLF to occupy the entire province. By the end of the year, it had penetrated parts of Wollo, Gondar and Shoa Provinces, and it tried to use these successes to present itself as an alternative to the Mengistu regime. This claim might have been more believable if it had not become clear that some of the military successes in late 1989 and early 1990 had been exaggerated. Outside Tigray Province, the TPLF used 'hit-and-run' tactics and did not hold any territory or town for long. Threats that the TPLF would take the war to Addis Ababa were also exaggerations.

By moving out of Tigray and spreading its fighting force thinly in neighbouring provinces, the TPLF appeared to have overreached itself. Although aware that it did not have the capability to engage in full confrontation with government forces, the TPLF made several unsuccess-

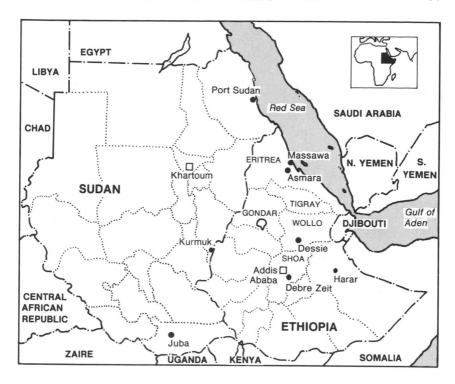

ful attempts in late 1989 to capture Dessie, the capital of Wollo Province; nor was the TPLF able to disrupt the strategic Addis Ababa–Assab highway. Given these limitations, its demands for an immediate cease-fire, the restoration of democratic rights, dismantling of security organizations, expulsion of foreign forces, and the establishment of a provisional government made up of all political organizations were unrealistic. The government did agree to talks with the TPLF which began in Rome in early November 1989 under the chairmanship of Alberto Solera, the Italian ambassador to China, but they ended inconclusively. Further talks started in Rome on 20 March 1990.

That Mengistu was beginning to feel the weight of internal and external pressure was reflected in the reforms he set forth in a six-point report to the plenum of the Workers' Party of Ethiopia (WPE) on 5 March 1990. He suggested changing the name of the party to the Ethiopian Democratic Unity Party, expanding it to accommodate opposition groups, and recommended a gradual shift from a centrally-planned to a market economy. The EPLF and TPLF, however, immediately dismissed the proposals as a transparent effort by Mengistu to buy more time.

The war in Eritrea and Tigray, and a lack of sufficient rain during the year, led to crop failure in both provinces. With harvests only 15% of what was expected, Ethiopia's already severe economic problems were

seriously exacerbated. According to international aid agencies, more
than four million Ethiopians, especially those in the war-ravaged north,
faced starvation unless the international community took urgent steps
to avert the crisis.

By early 1990, it was estimated that Ethiopia needed about 600,000
tonnes of food in addition to the 450,000 tonnes it needs annually to
cover its chronic food deficit. Even with the international community
supplying these amounts of food, it was clear that many thousands
would starve. As has been true for many years, both the Ethiopian government and some of the guerrilla groups with which it continues to
fight were not loath to use food aid to advance their political goals.
Without 'open road' channels throughout the country, some of the
starving population are unable to reach main distribution centres in
either government-controlled or guerrilla-held areas. The situation has
been worsened by the rebel seizure of the port of Massawa. Some relief
agencies attempted to surmount this problem by using cross-border
operations from Port Sudan to deliver food to the needy in Eritrea and
Tigray, but this resulted in long delays, and long delays meant disaster
to hundreds of thousands who needed food immediately.

Sudan

Major developments in Sudan in 1989 revolved around the search for
two apparently elusive political goals: an effective and democratic government in Khartoum; and a peace formula to end the seven-year-old
war in southern Sudan. The successful pursuit of both goals depended
on agreement about the future of the *Sharia* (Islamic law), but by early
1990 no agreement had been reached and both goals appeared as far
from attainment as ever.

The three-year-old coalition government of Prime Minister Sadiq
al-Mahdi – which at various times included Mahdi's own Umma Party,
the Democratic Unionist Party (DUP), the National Islamic Front
(NIF) and minor southern parties – had proved ineffective and indecisive on the interrelated and sensitive questions of Islamic law and
the civil war with the Sudan People's Liberation Army (SPLA) in the
south. The government's inability to reach even limited agreement was
hardly surprising for the three major parties that made up the coalition
hold virtually irreconcilable views on these problems, particularly that
of the future of the *Sharia*. For instance, the SPLA and the DUP had
signed a draft peace agreement in Addis Ababa in November 1988
under which the *Sharia* would not be extended to the largely Christian
south, but Mahdi's refusal to endorse it prompted the DUP to withdraw
from the government in December 1988.

Early in 1989, the Sudanese Army, which had been frustrated by a
lack of equipment and by the military victories achieved by the SPLA,
tried to make the Prime Minister re-examine the role of Islamic law and
end the civil war. It sent him a memorandum on 20 February demanding, within one week, an end to the government's pro-Libyan policy,

the formation of a broad-based government, the reduction of Islamic fundamentalist influence, and initiatives to end the civil war. Mahdi, as usual, hesitated, but after meeting with Armed Forces Commander-in-Chief Gen Fathi Ahmed Ali on 2 March, he accepted the general thrust of the memorandum. As a result, the NIF left his government. Mahdi had to form another coalition government with the DUP and the minor southern parties, which he managed to do in March. This vacillation on his part made any positive action impossible. Not only was the government unable to operate with any efficiency, he appeared to be seeking compromise with other political parties as an end in itself, rather than as a means to some larger end.

The era of indecisiveness came to an abrupt end on 30 June when the Mahdi government was overthrown in a military coup led by Brig Gen Omar Hassan al-Bashir, who promoted himself to Lt Gen a few days later. Bashir claimed that he had no affiliation with any political party, but some of his colleagues on the 15-member Revolutionary Command Council (RCC) for National Salvation – the military junta – have sympathies with the Islamic fundamentalist NIF. Mahdi's cabinet had been set to debate, and probably would have ratified, the SPLA–DUP draft agreement on 30 June, and a date had been fixed for a constitutional conference to bring together all political forces and groups to discuss the nation's future, when the coup took place. The emerging peace process was effectively derailed when Bashir rejected the November 1988 initiative, ignored the February demands of the armed forces and relied heavily on NIF supporters. The circumstances under which the coup took place, and the general orientation of its leaders' policies, especially their determination to preserve the *Sharia* at any cost, strongly suggests that Bashir's move was a fundamentalist-inspired one, partly designed to prevent the suspension of Islamic law.

The NIF, by far the best-organized and most highly-motivated political party in the country, saw the Bashir coup as a turning-point in the civil war, hoping that the army would either negotiate from a position of strength or launch an offensive. The NIF leader, Hassan al-Turabi, had warned in March that his party would use extra-parliamentary power to frustrate any government policy designed to limit the scope or operation of Islamic law.

The coup ended any hopes the Sudanese might have had not only of making their multi-party system function effectively, but also of reverting to secular politics. Bashir suspended the constitution, detained the former prime minister and other leading politicians, dissolved the National Assembly and banned political parties, trade unions and civil newspapers. In July, he also dismissed more than 400 officers; they apparently had been involved in planning a secularist coup.

The RCC claimed that one of its reasons for intervening in politics was to work out an acceptable formula for ending the civil war with the SPLA, which is led by Col John Garang. The SPLA, established in 1983, has its main base in, and gets support from, Ethiopia (in retaliation for

Sudan's offer of sanctuary to the EPLF). Its aim has been to unite Sudan under a secular government, but it is a distinctly southern group which draws almost all of its support from that region, although the southern Sudanese are not a homogeneous group and small tribes fear domination by the numerically preponderant Dinka, who also control the SPLA. Thanks to the apparent political chaos in the government, and the confused signals emanating from Khartoum, the SPLA's morale, arms supplies and international profile were at an all-time high.

Bashir's peace plan envisages a federal arrangement which was reflected in the scheme drawn up in Khartoum during September and October at a conference organized by the Committee for National Dialogue (which was boycotted by the SPLA). The main thrust of the government's proposal is that any unit in the federal system would be free to opt out of Islamic law, and further appears to suggest that Sudan could be partitioned, but the *Sharia* would not be abolished. If implemented, the scheme effectively means that Khartoum and the rest of the more developed northern Sudan would be governed by the *Sharia* and any non-Muslim southerner who worked there would be subject to these laws. This was unacceptable to the SPLA, which reiterated its demand for the abolition of the *Sharia*, the formation of an interim government, the lifting of bans on political organizations and the reconstitution of the Sudanese army to include SPLA troops. It also has called for the termination of Sudan's military pacts with Egypt and Libya.

In spite of their wide differences, representatives of the SPLA and the Bashir regime held a first unsuccessful round of preliminary peace talks in Addis Ababa in August 1989. Another round of negotiations was convened in Nairobi in December, under the aegis of Jimmy Carter, but they too broke down because of the basic disagreement on the *Sharia*.

In November 1989, just a few weeks before the Nairobi meeting, serious fighting broke out between government troops and SPLA guerrillas around the town of Kurmuk, ending the cease-fire which both sides had observed since May. Government forces were driven out of the town, but recaptured it a week later. During most of the rest of the year fighting was sporadic, but it intensified around Juba in January 1990, forcing UN and other international relief teams to withdraw.

Bashir's other most pressing internal challenge has been the deteriorating economic situation. Sudan's economic problems include shortages of food, petrol and other essential commodities, declining agricultural production, drought and more than one million refugees from Uganda, Ethiopia and Chad. The economic measures Bashir attempted, especially his determination to maintain rigid price controls, were simplistic and appeared designed basically to address the symptoms rather than the roots of the country's economic malaise. Ignoring the fundamental mechanisms of the market, the government forced traders at gun point to sell goods at unrealistically low prices, leading inevitably to considerable losses and widespread hoarding, and virtually paralysing the economy. Greater shortages developed as a result of an almost complete halt in imports by private businesses because of the strict foreign currency regulations introduced in July. With these shortages, inflation by the end of 1989 was running at 100% per year, far ahead of any of the neighbouring countries.

Sudan's external debt, which reached $13bn in 1989, was one of the largest in sub-Saharan Africa. The IMF, the World Bank and some Western creditors accordingly demanded severe belt-tightening.

More of the Same to Come?

In early 1990, the security situation in the three countries of the Horn shows no sign of settling down. Each of the existing governments is in a weakened state, but there are as yet no clear signs that the opposition forces are either strong or united enough to topple any of them soon. Indeterminate negotiations continue, some under international auspices, but the lines of cleavage are so great that it is difficult to see any of them succeeding.

In Sudan, government forces are still engaged in fighting with SPLA guerrillas. Although neither side appears to be able to overcome the other, the course of the talks they held in 1989 indicates that there is little basis for a renewal of negotiations between them. Bashir's power base appears to be very fragile; since he relies increasingly on Islamic fundamentalists for support, there seems scant opportunity of replacing the system of Islamic law. With the Sudanese economy still in a shambles, and little reason to expect further foreign investment, the possibility of meaningful recovery is remote. At best, the government and the country seem condemned to merely stumble along.

The government in Ethiopia is also still at war with its internal opposition: the TPLF and other opposition groups which include the Oromo Liberation Front (OLF) and the Afar Liberation Front (ALF). The OLF and ALF, formed in the mid-1970s, were virtually moribund until late 1989, when they realized that Mengistu was under great pressure. The EPLF, which has maintained a cease-fire since mid-1989, appears to be collaborating with, and lending support, to the minor liberation movements. Here, too, the outlook for negotiations is poor, and the future of the government looks shaky. It may be able to hang on, but it will neither govern much of the country nor be able to provide much of a life for those still under its control.

Somalia remains economically poor and politically unstable. It also looks as if it has been abandoned by the international community. The strength of the Somali opposition groups is difficult to gauge and some of their claims very hard to verify. They still talk of plans to form a united front, but they seem to distrust and hate each other as much as they do the government. Unless they can bury their differences at least temporarily, Barre's instinct for survival may continue to astound many observers throughout the coming year.

The Middle East

During 1989–90 relations between the Arab states of the Middle East were dominated by the questions of Lebanon and of the Palestinians – both situated symbolically and literally at the heart of the Arab world. This preoccupation was hardly surprising in the aftermath of the Gulf War. Iran was turned in on itself, as various factions sought to wrestle with the problems of economic reconstruction and of the succession to Ayatollah Khomeini. Iraq was also focusing much of its attention on the legacies of the war, as its President tried to demonstrate that he could deliver a future that made the sacrifices of the past worthwhile. Consequently, the elimination of the last vestiges of constitutional order in Lebanon and the continuation of the *intifada* in the West Bank and Gaza thrust these issues upon the attention of the other Arab states.

With this shift in attention and concern came a shift in the centre of gravity of Arab politics – or, perhaps more accurately, formal recognition of a shift under way for some years. This was the reassertion of Egypt's relative pre-eminence in Arab affairs and the simultaneous decline and isolation of Syria. The Casablanca Summit of May 1989 formally marked this reversal of roles. Egypt was re-admitted to the Arab League, having finally overcome Syria's hitherto adamant insistence that it must first renounce the peace treaty it had signed with Israel. The Summit endorsed the Egyptian-supported efforts of the PLO to pursue a strategy aimed at eventual direct negotiations with Israel, despite Syria's vocal opposition to these efforts and to the PLO leadership. Even on Lebanon, where Syria's military strength gave it a veto over Arab League moves to impose any solution, Syria's intransigence led to the setting up of a committee which, by including Saudi Arabia, had some effective leverage over Syria. Here too, Egyptian backing of this initiative by the traditionally cautious Saudi government appears to have emerged from a developing Egyptian–Saudi relationship and a mutual concern that the antagonisms of the two Ba'athist regimes in Syria and Iraq should not dominate and disrupt inter-Arab relations.

The re-establishment, by the end of 1989, of formal diplomatic relations between Syria and Egypt could ironically be portrayed, therefore, as Syria's attempt to break out of its own isolation. Syria seemed to be acknowledging that it needed strong regional allies at a time when its own strategies had been frustrated. The alliance with Iran had not succeeded in dislodging Syria's hated rivals in Baghdad. On the contrary, it had led to widespread condemnation and sanctions in the Arab world, as well as to a series of complications in its dealings with Western states concerned about Iran's role in supporting acts of terrorism. The cultivation of a rival leadership to Arafat within the PLO had also failed to produce anything but condemnation of Syria's attempt to divide and weaken the movement during this crucial juncture. The stalemate in Lebanon was no more amenable to Syrian direction than it had been during the past ten years. Instead, it kept alive regional suspicions, actively fuelled by various players in the Lebanese game, about Syria's long-term intentions in the country.

Militarily, economically and politically, Syria was being weakened by other developments within the region and beyond. Regionally, Syria relied more than ever on financial aid from the Gulf states to shore up its own crumbling economy. Its government was further perturbed by the implications of Iraq's bid for regional military supremacy. Internationally, the changes in the USSR and in its policies towards the Middle East made Syria's quest for strategic parity with Israel unachievable and weakened its political position in the Arab world. By the beginning of 1990, therefore, recognition of this situation by the government in Damascus was leading to a relative *rapprochement* with Egypt. This was not a recognition of Egyptian pre-eminence, so much as a belief that, in the changed patterns of Middle Eastern politics emerging during 1989–90, Syria would have more to gain by co-operating with, than by confronting, Egypt. Similar views appear to have been widespread. They contributed to Egypt's diplomatic successes during the year and to the consequent shift in the region's centre of gravity. It was a shift of considerable symbolic importance, but it was also one which was caused by very practical considerations of states' interests by most Arab governments.

LEBANON AND THE ARAB WORLD

With regard to Lebanon, the symbolic aspect was evident in the increasing concern that the continued existence of two governments in the country – one led by General Michel Aoun, a Maronite Christian and the other by Selim al-Hoss, a Sunni Muslim – represented a step closer to the point where the fragmentation of Lebanon would be given formal recognition. Although the actual fragmentation of Lebanon had been developing for some years, the Arab League states feared the precedent that might be set by its *de jure* acceptance.

On a more practical level, the existence of two rival administrations in Lebanon suggested a number of possibilities which alarmed a range of Arab states: it seemed to bring closer the day when Syria would use its 30,000 troops in the country to annex the areas outside Aoun's control; it seemed to provide Israel some justification for maintaining the separate 'principality' of the southern zone controlled by the South Lebanon Army; the creation of two states – one inhabited largely by Christians, the other by Muslims – would, it was believed, give new impetus to Shi'ite based groups, such as *Hizbollah*, determined to ensure that the state which included a majority of Muslims would indeed be an Islamic state of the kind prescribed by *Hizbollah*'s Iranian mentors. Formal division of Lebanon seemed likely to reinforce involvement by those states (Syria, Israel and Iran) whose activity during the past few years in the same area had been regarded by many Arab rulers as directly contrary to their own interests.

In March 1989, Gen Aoun tried to enforce his claim to be the sole legitimate government of Lebanon by imposing a sea blockade on those ports which he declared to be 'illegal' – that is, those run by groups and organizations which refused to recognize his, or indeed anyone's, authority. He followed this with a demand that Syria withdraw all its forces from Lebanon, declaring that he would wage a 'war of liberation' against them until Syria complied. Inevitably, this set off a bout of renewed fighting, including, for the first time in three years, a series of intense bombardments between East and West Beirut. Reports of quantities of weapons being shipped to Aoun by Iraq reinforced Syria's determination to impose a blockade of its own and to step up its support for its allies in Lebanon. This aspect of the fighting strengthened the fear of many Arab rulers that the most enduring and dangerous conflict in the Arab world – that between the rival Ba'athist regimes of Syria and Iraq – having found a new terrain and new fuel in Lebanon, was set to escalate. This fear spurred the Arab League Committee on Lebanon, headed by Kuwait, to call for an immediate cease-fire. Some of the parties agreed to this at the end of April, but it had little noticeable effect on the scale of the fighting. Indeed, it could be said to have claimed the life of at least one prominent Lebanese – the Lebanese Grand Mufti, Sheikh Hassan Khaled, the most senior religious dignitary of the Sunni Muslim community – who was assassinated in May, after publicly expressing his support for the Arab League cease-fire plan.

These developments contributed to the Arab League's call for the Arab Heads of State to meet in Casablanca on 25 May. There the disarray over the question of Lebanon became evident: Syria declared that it had no intention of relinquishing its pre-eminent position in Lebanon, guaranteed on the ground by the 30,000 troops it had stationed there. This led to the abandonment of a plan, proposed by Iraq, for replacing all the Syrian troops by a genuinely mixed Arab League force. Saddam Hussein of Iraq reacted angrily and threatened reprisals against Syria. Faced with this impasse Kuwait abandoned its chairmanship of the committee which then promptly dissolved.

The collapse spurred the Arab League to set up a more formidable committee to 'rescue Lebanon', composed of King Hassan of Morocco, President Chadli Benjedid of Algeria and King Fahd of Saudi Arabia. Given the scale of Saudi subsidies to the ailing Syrian economy, it was evidently thought that the new committee stood a greater chance of success, since it would have some means of bringing effective pressure to bear on the Syrian government. It thereby signalled Saudi Arabia's increasing and unusually high-profile involvement in this particularly thorny question of inter-Arab politics.

In the immediate aftermath of the Casablanca Summit and during much of the summer of 1989, there was no appreciable difference in the situation in Lebanon itself. The blockades remained in force, leading to increasing isolation of the Christian areas of Lebanon as the weight of Syrian power began to tell against them. Shelling continued across the border between the territory held by Aoun's forces and that held by the Syrians and their Lebanese allies. The exodus from Beirut continued and, by July, it was estimated that some 500,000 had fled the city. Attempts by the Syrians' allies to invade the territory held by Aoun were repulsed, leading to direct clashes between Aoun's forces and units of the Syrian army. This, in turn, led to warnings from Iraq and an increase in Iraqi aid to Aoun.

The new Arab League Committee was meanwhile seeking to devise a plan which would persuade all sides to implement a cease-fire more durable than the many short-lived schemes periodically declared during the summer. By September, there were signs that the major parties to the conflict might be persuaded to accept such a cease-fire. Syria was increasingly isolated in the Arab world, and there seems little doubt that considerable Saudi pressure – in the form of financial rewards or threats – was brought to bear in order to induce Syria to accept the Arab League plan. On the Christian side, Aoun appeared to be as adamant as ever in his public determination to maintain his vision of the state of Lebanon. However, he was facing increasing criticism from within the Christian community – from sources as diverse as the Maronite Patriarch and the commander of the Lebanese Forces militia, Samir Geagea. At the same time, Iraq appears to have been subjected to some pressure within the Arab world to reduce its level of support for Aoun.

In September, the combined force of these developments led to Syria's acceptance of the Arab League seven-point peace plan – one significant feature of which was a partial withdrawal of Syrian forces, albeit linked to certain political reforms in Lebanon. Aoun evidently had reservations about the plan, but he called off his 'war of liberation' against Syria and agreed to the cease-fire terms. This meant an end to the fighting and the reopening of Beirut airport. It also opened the way for the next stage of the Arab League plan: to convene the surviving 62 members of Lebanon's 99-member parliament (last elected in 1972) at Taif in Saudi Arabia to discuss the political future of Lebanon.

From 30 September to 22 October the 62 deputies, isolated in Taif, were obliged to work their way through a proposed 'Charter for National Reconciliation'. Despite heated argument and the occasional threatened breakdown of the talks, by 22 October 58 deputies were able to agree on a plan for the re-establishment of the Lebanese constitutional state. Known as the Taif Agreement, its most important elements were the transfer of executive power from the (Christian) President to a Cabinet with equal numbers of Christian and Muslim ministers. This body would be responsible to a parliament which was also to have equal Christian–Muslim representation (as opposed to the present 6:5 ratio in favour of the Christians). However, the existing confessional distribution of the principal offices of state was to remain unchanged. At the top this meant that the President would remain a Christian, the Prime Minister a Sunni Muslim, and the Speaker of Parliament a Shi'ite Muslim. A further feature of the Taif Agreement was that the Syrian government would agree to redeploy its troops to the Beka'a valley within two years of the beginning of the process of reform. In addition, the assembled deputies agreed to reconvene in Lebanon in order to elect a new President of Lebanon who would be responsible for the implementation of the reforms.

Reactions to the Taif Agreement in Lebanon itself were predictable. The Druze leader Walid Jumblatt criticized it as an abject surrender to Christian pressure, since, in his view, the dismantling of Christian power had not gone far enough. The Shi'ite leader Najib Berri criticized it on similar lines, since it failed to accord the Shi'ite community a share of power proportional to its numerical weight. *Hizbollah* naturally criticized it since it did not even come close to laying the foundations for the Islamic state which was their own favoured future for Lebanon. More seriously, General Aoun rejected the Agreement outright. He sought to assert his claimed authority as the acting government by issuing a decree dissolving parliament. This, he declared, would render null and void all further decisions it was to take. Furthermore, he threatened to bombard the parliament building itself should the deputies attempt to convene there.

These reactions did not prevent the deputies from reconvening in Lebanon, although they had to do so at Qlaiaat air-base in Syrian-controlled northern Lebanon. On 5 November they elected one of their number, the Christian René Mouawad, as President and ratified the reform plan agreed at Taif. This was followed by violent demonstrations in East Beirut whence the Maronite Patriarch, who had been generally supportive of the scheme to end the civil war, was forced to flee.

President Mouawad appointed Selim al-Hoss his Prime Minister, but found it nearly impossible to persuade any Christians to join the cabinet. The stalemate which followed was broken on 22 November: President Mouawad and 17 others were killed when his motorcade was devastated by a massive explosion in West Beirut. However, within two days the deputies of the Lebanese Parliament reconvened and on 24 November they elected the Christian Elias Hrawi as President of Lebanon. In the shock which had followed the murder of his predecessor, Hrawi succeeded in forming a 14-member government, composed equally of Christians and Muslims. The new government dismissed General Aoun from his post as Commanding Officer of the Lebanese Armed Forces and appointed General Emile Lahoud in his stead. The latter, however, had virtually no army to command since the bulk of the armed forces remained loyal to Aoun.

General Aoun refused to recognize the authority of the new government and reinforced his position at the presidential palace of Baabda. Syria brought in reinforcements and President Hrawi issued an ultimatum stating that Aoun had 48 hours in which to leave the palace.

Thousands of civilians thereupon converged on Baabda to form a human shield around the palace, obliging Hrawi to reconsider the use of Syrian troops to enforce his ultimatum. In such a situation, which seemed likely to pit the Syrians directly against the Lebanese, Aoun was able to rally a show of support within the Christian community, even amongst his potential rivals.

Consequently, a new stalemate developed. Aoun refused to recognize the new government and the authority of President Hrawi and thus refused to relinquish either his army command or the presidential palace. For his part, Hrawi had no means of enforcing his authority save through the Syrian armed forces. Yet to have done so, would have been automatically interpreted as having undermined his own tenuous authority.

It appears that Hrawi and others were waiting for, and possibly encouraging, developments within the Christian community to unseat Aoun. In this respect, their hopes were pinned on Samir Geagea and the Lebanese Forces militia under his command. Geagea's relations with Aoun had never been easy. Although they shared a common hostility to the Syrian military presence in Lebanon and disliked the Taif Agreement, they were both rivals for the leadership of an essentially Christian constituency. Clearly, Geagea believed that Aoun's methods were likely to be both self-defeating and destructive of Geagea's own ambitions.

The rift within the Christian area quickly became apparent. In early February 1990, Aoun, suspecting that Geagea would seek to oust him, went on the offensive, moving his forces against the Lebanese Forces militia, determined to beat them into submission and to neutralize the threat they posed. During the first half of February, Aoun's forces overran some of the strongholds of the Lebanese Forces, although at a heavy cost. Aoun seemed to be running the risk of direct intervention by Syrian forces acting on President Hrawi's – unredeemed – pledge that outside assistance would be forthcoming if Geagea were to request it. In fact, reluctance to give the Syrians licence to involve themselves more deeply in Lebanese affairs appears to have prevented both Geagea and Hrawi from requesting Syrian support against Aoun.

The ensuing circumstance highlights the paradox that maintains a bloody stalemate in Lebanon. The Syrians remain the most powerful military force on the ground. Equally, in their hostility to Aoun, they can count on a large number of sympathizers among those who are seeking to reconstruct the Lebanese political order. Yet these same Lebanese are deeply mistrustful of the Syrians and want to do nothing that might seem to legitimize or perpetuate their presence in the country, since that would be to acquiesce in the vassal status of Lebanon. It is here that Aoun's emotional appeal to a sense of specifically Lebanese pride creates a sympathetic echo even among Muslim Lebanese beyond the frontiers of the fraction of the Christian enclave he dominates.

Consequently, in the face of Aoun's defiance and the still relatively well-equipped and well-trained forces at his disposal (one third of whom are Muslim), those who constructed the Taif Agreement are powerless to enforce their newly claimed authority. There are many in the Arab world who are tempted to support Aoun, if only as a way of frustrating Syria. There are others who also do not wish to see Syria become the uncontested master of Lebanon and who will try to exert external pressure on Damascus to prevent this from happening. The result has been to create a space in which the commanders of armed forces can flourish behind their ramparts. As the newly formed government of President Hrawi seeks to exert its control from temporary and insecure accommodation in West Beirut, it must begin to suspect that there is no longer much possibility of establishing a unitary Lebanese state. Whatever constitutional arrangements may have been devised, it seems that the space which is intended to accommodate them has already been occupied by others – *de facto* if not yet *de jure*.

Egypt and the Arab World

The Casablanca Summit of May 1989 which had produced such meagre results for Lebanon did, however, produce considerable satisfaction for the Egyptian government. It was at Casablanca that Egypt was re-admitted to the Arab League, ending ten years of exclusion which had followed Egypt's signing of the peace treaty with Israel in 1979. This was the culmination of several years of active Egyptian diplomacy during which Egypt had re-established diplomatic relations with the great majority of the member states of the Arab League. Symbolically, therefore, Egypt's re-admission was of considerable significance for the authority and prestige of the government of President Hosni Mubarak. In reality, however, Egypt had already profited from all the advantages which Arab League membership is supposed to confer. In addition, the League, as a regional grouping , is no longer what it was when it represented the sole forum of inter-Arab co-operation. Its former pretensions to pan-Arab unity of purpose have been repeatedly exposed during 45 years of discord among its member states, jealous of their own sovereignty. More recently, regional sub-groupings have emerged amongst its members, reflecting the more pressing requirements of intra-regional co-operation.

In February 1989, Egypt had been a founding member of one such grouping – the Arab Co-operation Council (ACC). This brought together Egypt, Iraq, Jordan and North Yemen into an organization which supposedly had been set up to further economic co-operation amongst its members. Given the low volume of trade among the four states and the structures of their economies, this was never a very convincing reason for its establishment. It is true that the three summit meetings of the four heads of state held during 1989 – in February, June and September, respectively – did produce some economic, cultural and commercial agreements. However, it is more probable that each country joined the ACC for reasons that owed more to their current fears and ambitions within Arab regional politics than to any realistic hope of establishing a workable economic community.

For Egypt, the ACC was a means of capitalizing on the relationship established with Iraq during the years of the Iran–Iraq War. Egypt probably hoped it would provide a framework for a post-war relationship that might guarantee some measure of Egyptian influence over a frustrated and disappointed country. This was important for Egypt in a number of ways. Firstly, by claiming to moderate Iraqi ambitions, Egypt could serve as a mediator between that country and Saudi Arabia. The pattern of the latter's nervousness was demonstrated in March 1989, when King Fahd visited Iraq to sign a non-aggression pact with Saddam Hussein – a curious move between ostensibly allied rulers – and then proceeded directly to Egypt, as if to seek reassurance that Egypt would keep Iraq to its word. A second aspect was Egypt's determination to encourage Iraq to maintain the tone of moderation that had pervaded Saddam Hussein's pronouncements on the Arab–Israeli issue during recent years. At a time when Egypt was engaged in the delicate task of encouraging a Palestinian–Israeli dialogue, it was vital to ensure that any possible support for rejectionism should be neutralized.

A related issue may have provided Egypt with a third reason for participating in the foundation of the ACC. This was the question of Syria, and specifically of Syria's attitude towards any developing peace process. The grouping of the ACC states could be seen as a way of bringing home to Syria its relative isolation in the Arab world. However, a possibly more important consideration was Egypt's hope that the ACC would become a means of reassuring Syria that Egypt might be able to mediate in the long-running dispute with Iraq. Egypt could offer to restrain the latter through the mechanism of the ACC and could hold out the possibility of some face-saving means of reconciliation in the future should Syria eventually wish to join the organization.

It was certainly noticeable that contacts between Syria and Egypt increased during the early part of the year and that Egypt discontinued its verbal support for Gen Aoun's administration in Lebanon. In mid-May Syria withdrew its objection to Egypt's attendance at the Casablanca Summit and, when Egypt was re-admitted to the Arab League, gave it a warm welcome. Partly because of its stance in Lebanon, Syria was feeling weak and isolated by the end of 1989. It was unable to use its military superiority to any great effect in Lebanon, either because of local resistance or because of external constraints; in addition, the regime in Damascus had reservations about the cost of the venture. On its eastern flank, the dispute with Iraq was as bitter as ever and Syrian anxieties can only have been underlined by Saddam Hussein's apparent determination to develop devastating weapons systems, regardless of cost or of international concern. Iraqi announcements near the end of 1989 of tests of missiles with ranges of around 2,000 km will increase Syrian concerns, and the claimed launch of a rocket capable of carrying satellites into orbit will not mitigate them. At the same time, developments within the USSR, Syria's major weapons supplier, made it clear that Syria could no longer believe it could develop 'strategic parity' with Israel.

It was perhaps not surprising, therefore, that the Syrian government should have been more receptive than ever to Egyptian overtures. Although reconciliation with Egypt might not have corresponded by any means to the preferred objectives of the Syrian government, it did seem to provide one route out of Syria's isolation – and might also be well rewarded by those, such as the US and Saudi Arabia, who wished to encourage precisely such a form of reconciliation. The result was that on 27 December Syria and Egypt declared that they were to restore full diplomatic relations, bringing to an end ten years of formal estrangement.

For President Mubarak of Egypt, therefore, 1989–90 represented a year of considerable diplomatic achievement in the Arab world. It was also a vindication of the foreign policy pursued by Egypt for the past ten years. On the one hand, Egypt was re-admitted unconditionally to the Arab League. On the other, not only was Egypt actively pursuing the peace process in negotiations with Israel and the US, but this activity was now regarded as fundamental to the strategy of the PLO itself. Egypt was consequently able to demonstrate that there was no incompatibility in maintaining a dialogue with the Arab states and with Israel. On the contrary, as Egypt's own experience had shown, only by so doing could the sacrifices associated with open conflict – in this case the *intifada* – be transformed into political successes, uncertain as the outcome of the process might be. Egypt had therefore emerged once again a dominant power in the Arab world. The foundations of this pre-eminence are very different to that of the 1950s and 1960s, when political intimidation and the illusion of military superiority had won for it the leadership of the Arab states. In the 1990s it is Egypt's capacity to moderate and mediate between the Arab states and outsiders, as well as between the insecure Arab governments themselves, which will be put to the test. The outcome will set the pattern for Egypt's future and for the shape of the region in the coming decade.

ISRAEL AND THE PLO: THE SEARCH FOR PEACE

The Palestinians in the Israeli-occupied territories of the West Bank and Gaza Strip maintained their pressure on Israel through the *intifada* during 1989. While the uprising itself continued to display many of the characteristics of the previous year, levels of public participation and insurgent activity clearly declined; nevertheless, in 1989 it generated a new Israeli–Palestinian political process which developed around an Israeli plan for an interim settlement.

Both the peace plan and the *intifada* survived the calendar year, though neither registered any notable progress towards a resolution of the Palestinian issue. What constrained the peace process in particular was the reluctance of the three parties primarily involved – Israel, the

PLO and the United States, each for different reasons – to make significant concessions or to take dramatic initiatives. Even though Egypt played a remarkably innovative role it could not significantly shift entrenched positions.

The *Intifada* Continues

The second year of the Palestinian uprising in the West Bank and Gaza ended in early December 1989. In terms of total Palestinian casualties, both Israeli and Palestinian statistics indicated that the second year had produced numbers similar to the first – between 300 and 400 killed, and around 40,000 wounded (most superficially). But the second year's statistics in fact reflected a considerable decline in the scope of low-level violence. This year a far larger portion of those killed were in fact murdered as 'collaborators' by fellow Palestinians; Associated Press statistics listed 131 such deaths in the second year, compared to 22 in the first. Then too, during the second year the violence was largely restricted to small groups of youths, some masked and armed with hatchets and even guns, rather than large crowds. This reflected both Palestinian civilian fatigue and the effectiveness of escalating Israeli army rules of engagement, which now emphasized use of the plastic bullet on crowds and of live ammunition against masked youths. The political breakthrough the PLO had made in late 1988 – inspired not a little by the *intifada* – and the subsequent start of a political process early in 1989, may also have reduced the scope of Palestinian violent demonstrations – but only temporarily, as residents of the Occupied Territories soon resigned themselves once more to a prolonged struggle of attrition.

There were a number of specific developments in the Israeli–Palestinian struggle during 1989 that may have continuing effects. One was a brief escalation of clashes between Arabs and Israelis throughout the country, provoked in part by acts of extreme violence by Arabs, particularly the murder of Jews inside Israel, in part reflecting growing Jewish frustration with the security forces' perceived inability to protect Israelis and their property, with government restraint in dealing with the uprising, and with the prospects for a political settlement that would fail to satisfy extremist Jewish aspirations.

By mid-May, Israeli mob violence against Gazan Arab commuter workers in the Ashdod and Ashkelon areas (along the southern Israeli Mediterranean coast) so alarmed the police that all Gazan workers were ordered to return to Gaza and remain there temporarily. At the same time, Israeli settlers in the Occupied Territories launched vigilante attacks on Arab villages. On more than one occasion Israeli Defense Force (IDF) officers who sought to intervene were themselves attacked by fellow Jews. Israeli leftist groups began taking unilateral actions in the Territories to counter the violence of the settlers and to offer support for the Palestinians. By the end of May most Israelis, including the Council of Settlers in the Territories, were sufficiently alarmed by these events to produce near universal condemnation of vigilante acts, and calm was restored. But the escalation had spotlighted more than ever before the incapacity of the Israeli army, and in a broader sense of Israeli society, to deal with a civilian uprising.

One obvious security problem with strategic ramifications for any future political resolution was the presence of the Israeli settlers in the Territories. The army claimed it was impossible to protect all 70,000 Jewish settlers while the settlers demanded protection. Another issue was the degree of force to be used. The Israeli right was nearly unanimous in arguing that if the IDF were more aggressive and less sensitive to human rights in dealing with the *intifada*, security could be restored; Rabin and the IDF senior staff responded that the uprising would merely escalate, and a political settlement would become more difficult – while the left, and the international community, argued against a heavier crackdown for political and humanitarian reasons.

One result for the army was ambiguity: orders to soldiers tended to obfuscate the bounds of permissible force. This was clearly illustrated by a military court decision in late May that found four soldiers guilty of failing to realize that their orders – to beat an unarmed Arab civilian who did not oppose arrest – were 'clearly illegal' (the man died of his injuries). But the court also pointed an accusatory finger at the senior officers who had allowed such orders to go unchallenged.

If this case was widely seen as symptomatic of the IDF's day-to-day dilemma, several more probing assessments in the Israeli press and by strategists suggested that the army's unsuitability – in terms of morale and personnel – for extended riot control duty against an essentially political uprising, was eroding its cohesion and combat-readiness, and brutalizing Israeli society. Whether these opinions were accurate or not remains to be seen; for the moment they provoked a debate concerning the overall effect upon Israel of an extended confrontation with highly motivated and aggressive Palestinian civilians.

One dramatic indicator of a parallel predicament among the Palestinians was their growing reliance on violence. On the one hand, more lethal attacks by individuals were launched against Israelis, the most extreme being the attack on a bus near Jerusalem on 6 July, and the fatal petrol bombing of Israeli tax collectors in Ramallah on 14 August. On the other, the uprising increasingly turned upon itself. Brutal executions of 'collaborators' became more common. In January 1990, for example, more Palestinians were killed at Palestinian hands than by Israelis.

That about half of those Arabs murdered in this way were evidently not collaborators with Israel, but usually common criminals, reflected another key aspect of the *intifada*: the growing shift of Palestinian energies towards an effort to establish and enforce their own 'sovereign' institutions under, and despite, Israeli rule. Thus people's committees organized private hospitals, key industries (such as dairies), and local self-rule institutions (like neighbourhood patrols), while boycotting

Israel's economy and its institutions, and new women's, students' and workers' organizations were institutionalized.

Another concerted Palestinian attempt at civil disobedience suffered a more ambiguous fate. This was a tax rebellion in the largely Christian town of Beit Sahur, near Bethlehem, a revolt that was suppressed in October through massive expropriations of goods and property by the IDF. While this deterred Palestinians elsewhere in the Territories from joining the tax rebellion, the entire affair also constituted a public relations victory for the Palestinians, as Israel came under sharp international criticism for its heavy-handed tactics.

Yet another key development of 1989 was the rise to prominence of *Hamas*, the 'Islamic Resistance Movement'. Surprisingly, this Muslim fundamentalist wing of the uprising was not declared illegal by the Israeli authorities until August 1989 – fully a year after it had published a charter rejecting Israel's right to exist. This presumably reflected traces of Israeli policies that, prior to the uprising, had considered the fundamentalist trend in Gaza as a counter to the PLO. During 1989 *Hamas* was implicated in the abduction and murder of two Israeli soldiers, and its leader, Sheikh Ahmed Yassin, was put on trial. By the end of 1989, Israeli and Palestinian sources alike assessed the potential electoral strength of *Hamas* as at least 25% of the vote. While *Hamas* was still not represented in the Unified Leadership of the Uprising, and continued to issue its own directives to the population, its adherents did express support for dialogue with Israel and for elections in the Territories. The PLO might allow it to be represented on a Palestinian delegation to the Cairo talks with Israel, if only in the hope of neutralizing its potential for sabotaging the dialogue.

Finally, inside Israel, the uprising continued to permeate the fabric of Israeli Arab society: during the first half of 1989 incidents of stone-throwing, Palestinian flag raising and arson doubled, and summer '*intifada* camps' and anti-Israel video cassette programmes mounted. This appeared to presage increasing 'Palestinization' of Israeli Arabs, who make up 18% of the Israeli population and can vote, unless a political solution could be found in the Territories.

Many of these developments may have offered considerable moral satisfaction for the Palestinians, but in the short term they barely affected the lives of most Israelis; indeed, the continued readiness, despite death threats, of around 90,000 Palestinian workers from the Territories to commute daily to Israel appeared to offer dramatic proof that most of the hardship generated by the uprising was borne by the Arabs, with few political results to show for it. As for Israel, its construction and tourist industries suffered, and it was hard put to find budgetary appropriations for the additional costs incurred by the IDF in policing the Territories. But the total economic damage to Israel engendered by the uprising was estimated at no more than one or two per cent of GNP, and the economic factor remained secondary in any evaluation.

One indication that the *intifada* may have been becoming less intense – though by no means ending – was the increasing effort made by the Islamic *Jihad* (a Palestinian fundamentalist terrorist group) along with the more radical secular Palestinian organizations supported largely by Syria and Iran, to develop an alternative focus of struggle across Israel's borders. This took the form of attacks on Israel from Jordan and Egypt and, most spectacularly, the 4 February 1990 attack on a busload of Israeli tourists in Egypt.

A strikingly different indication of the same Palestinian frustration was the declaration by Faisal al-Husseini, perhaps the most prominent of Palestinian leaders in the Territories, that the third year of the uprising would focus on influencing Israeli public opinion. This appeared to reflect the Palestinians' recognition that Israelis remained relatively unmoved by the Palestinian cause as expressed in the uprising.

The Israeli Plan

By spring 1989 two developments had combined to generate a new Israeli government proposal for a peace process on the Palestinian issue. One was the continued pressure generated by the *intifada*. It had become clear to the Israelis that, unless they were to transgress their own self-imposed moral constraints they could, at best, only contain the uprising and limit its scope. The second development was a new administration in Washington that sought to exploit its dialogue with the PLO, and its influence over Israel, to generate momentum for a peace process. As early as February, US Secretary of State Baker called upon Israel to produce new and effective ideas towards that end; and it soon became apparent that the Bush Administration would neither advance a plan of its own nor offer the Israelis and Palestinians far-reaching guarantees to entice them into a dialogue.

Even the *Likud* bloc in the Israeli government now recognized, as the Labour contingent had long ago, that the *status quo* in the Territories had become untenable, at least as the foundation for a political position *vis-à-vis* the US. Both *Likud* and Labour, however, continued to maintain the Israeli mainstream political rejection of direct dialogue with the PLO and of the establishment of a Palestinian state. Beyond this, such innovations and concessions as they offered reflected primarily an Israeli readiness to talk with local Palestinians, and a recognition of the need to improve Israel's image in the world.

What came to be known as the Shamir Plan evolved from ideas first mooted in late January by Defence Minister Rabin. Prime Minister Shamir unveiled the outlines of his own plan in Washington and had it approved in final form by the Israeli government on 14 May. The Plan comprises four steps to 'be dealt with simultaneously': a mechanism for carrying out the Palestinian autonomy provisions of the Camp David Accords; a provision for enhancing relations between Israel and Egypt; a call for rehabilitation of the Palestinian refugees in camps in the West

Bank and Gaza; and expansion of the peace process to include all Arab states still at war with Israel.

Of these four elements, the Plan goes into detail only regarding the autonomy phase, and then only after setting forth the twin premises of Israeli rejection of the establishment of a Palestinian state in the Territories and Israeli refusal to negotiate with the PLO. It proposes that the residents of the Territories freely elect representatives to negotiate a five-year transition period of autonomy. After three years of autonomy, a permanent political solution would be negotiated, with the new self-governing authority constituting the Palestinian delegation in these negotiations. At that time any and all proposals could be tabled for discussion. This final stage would also include 'arrangements for peace and borders between Israel and Jordan'.

The Israeli proposal was essentially the Camp David autonomy arrangements agreed upon in 1978 between Israel, Egypt and the US, with elections introduced as a means of selecting the Palestinian delegation. It referred only to Palestinians in the West Bank and Gaza – not to members of the exile community, nor even to Palestinian residents of East Jerusalem. Its great advantage from the Israeli domestic standpoint was its acceptability to both Labour leaders Rabin and Shimon Peres and to the *Likud*. Shamir argued that the proposal accommodated the *Likud* position – i.e., the Territories must never be delivered to non-Israeli rule – in that Israel would be free, in the second-stage negotiations, to reject proposals for Arab sovereignty, thereby perpetuating autonomy. Rabin and Peres, who continued to seek Jordanian involvement in a final settlement, argued that they would be free to proffer their 'territories for peace' formula when, after three years, final-stage negotiations began.

Meanwhile, both the *Likud* and Labour leaderships recognized that the key to maintaining a consensus over the proposal lay in avoiding the necessity of dealing with details that might reveal their differences. Presumably, they had produced the plan on the assumption that it would be possible to persuade local Palestinian leaders to run in elections without the direct involvement of the PLO. Yet, because Shamir and Rabin disagreed over even 'local' issues such as the right of East Jerusalem Palestinians to vote (Shamir was opposed, Rabin in favour), they sought to avoid tackling these questions at least until the Arab side had agreed on the principles they had put forth.

Initial Reactions

Herein lay the first difficulty. Most local Palestinian leaders rejected the very idea of elections held without PLO involvement, and prior to some form of IDF withdrawal from polling areas. The PLO was more explicit. Bassam Abu-Sharif, who regularly 'tested' new ideas for Arafat, published an initial PLO response in *The Washington Post* insisting on at least partial IDF withdrawal before elections, international monitoring of the electoral process, and ultimately an international conference based on 'the Palestinian right to self-determination'. He made clear that East Jerusalem Arabs must participate in the initial stage, and the PLO in the final stage; but did not totally reject the Plan.

The Shamir–Rabin team would indeed prove flexible on some of these questions, such as monitoring and partial withdrawal. Yet the agreement to their Plan on the part of 'the Arab side' could not, from their standpoint, come from the PLO. Thus US Secretary of State Baker and his Director of Policy Planning Staff Dennis Ross, began playing an active role in April and May in seeking clarifications on the Israeli plan and the PLO attitude. Ross visited the region in mid-May for discussions with Israel. President Bush and Secretary Baker publicly praised the Israeli initiative while pressing for a 'fleshing out' of the proposal, and they outlined positions that were clearly unacceptable to the *Likud* half of the government. In effect, Washington had seized upon a fairly minimalistic Israeli initiative, produced at its behest, with the clear aim of developing it into a formula for progress – but only by mediating, not by offering a commitment of its own.

This process came to a head in Baker's speech to the American Israeli Political Action Committee (AIPAC) convention in Washington on 22 May – the only detailed high-level enunciation of American policy on the Palestinian issue that was made throughout 1989. Baker offered a carefully balanced prescription of the many policy changes the US sought from both the Arab and the Israeli sides. In particular, he appeared to move away from his predecessors in elaborating US positions that conflicted with those of the *Likud*. He argued that negotiations for Israel would have to 'involve territorial withdrawal and the emergence of a new political reality'; Israel must abandon 'the unrealistic vision of a greater Israel. . . . Foreswear annexation. Stop settlement activity. . . . Reach out to the Palestinians as neighbors who deserve political rights'. In a variety of references to the Palestinians' rights and status, Baker appeared to be describing an entity that approximated the state the PLO sought. In ascribing PLO positions to 'Palestinians', he seemed to equate the two and indirectly recognize the PLO's role in a settlement. Baker's speech was greeted angrily by Shamir, who called its innovations 'useless' (they obviously went beyond his own vision of his own plan), and stonily by Rabin, who probably felt that it was counterproductive to dwell at this stage on issues on which *Likud* and Labour were divided.

One of Baker's principal target audiences was probably the Arab League Summit which met shortly thereafter in Casablanca. There, in return for Arab readiness to avoid pressuring Syria over its role in Lebanon, Damascus was persuaded to endorse the PLO position on a settlement, and to allow Egypt to return to the Arab League, despite its peace with Israel. While these measures hardly added up to an Arab endorsement of either the Israeli or the American positions, they gave implicit Arab support to the notion of a negotiated compromise Palestinian peace with Israel.

A coalition of forces within the *Likud* soon tried to place clear constraints on Shamir's freedom of manoeuvre. On 5 July Cabinet Ministers David Levi, Yitzhak Modai and Ariel Sharon forced Shamir to convene the *Likud* Central Committee to discuss their insistence that East Jerusalem Arabs not be allowed to participate in autonomy elections; that terrorism and violence cease before any negotiations with Arabs begin; that no foreign sovereignty be applied anywhere within the bounds of the 'Land of Israel'; and that no negotiations be held with the PLO.

After considerable political manoeuvring, Shamir adopted these four principles in his policy speech to the *Likud* caucus. Indeed, it was clear that in terms of his personal views regarding his peace initiative, he was merely rendering explicit those constraints that had determined his position all along, but which had been omitted from the Israeli plan in deference to the need to maintain a consensus with Labour. Hence Shamir hastened to clarify, after the caucus, that his acceptance of these constraints had in no way altered the *Likud*–Labour consensus over the peace plan. Shamir's ambivalence was to prove a strain on the minimal coalition consensus needed to maintain the saliency of the Israeli peace initiative.

By the end of May there appeared to be a distinct possibility that the demands on Israel to elucidate key aspects of the Plan in order to make it acceptable to the Palestinians – or even to the US – would not only cause friction in US–Israeli relations, but an Israeli government crisis as well, insofar as Labour and *Likud* had diverging views on the need to make further concessions.

When the US sought to elicit a Palestinian response – primarily by contacting the West Bank and Gazan leadership and via the direct channel opened up in Tunis in December 1988, but also, and increasingly, through Egyptian good offices – it found that the mainstream PLO objections centred on all the elements that the Israeli proposal clearly did not contain. Hardliners within the PLO rejected the Plan totally. Beyond the PLO, it was opposed by Abu Musa's *Fatah* rebels, Abu Nidal, the PFLP-GC and other pro-Syrian groups in Lebanon, Syria and increasingly Iran, and by the *Hamas* movement in the Gaza Strip.

Hence PLO leader Arafat was also subject to conflicting pressures that caused him to walk a political tightrope in responding to American and Egyptian demands for greater flexibility. He produced a number of ideas in response to the Shamir Plan; none were acceptable to the US. Nor, obviously, were they acceptable to Israel, or endorsed even by Egypt and Jordan. By summer 1989 the entire cumbersome process appears to have caused Arafat to drop the flexible and moderate attitude he and the mainstream PLO had been showing. At the Fifth *Fatah* Congress held in Tunis in early August, Arafat accepted a formulation of Palestinian policy that was verbally far more extreme than anything enunciated by mainstream PLO spokesmen for the past year. It emphasized 'all means of armed struggle', and used language ('Zionist entity') that was thought to have been relegated to history.

To break the summer deadlock, President Mubarak of Egypt weighed in with his own plan. By now Egypt, with increasingly comprehensive inter-Arab and superpower backing, had assumed the role of official presenter of the PLO viewpoint to Israel, thereby circumventing, to the satisfaction of all parties, Israel's objections to being addressed directly by the PLO, and allowing Jerusalem to ignore its own inability to elicit independent responses from the West Bank and Gazan leadership to whom it had sought to address its initiative. Rather than describing a comprehensive peace, Mubarak sought to lay down a set of ten compromise principles aimed at facilitating the Israeli election plan. Once accepted by all, they were intended to enable the parties to begin active negotiations over implementation of the Israeli plan.

Mubarak's ten points sought to bridge two key gaps between Israel and the Palestinians. First, the 'territories for peace' principle – roughly equivalent in the eyes of the PLO mainstream to its demand for an ultimate stage of Palestinian sovereignty – was enshrined in UN Resolutions 242 and 338, both of which Israel had long since accepted. Secondly, the Egyptian plan specified that the Palestinian delegation would be composed of residents of the Territories and East Jerusalem, it being understood (in verbal clarifications) that this could include two Palestinians who had been exiled by Israel from the Territories. In this way, a key PLO demand – that the Palestinian diaspora be represented in the process from the beginning – would be met, yet in a way that did not explicitly contradict Israel's refusal to involve the diaspora in negotiations, since the additional Palestinians could be considered legally to be residents of the Territories.

The Egyptian plan was endorsed by the US. By mid-September the official PLO position on the plan remained ambiguous, but Cairo and Washington appeared confident that they could elicit a favourable response from Arafat if Israel were to concur. It was accepted on a limited basis by Rabin and Peres: they specified that they had no objection to meeting a Palestinian delegation in Cairo that adopted the ten points as its opening position, while Israel held fast to its own four-point plan. The *Likud*, however, objected, claiming that the Egyptian plan opened the way for PLO representation in the process, which both *Likud* and Labour had opposed. Accordingly, in early October the Israeli Inner Cabinet, in which the *Likud* and Labour had equal representation, failed to endorse the plan.

The tie vote in the Cabinet generated considerable tension within the *Likud*–Labour coalition. It also revealed the first clear signs of a difference of tactics within the Labour Party, between Rabin and Peres. Rabin held to a view that only a broad coalition could move Israel into genuine negotiations over a Palestinian settlement; Labour would be foolhardy to leave the government, try to set up an alternative narrow-based coalition, or precipitate elections, unless it could appear as the champion of a peace process that was in place and on track. Peres began actively to pursue negotiations with several small dovish ultra-orthodox and leftist parties with a view to forming an alternative coalition if and when the government reached a stalemate, even if this occurred before a peace process began – which is indeed what eventually happened.

The impasse that had been reached was a result of the incompatible views held by the six actors in the drama: *Likud* refused to countenance any PLO role in the process or mention of a territories for peace stage, insisting that the process should involve Israel and the 'local' Palestinians (i.e., residents of the West Bank and Gaza) in autonomy arrangements alone. Labour would accept some form of symbolic representation of the Palestinian diaspora, as well as East Jerusalem Palestinians, in the Palestinian delegation, and was prepared to countenance some form of discussion of the ultimate, post-autonomy territories for peace issue. The PLO refused to sanction any process in which it did not participate. The 'local' Palestinians were adamant in refusing to enter a process without the PLO, though no doubt some felt that as the initiators and sufferers of the *intifada* they had impeccable credentials to negotiate for themselves. Egypt was exploiting its contacts with both Israel and the PLO, and its enhanced inter-Arab status, to pressure a reluctant Arafat into making the concessions required to enter the American-sponsored process. And the US was negotiating with the PLO in Tunis and through Egyptian good offices on the basis of the Israeli plan, searching for a formula that would satisfy all parties sufficiently so as to move them into the first crucial stage of a peace process – where, it hoped, a 'peace dynamic' would develop that would commit all the parties to modifying their views.

The Baker Plan

On 1 November Secretary of State Baker stepped in with a five-point formula of his own to encourage the *Likud*'s agreement to begin negotiations in Cairo: the formula tried to emphasize those parts of the process to which all sides appeared to agree and ended by suggesting that the foreign ministers of Israel, Egypt and the US meet a fortnight later.

Initially, this plan, too, failed to satisfy the *Likud* on the key issues of preventing 'outsider' Palestinian participation and restricting negotiations to the modalities of elections. This contributed to a growing assessment in Washington that Shamir was intent on preventing his plan from being implemented according to any but the most narrow of premises. The result was a period of US–Israeli tension, beginning in the second half of October: on 17 October Shamir declared that Israel would 'stand firm and not give in' to American pressure over the issue, even 'if we must face a clash . . . in which case our relations will change'. *Likud*–Labour tensions reached a point where most of the Labour *Knesset* members walked out of a vote of non-confidence on October 23 rather than vote for the government.

By early November a way out of the impasse appeared to be developing. Baker agreed to a few small changes in the five points, which were seen by Shamir and Arens as face-saving concessions, and it was also tacitly agreed that both Israel and the PLO would seek to resolve their remaining reservations in the form of unilateral US assurances to them. This enabled the Israeli Inner Cabinet, on 5 November, to approve the Baker Plan, along with a list of requested 'assurances' that were 'assumed' to be forthcoming, by a 9 to 3 vote. Only the three *Likud* hardliners – Sharon, Modai and Levi – voted against the proposal.

The assurances, like the alterations to the Baker Plan that preceded them, by now appeared to many to be an exercise in the diplomatic art of splitting hairs. They were essentially throwbacks to *Likud* demands to exercise a veto over 'outsider' and East Jerusalem Palestinians in the Palestinian delegation to the Cairo meeting, and over the discussion in Cairo of issues (territories for peace) not directly related to the autonomy elections issue, coupled with a rephrasing of the hoped-for American promise that Israel would not be urged to negotiate with the PLO at some later stage. Their relevancy to the process was assessed very differently by Baker, who refused to treat them as a condition for moving the process forward, and by Shamir, for whom they appeared to provide another brake upon a process that was placing growing constraints upon his political freedom of manoeuvre. Shamir could now expect to confront a vigorous campaign within his own party, spearheaded by Sharon, Levi and Modai, to negate what they saw as new policy compromises on his part. In parallel Rabin and Peres, each with a slightly different party political agenda within Labour, would now seek, in contacts with Washington and Cairo, to refine the modalities of the Baker Plan so as to present Shamir with a formulation that he could not refuse without abandoning the peace plan that bore his name.

As for the Arab side to the process, in early November Egypt's President Mubarak initiated a meeting of the PLO Executive Committee in Cairo to formulate the conditions for PLO acceptance of the Egyptian Ten-Point Plan and the Baker Five-Point Plan. The PLO's response fell short even of Israel's ambiguous decision to join the process. The PLO avoided taking a clear-cut stand – with PLO 'Foreign Minister' Farouk Kaddoumi joining George Habash's PFLP in the Cairo meeting in opposing the plans – preferring only to reiterate its position that 'it was the only party responsible for the composition of the Palestinian delegation'. However, it was also reported from Cairo that the PLO intended to seek its own parallel set of assurances from the US as a condition for entering the process.

The prospect of two parallel (and possibly contradictory) sets of American assurances, to Israel and the PLO, suggested that either a great deal of constructive ambiguity would be required by US State Department specialists to keep both sides 'in' the process, or that this new hope of progress, such as it was, would soon dissipate. From a broader perspective, the process could be assessed in terms of either (or both) of two radically different approaches. Looked at positively, perhaps once the sides entered the process, however tenuously, a dynamic of negotiation would develop that would make three months of haggling over details and endless 'point plans' seem worthwhile. On the other hand, the process could also be described as moving continuously backward, not forward, from the starting point of Shamir's 14 May plan. As Tom Friedman put it in *The New York Times*, the entire effort had come:

> perilously close to the line between serious diplomacy and farce. Mr Baker is now negotiating with Egypt and Israel on how to get a dialogue going between them for the purpose of organizing a dialogue between Israelis and Palestinians for the purpose of organizing elections in the West Bank and Gaza Strip for the purpose of electing Palestinian representatives who would negotiate with Israel on an interim settlement.

Certainly it remained possible that, if the process did not soon develop some momentum of its own, the US would abandon its mediation efforts and at least partially blame Israel.

Baker, faced with the two sides' contradictory reservations, in effect refused to grant most of their requests for reassurances. He was reportedly willing to promise Shamir only that Israel would not be pressured to deal directly with the PLO 'at this stage'. Baker also reportedly assured the PLO of the US commitment to a territories for peace solution and to a final settlement in which Palestinians realized their legitimate political rights. The first concrete step would be a meeting of the American, Egyptian and Israeli foreign ministers, to prepare the Cairo conference of Palestinians and Israelis. In response to an admonition from Shamir that he was not trying hard enough, Baker indicated that, given the press of momentous world events, he was close to a decision to abandon his efforts. This was accompanied by hints that the Bush Administration might not oppose a move to cut aid to Israel, if only symbolically.

By early February 1990 the scene appeared to have been set for a showdown among the various protagonists over the key remaining issues of contention. The PLO, Egypt, Peres and Rabin had signalled their acceptance of a compromise in which the Palestinian delegation to Cairo would be announced by the Egyptians, and would include two exiles (who would be allowed to take up residency in the Territories again) and two residents of East Jerusalem who also maintained homes elsewhere in the West Bank. Baker travelled to Moscow, where he obtained Soviet agreement to the prospective process.

Another *Likud* caucus was held on 12 February, again at the initiative of Sharon, Levi and Modai, to formulate Likud's position. Hardliners attempted to force Shamir to take a platform that would have obliged him to abandon his plan and probably to resign as well. The result was a serious split within *Likud*, with Sharon tendering his resignation in protest against Shamir's readiness to compromise. At this stage, the faltering process broke down: Shamir appeared to have emerged from his party infighting no more ready to compromise on the key remaining

issues than he was before Sharon's resignation. Indeed, Shamir's efforts
to restore party unity even at the expense of progress in the peace process seemed to confirm the suspicion that he had been using his proposal all along to buy time.

These suspicions lay behind the successful outcome of a vote of no
confidence in the *Knesset* on 15 February. Earlier in the week Shamir
had dismissed Labour's leader Peres from the cabinet when Peres tried
to force a positive response from the government on the peace issue.
Labour then gained the support of key small religious parties to topple
the Shamir-led government. In mid-March Peres was attempting to put
together a new government dedicated to re-invigorating the peace process. Even if he were successful, however, there was little certainty that
any resulting negotiations would move much beyond the present
agenda of preliminary rather than substantive issues.

Inter-Arab and Superpower Influences

The Egyptian reintegration into the Arab League during 1989 gave
President Mubarak confidence that he could not only 'represent' the
PLO in prenegotiations with Israel and the US, but could proffer his
own Ten-Point Plan for advancing a Palestinian settlement. Syria's
rapprochement with Egypt in late 1989 reflected the extreme isolation
Damascus felt towards the rest of the Arab world, and Soviet pressures.
In Syria's case (and that of the PLO), *perestroika* meant pressure to
abandon the military option and move towards a political option in
dealing with Israel. By 1990 the notion of a Syrian–Israeli peace was
hardly a concrete possibility, but at least Syria, and its Palestinian prox-
ies, were put on notice by the Soviet Union and the moderate Arab
camp not to sabotage a Palestinian settlement, if one could be arranged.

Jordan was adversely affected by the peace process. King Hussein was
sufficiently wary of the *intifada* spreading to his territory to encourage
democratization, only to find that in parliamentary elections 40% of the
votes went to Islamic fundamentalists – for the most part Palestinians
with links to *Hamas* in the West Bank and Gaza Strip. What appeared
to concern the Jordanian monarch most, however, were the voices from
circles on the Israeli right and left advocating 'Jordan is Palestine' as a
panacea for Israel's Palestine problem.

One of Hussein's remedies was to call in the Iraqis. Saddam Hussein,
now at least temporarily free of his war with Iran, despatched planes
and infantry officers to patrol the Jordan River border with Israel in
July. Like Saddam's venture in supporting the Maronite Christian
Phalangists in Lebanon against Syrian pressure, his reappearance after a
decade as a major player in the Arab–Israeli geographic arena appeared
directed essentially towards signalling Iraq's status as a regional power,
rather than against any particular party. Still, both efforts, when taken
together with Iraqi plans to develop medium-range missiles and to
maintain the Middle East's largest military force, gave cause for concern
not only in Iran, but in Syria and Israel as well.

The USSR was essentially a passive actor in the process throughout the year. In view of its preoccupation with internal and Eastern Bloc events, Moscow did not do much more than exercise diplomatic pressure on Syria and the PLO to abandon any thought of armed conflict as a means of solving their problem with Israel. While indicating a strong desire to participate in the process, it was not yet prepared to offer Israel (and the US) the one essential concession required for its entry – restoration of diplomatic relations with Israel – even though its readiness to allow tens of thousands of Soviet Jews to emigrate to Israel was at least as vexing to the Arabs.

Finally, Israel's relations with the US showed signs of strain during 1989. Administration and Congressional anger at instances of independent Israeli initiative directly affecting US interests, such as the abduction of the extremist Shi'ite leader, Sheikh Obeid, from southern Lebanon in July, and the revelations in November regarding Israeli–South African collaboration in ballistic missile development, seemed to dovetail with the perception of Israeli intransigence over the Palestinian issue and brutality in dealing with the uprising. An added factor was the new policy and aid priorities generated by the emergence of fledgling democratic regimes in Eastern Europe and US irritation at the possible settlement of Soviet *emigrés* in the Occupied Territories.

These developments seemed to be eroding Israel's image as both a democracy and a strategic ally, thereby increasing the possibility that the close ties between the two countries would be attenuated during the early 1990s. One indication of things to come may have been Washington's persistence in pursuing its dialogue with the PLO. Superficially, this may be seen to have been balanced by the USSR's readiness to permit mass immigration of Jews to Israel, and to admonish Arab leaders who protested against the necessity of dealing with Israel. But whereas, in early 1990, the direct relationship between events in Eastern Europe and the USSR and the future of the Arab–Israeli conflict was difficult to assess, it seemed quite possible that progress by Israel towards a Palestinian settlement would soon become vital to the maintenance of its alliance with the US.

IRAN AFTER KHOMEINI

The architect of the Iranian Islamic Republic, Ayatollah Ruhollah Khomeini, died on 3 June 1989. His death threw the system that he had created for that republic, the idea of the *velayat-e faqih*, or 'rule of the jurisprudent', into disarray, for the system requires the existence of a highly respected and senior clerical leader to rule in the absence of the last Shi'ite imam. With Khomeini's death the immediate problem was the selection of a clergyman senior enough, and respected enough, to assume this leadership role. President Ali Khamenei was chosen, despite his relatively junior religious standing as a Hojatoleslam.

The problem of reconciling political ability and activism with religious seniority in one man is a very real one. The current concept of the *velayat-e faqih* was tailor-made to suit Ayatollah Khomeini himself; without it, the basis for Islamic rule in the country would be undermined. Another structural problem lies in the dual nature of authority implied by this system. The President is head of the executive, but the Leader can override the decisions not only of the President, but those of parliament and the judiciary. It is a case of one man effectively ruling a country both as Pope and King.

With Khomeini's death, one danger for the government was that the loss of the country's final arbiter would mean that intra-governmental disputes could not be settled. Political views in Iran fall broadly into two camps: pragmatic and radical, though these are not watertight categories. These views are represented both by individuals and through associations and the media. During his lifetime, Khomeini was able to settle arguments between the two, but, with his death, the danger of more open disagreement and a potential for outright attack, or conversely for government inaction, has heightened.

Personalities and Policies

Within such a system, the politics of personality dominates, and the clash of personalities over the past year was particularly pronounced. The former heir-designate, Ayatollah Hossein Ali Montazeri, a respected and senior clergyman, might have been able to mediate the differences that now exist. But he had lost Khomeini's trust and his own position in March 1989 after he publicly denounced executions which took place in the wake of the 1988 cease-fire in the Gulf War.

In the last years of Khomeini's life, the country's effective number two was the parliamentary speaker, Hojatoleslam Hashemi-Rafsanjani, who was elected president in the middle of July. Rafsanjani's broadly pragmatic views predominated and his cabinet contained a number of technocrats better known for their experience and qualifications than for their ideological commitment. Three of the leading pragmatists in the government are the Foreign Minister Dr Ali Akbar Velayati, the Economics and Finance Minister Dr Mohsen Nurbakhsh, and the Oil Minister Gholamreza Aqazadeh.

Deeply suspicious of the views of this group are the radicals, most visibly represented by former Interior Minister Hojatoleslam Ali Hossein Mohtashemi, who was dropped from Rafsanjani's cabinet. He has repeatedly drawn attention to policies he opposes by insisting that they deviate from Khomeini's legacy, a potent accusation. Other radicals include the former prime minister Hossein Mussavi, whose post was abolished in constitutional changes which took place in the summer; the former intelligence minister Hojatoleslam Mohammad Reyshahri, who was made Prosecutor-General, replacing another radical Hojatoleslam Khoiniha. There are also ideological militants in sections of the Revolutionary Guards, universities and the media.

Despite the setback that these groups have suffered because of the death of Khomeini and rise of Rafsanjani to the presidency, their influence should not be ignored. For this reason the political situation since Khomeini's death has remained a volatile one.

Rafsanjani's main aim, particularly after the death of Khomeini, was to put into motion a reform programme aimed at centralizing executive authority. Greater centralization would curb the activities of the radical groups, which benefit from a weak executive structure, by fitting them into a bureaucratic system which makes them responsible to those higher in the chain of command. In this effort Rafsanjani was backed by the new Leader, now known as Ayatollah Khamenei, and attention focused on making these changes through a revision of the constitution. Rafsanjani set out his position in an interview: the government's lack of administrative experience, he said, had led to an incomplete constitution being drawn up in 1979; the parliament makes laws but could not decide on the direction of state policy, while the government, which did direct policy, was headed by a president who was not in charge of policy-making either.

When the final changes to the constitution were brought before the parliament dissenting deputies objected to the sweeping powers that would be concentrated in the presidency as a result. One deputy resigned after warning that the new measures would 'accumulate power in the hands of the few'. Nevertheless, the new constitution was approved by parliament and then by a public referendum on 29 July, the day of the presidential elections.

The main elements of the new constitution include the abolition of the post of prime minister and the creation instead of an executive with the president at its head and two vice-presidents. Because of the difficulty of finding religiously qualified spiritual leaders, the requirement that such a leader be *amarja*, or Source of Emulation (a form of Grand Ayatollah) was also abolished. An existing body, called the Assembly for Deciding What is Best (also known as the Expediency Council) was expanded and written into the constitution. It had been created by Khomeini in 1988 to break the legislative deadlock between parliament and the 12-man Council of Guardians, the body responsible for vetting legislation to see that it complies with Islamic law. A National Security Council (NSC), headed by the president, was created, and centralization was introduced in the judiciary through the stipulation that one man, rather than the 5-man Supreme Judicial Council, should be at its head. This corpus of reforms represented a considerable victory for Rafsanjani and it is highly unlikely that he would have stood for president if parliament had failed to pass them.

Trying to Control the Military

Although Rafsanjani had been appointed acting commander-in-chief of the armed forces by Khomeini and had been in that position for 15 months, in September 1989 he resigned in favour of the new leader,

Ayatollah Khamenei. (The constitution stipulates that the Leader is the head of the armed forces.) Rafsanjani might have tried to maintain himself in the position, but he probably felt obliged to relinquish command to deflect further criticism of his extensive powers as president.

Rafsanjani, backed by Ayatollah Khamenei, has been attempting to merge units of the two main fighting forces: the army and the Revolutionary Guards. This merger would have the advantage of greater control and accountability. The Revolutionary Guards, as the ideological arm of the military, form a crucial base of government support, and they have been given many privileges as a result. With the Gulf War at an end, the administrative difficulty and the costs of running two parallel organizations have provided the incentive to restructure the army and the Revolutionary Guards.

While the leadership desires the merger, it has also made it clear that the military must remain strong enough to deter Iraq from launching another invasion, which will continue to involve a heavy financial commitment. With the cease-fire, the government has felt secure enough to ease military conscription and to raise extra revenue by giving Iranian men abroad the option of deferring military service through payment of $13,500.

Attempts to merge the two military organizations have proved extraordinarily difficult and the government has come under attack for planning to do away with one of them. In November, Ayatollah Khamenei felt it necessary to deny strongly that the government was considering dissolving one or other of the forces. Yet neither organization wishes to be merged with the other, and both have intrinsic value to the government – the army for its professionalism and the Revolutionary Guards for its ideological support.

Instead, piecemeal moves have been under way to merge the overlapping non-combatant units of the two organizations. A bill abolishing the Ministry of the Revolutionary Guards, the body responsible for the Guards and administering its armaments and production factories, was finally approved by parliament. These responsibilities have been assigned instead to the Ministry of Defence, which has been renamed Defence and Armed Forces Logistics. Another potentially important change to the Revolutionary Guards was the decision to introduce military ranks; this has still to be approved by the parliament. It is a controversial move that has been heavily criticized by hardliners as diluting the 'fraternal spirit' of the corps. Through such moves, the government hopes to introduce greater professionalism to the corps as a step towards an eventual merger.

The danger for the government lies in the possibility of an erosion of support by the Revolutionary Guards or even of open confrontation. It has therefore balanced such moves with frequent and public declarations of praise for the Guards and has maintained their privileges, in terms of private facilities such as hospitals and shops. The government has also ensured that some changes in the regular military redound to their advantage. In October 1989, a former Minister of the Revolutionary Guards, Ali Shamkhani, was made commander of the navy. The navy had been the target of a series of military purges during 1989 because of fears that US intelligence had penetrated it more extensively than other arms of the military.

A Struggling Economy

The economy continues to be plagued by high inflation, a lack of investment because of insufficient oil revenues, and low productivity. According to the government, factories were working at only 20 to 30% of productive capacity, a reflection of the difficulty in obtaining raw materials and machinery from abroad. Measures to attract the private sector into productive investment have not proved successful because of a continuing belief that government moves were unpredictable and legislative guarantees were inadequate. In November Rafsanjani summed up the difficulties: 'We are still entangled with the problem of people who have gained money easily and are not prepared to invest their money in production. They want to profit through investing in the black market, hoarding, being middle-men and making profits by illegal means.' An offer to sell off state-owned factories did not have many takers, with the private sector preferring to put money into commerce and property rather than industry.

The government admits to a yearly inflation rate of 30%, but in some areas it is well above that. In Tehran property prices doubled during 1989. While many goods are available, most can only be purchased on the black market at prohibitively high prices. The black-market dollar rate fell in October after the government announced a new official rate of Rs1,000 to the dollar, available to importers of state goods, against the black market rate of Rs1,250 (the official exchange rate was Rs71 to the dollar). By December, however, the black-market rate had again begun to creep upwards and there is considerable speculation concerning new moves to devalue the rial.

Oil income, which was some $12bn in 1989, was barely high enough to prevent the breakdown of the economic system. Greater productivity in all sectors of the economy is dependent on higher levels of investment – for example, it has been estimated that $8bn is needed to sustain Iran's present productive capacity of a maximum of three million barrel/day, yet the country remains dependent on oil for over 90% of its foreign-exchange earnings. Investment might be obtained from abroad, but this is a sensitive subject since foreign loans have come to be equated with foreign domination. Many projects have been implemented on short-term credit rates, however, and in December Rafsanjani reported that these amounted to $10–12bn. A further $27bn of foreign capital investment is provided for in the five-year plan, which had a stormy passage through parliament and which was cleared in January 1990 only after extensive revisions.

Troubled Foreign Policy

President Rafsanjani's foreign policy has been characterized by an effort to reintegrate Iran into the international community and to obtain support for Iran's position on a peace settlement with Iraq. Moves towards these two goals were under way when they were jeopardized in February 1989 by Ayatollah Khomeini's imposition of a decree (*fatwa*) sentencing the British author Salman Rushdie to death for blasphemy for his novel, *The Satanic Verses*. Although both Khamenei and Rafsanjani subsequently endorsed the move, it thoroughly disrupted their policies by precipitating a new diplomatic crisis. Indeed, Khamenei appeared to be looking for a way out when he implied a few days later that should Rushdie repent, he might be forgiven. He was almost immediately overruled by Khomeini.

The Rushdie death sentence, which came immediately after the death of six men in riots during an anti-Rushdie demonstration in Pakistan, represented Ayatollah Khomeini's determination to reassert the primacy and centrality of Islam to the country's political system. The move underlined the government's difficulty in trying to pursue realism without losing its ideological constituency. It was also another example – along with the issue of the Western hostages held by pro-Iranian radicals in Lebanon – of the contradictory policies which resulted from the dual leadership structure. Although foreign policy has been more consistent since Khomeini's death, walking the tightrope between ideology and pragmatism continues to produce evident contradictions and severely limits the foreign ministry's room for manoeuvre.

Regional Relations

Although Iran and Iraq continued to meet in New York and Geneva under the auspices of the UN in an effort to implement the negotiating package incorporated in UN Security Council Resolution 598, no progress has been made. The main stumbling block continued to be the preconditions established by each party. Iran insisted that the Resolution be implemented in the order of its paragraphs; paragraph one calls for a complete withdrawal of troops to the internationally recognized frontier. Iraq, loath to give up its occupation of some 1,000 sq km of Iranian soil because of its possible use as a bargaining chip, called instead for the repatriation of POWs. Although Iran has compromised by proposing a simultaneous Iraqi withdrawal and an exchange of prisoners, Iraq has deemed this unacceptable and there is little sign of a breakthrough.

Since the end of the Gulf War, Iran has sought to mend relations with the smaller Gulf states. Officials frequently mention the need to leave old grudges behind (i.e., Arab support for Iraq during the war) and have proposed a 'strategic plan' for the region that would reintegrate Iran into the area and leave local problems in the hands of the regional states. Iran also called for closer economic ties with the Gulf states, and in September announced that technical studies were under way for the export of natural gas to some of the southern littoral states. The main aim behind these moves was to enlist the support of the Gulf states in any eventual peace settlement with Iraq, but it was also clear that Iran hoped to reassert its own claim that it was the dominant power in the Persian Gulf. Its best relations continued to be with Oman and the UAE, whereas its attempts to restore relations with Saudi Arabia did not succeed. In December 1988 Rafsanjani had predicted that relations would be normalized, and in early 1989 Deputy Foreign Minister Besharati expressed the view that Iran would be participating in that summer's pilgrimage to Mecca. But nothing came of these moves and relations deteriorated even further after the execution in Saudi Arabia of 16 Kuwaiti Shi'ites for their role in a bomb attack on Mecca.

Wider Relations

The dichotomy between the pragmatic and fundamentalist strains in Iranian foreign policy was most evident in relations with Europe. They came under severe strain after Khomeini pronounced his death sentence on Rushdie, although most European countries returned their ambassadors to Tehran several weeks after recalling them in protest. In early March, however, Iran and the UK broke off diplomatic relations. In September the head of the judiciary, Ayatollah Yazdi suggested that a pardon was possible for Roger Cooper, a British businessman and journalist who had been imprisoned on espionage charges, but this idea was dropped in the face of sharp reactions from hardliners.

In February 1990, as the anniversary of Rushdie's death sentence approached, Rafsanjani hinted that under certain conditions the death sentence could be lifted. He was almost immediately countered by Ayatollah Khameini who played to the radical fundamentalists at home by reiterating the eternal validity of the death sentence. Another instance of the difficulty Iran has in pursuing normal foreign relations came in July 1989 when Iranian–Austrian relations were strained as a result of the detention of Iranian suspects by the Austrian authorities in connection with the assassination in Vienna of Dr Abdorrahman Qassemlou, the leader of the anti-Iranian Kurdish Democratic Party.

In January 1989, Khomeini sent a delegation to Moscow with a personal message for Mikhail Gorbachev. This was the start of a new diplomatic initiative aimed at improving relations with one of the superpowers, in the hope that pressure might be brought to bear on Iraq to implement UN Resolution 598. Rafsanjani went ahead with a planned visit to the Soviet Union on 20 June, less than three weeks after Ayatollah Khomeini's death. A wide-ranging series of economic and trade agreements, including the resumption of sales of Iranian gas to the USSR, were signed later in the year.

The disturbances in Azerbaijan in early 1990 threatened to disrupt these close ties; yet although the Iranian press deplored the despatch of Soviet troops to the region and often expressed sympathy with the Azeris, these comments were mixed with others supporting Gorbachev and *glasnost*. The Azerbaijan issue is not a simple one for the Iranian government. It might like to give encouragement to Soviet Azeris to assert their Muslim identity but this contains the danger of a nationalist movement for autonomy by Iranian Azeris.

By contrast to its success with the USSR, a breakthrough to restore relations with the US still eluded Iran. While Khomeini was alive, significant efforts to improve relations were scarcely possible. With his death, there were some indications of Iranian willingness to negotiate the release of the eight US hostages in Lebanon in exchange for the return of Iranian assets frozen in the US. A number of indirect contacts were developed, but they produced no results. It is clear, however, that without some resolution of the hostage question there can be no improvement in US–Iranian relations, and in the first months of 1990 Rafsanjani was again hinting at efforts by his government to seek the release of the Western hostages.

Moderation in the Future?

There was an unexpectedly smooth and peaceful transfer of power after Khomeini's death. Although the passing of the leader opened an opportunity for President Rafsanjani to confront the hardliners once and for all, he chose instead the less decisive politics of accommodation. Thus, for the moment, the Islamic Republic shows little inclination to abandon its ideological base, and the new Leader, Ayatollah Khamenei, has continued the tradition of rhetorical religious pronouncements and has emphasized Islam as the alternative ideology to communism.

Yet within these parameters a discernible pattern of introspection has emerged, with emphasis on the 'export of revolution' dropped in favour of rebuilding the country in an Islamic model. The moves towards centralization signal the government's determination to curb the revolutionary excesses of the previous decade if only to enhance its own authority. Moreover, even if ideology has not been abandoned, it has been shown that it can, to some extent, be revised to suit the needs of the time.

While Ayatollah Khomeini emphasized that the price of Iran's independence was isolation and poverty, President Rafsanjani instead avers that independence cannot be achieved unless the country is wealthy, and that for it (and therefore, Islam) to be influential it must be part of the world community. If the present group of pragmatic leaders can retain power, it seems likely that rhetoric will diverge increasingly from action, while ideology is revised to fit political necessity. Perhaps pragmatism will prevail.

East Asia

The desire for a loosening of the political and economic constrictions that have for so long stultified the lives of the people of communist-ruled nations was as manifest in East Asia as it was in Europe. Unfortunately, the outcome of demonstrations for greater freedom were very different on the two continents. In China an intransigent gerontocracy, fearful of losing power, called on an army willing to turn its arms against its own people to repress peaceful, unarmed demonstrations. The brutality of that June night and the subsequent and continuing repression may have cowed the people in the short term, but there are few who believe that either the desire or the ability of the people to stand up again for greater liberalization has been totally removed. In North Korea the regime is showing the strain of its isolated position, but the tight bonds of control that Kim Il Sung has woven have not yet begun to unravel.

In two other communist states, however, external pressures that have resulted from the changes in the Soviet Union, and internal ones caused by their deteriorating economies, have led their regimes to institute changes from above. Mongolia has moved very rapidly to multi-party elections and is trying to adopt its own *perestroika* to match that under way in the Soviet Union. In Vietnam, the regime has been systematically introducing a market-based economy in hopes of countering the difficult conditions that have resulted from its previous reliance on a command economy of the old Soviet model. Vietnamese leaders also hope to encourage investment, particularly from the West, and in part, this motivated the withdrawal of Vietnamese forces from Cambodia during 1989. With this obstacle out of the way, there have been a number of new efforts to negotiate a settlement to the Cambodian war, but they have all foundered on the irreconcilable positions of the four local factions.

The Philippines is undergoing a deep political and economic crisis. Mrs Aquino came to power four years ago as a result of 'people power' amid expectations that the peoples' lives would be vastly improved. Now, however, the Aquino government is heavily criticized for its corruption, she has lost the support of the peasants by failing to pass an effective land reform bill, the middle class has deserted her because of what it perceives as her indecisiveness, and the highly politicized officers of the armed forces are at odds with each other and with the government.

In December 1989 the sixth, most sustained and serious, coup attempt was launched by disaffected army officers and personnel against Mrs Aquino. Her government was saved only by a timely intervention by American jet fighters (although they did not engage in combat, their appearance in the sky provided air cover for the government ground forces) and by the continued loyal support of the Defence Minister Gen Fidel Ramos. Yet, although they were unsuccessful in their latest attempt, the rebels were more persuaded to move out of the positions they had seized than subdued by force. They are still at large and reportedly preparing their next attempt.

There is thus a serious question whether the increasingly fragile government can survive until the next presidential elections due in 1992. Eduardo Cojuangco, the very popular multi-millionaire crony of Ferdinand Marcos, who had left the country after being charged with a large number of crimes, has returned from abroad to a hero's welcome. He will be a formidable foe to Mrs Aquino; he is thought to have been involved in the last coup attempt and would not hesitate to bankroll another. There is also the question of whether Gen Ramos will be content to continue to bail out Mrs Aquino, or whether he will feel that a stronger hand at the tiller (his own, for example), would not benefit the country. In any event the situation in the Philippines remains among the most volatile in East Asia.

CHINA: YET AGAIN IN CRISIS

Every ten years or so China drives itself into yet another major crisis and change of policy. In its 40-year existence, communist China has careered from the Great Leap Forward of the late 1950s, to the Cultural Revolution of the late 1960s, and then to the adoption of the Four Modernizations in the late 1970s, without finding a stable road to development. Now it has created for itself yet another crisis, one whose climax was determined by the blinkered views of China's aged leaders and their fear of losing power. That climax, the massacre in Beijing (or less accurately, in Tiananmen Square) on the night of 3–4 June made front-page news around the world, and did more damage to China's international standing than any event since the Cultural Revolution.

The attention of the world had been focused on China, not because of student protestors, but because of the Sino-Soviet summit (15–18 May), arguably the largest shift in the East Asian strategic balance since President Nixon visited China in 1972. For a few brief moments between the departure of Mikhail Gorbachev on 18 May and the declaration of martial law in Beijing two days later, China achieved the international position that had eluded it for decades. By the time the Beijing bloodletting took place, however, China's leaders were far too blinded by their paranoia to appreciate the success of their foreign-policy initiatives, and to begin to reap any benefits from it. As part of the rationalization for the gravity of the domestic crisis, China began to blame Westerners for having fomented the unrest.

Crisis at Home
In the early days of the protests, there seemed little reason for China to have created such difficulties for itself. Student demonstrators first emerged on the streets after the death of former Party General Secretary

Hu Yaobang on 15 April. Hu, who had been purged in January 1987, ostensibly for having failed to take a firm line against student demonstrations, had become a symbol of shelved political reform and at least some toleration of the airing of more radical ideas. Thus initial student demonstrations, overwhelmingly in Beijing, were really about the failure of the leadership to contemplate wider reform in China, even though many of the specific demands were focused more narrowly.

The subsequent dilemma might have been avoided if it were not for the volatile combination of deep-seated problems with economic reform and pronounced divisions among China's leaders. An ill-judged sharp attack on the students in the *People's Daily* on 26 April was an attempt by the Party to avoid a re-run of the events which led to the purge of Hu Yaobang. This official condemnation of their actions served only to enrage the students; demonstrations resumed, now much larger and spreading to other major cities in China. On 27 April more than 100,000 took to the streets of Beijing, and daily demonstrations in the thousands were mounted. On 13 May some students went on hunger strike, thereby intensifying the emotional tension of the crisis even further.

It is possible that a firmer, but more careful and united Party leadership might have avoided a confrontation, but such a leadership did not exist. The reasons for the division, and indeed the deeper cause of the unrest, was the stalling of economic reform. As a series of Party and State meetings in late 1988 and the first quarter of 1989 made plain, the leadership was far too divided on how to proceed with economic reform to take any positive action. Price reform was postponed for three years, and speech after speech by China's top leaders indicated that they had no new ideas on how to break out of the doldrums. With the real rate of inflation rising to nearly 40% in late 1988, and the inevitable corruption that comes from trying to mix planned and market economies increasing, there was growing disquiet among many ordinary workers who yearned, unlike the students, for a more stable and fair system of government. China's approximately 800 million peasants, who still constitute some 70% of the population, had benefited most from the decade of reforms, but even they were now finding it harder to make profits at the same pace. Because of the broader economic problems, the central government was even unable to guarantee payment to the peasants for their grain production.

The most acute problems were in urban China. On the streets of Beijing, and to a much smaller extent in other Chinese cities, the demonstrations grew in size. Fed by apparent division in the Party hierarchy, and 'protected' by the presence of the Western media in China for the meeting of the Asian Development Bank in early May and then the Sino-Soviet summit in mid-May, first students and then workers expressed their loosely assembled complaints.

The mix of motives for the protestors, who eventually came to demand the resignation of the conservative Prime Minister Li Peng and even of the *de facto* paramount leader, Deng Xiaoping, reflected the fact that they drew inspiration from a number of sources. Some were students who had lived in the West, while others were counting on Filipino-style 'people's power'. Considering the range of demands and student groups involved, they were remarkably well organized in marshalling the crowds, even if they could not produce a coherent set of political demands. On 23 May there were over a million demonstrators on the streets of the capital, but still there was no violence.

The most important inspiration to the protestors, to everyone's surprise, came from the Soviet Union and Eastern Europe. It was not merely the fact that Gorbachev's visit provided a good reason for cautious behaviour by Chinese riot police; it was far more that Gorbachev had inspired a political reform within a communist system that was much harder for Chinese leaders opposed to similar liberalization to refuse. It was one thing to denounce Western pluralist democracy as unsuited to China, but far harder for a communist regime to reject the experiments with pluralism in one Party which seemed to be sweeping so many communist states in Europe.

By the time martial law was eventually declared on 20 May, against the advice of the moderate Party General Secretary Zhao Ziyang, the protests had gathered too much support to be easily subdued. Zhao's tearful apology to the students on 19 May for his inability to convince the Politburo of the need for compromise was a clear sign of major division at the top, and the fact that he had lost the battle. Yet, even with Zhao's loss of influence, it was made plain to the protestors that there was still considerable high-level opposition to a bloody imposition of martial law. During the ensuing fortnight, demonstrations continued, and often focused around marooned People's Liberation Army (PLA) convoys which had been brought in to intimidate the protestors, but which ended up as symbols of collapsed Party authority.

The government apparently tried to wait out the students and indeed the numbers on Tiananmen Square did begin to dwindle towards the end of May. The protests were recharged, however, by the erection on 30 May of a 'Statue of Democracy' modelled on the Statue of Liberty (but with two hands on the torch because the burden of democracy was so much heavier in China). A new hunger strike also brought increasing numbers of people back into the square and the authorities then decided to clear it. It now seems clear that the PLA forces, which had been gathered from most of the military regions and camped outside Beijing since 20 May, were not sent in to kill thousands of people, but they were determined to clear the streets and square and were prepared to kill if necessary. When they did move, very late on the night of 3 June, they did not come in with guns blazing, but soon after they were blocked on the outskirts skirmishes turned to warning shots and then deadly fire. Students fought back and many hundreds were killed.

The specific trigger for the determined action on the night of 3–4 June is not clear, much as it is uncertain whether a few hundred or up to 6,000 people died that night. A careful analysis by Amnesty International suggests about 1,300 people died. Whatever the specific death toll, this was the first time repression of peaceful protest by fire-power on this scale was seen on television screens around the world. Overnight, China lost its label as the 'good communist'. As communism collapsed in Eastern Europe later in the year, China's policies looked even more antiquated – relics of a harsher world.

The Consequences

The death toll and damage to China's image are the consequences most often noted. Foreigners were evacuated as rumours spread of civil war between rival factions and troops. Western countries swiftly imposed sanctions. And yet, from the point of view of those who gave the order to open fire, their immediate objectives were achieved. Order was restored to the streets, and quiet has since been maintained. Despite the revolution in Eastern Europe, martial law was lifted on 11 January 1990. Most foreign business personnel had returned to China by July 1989, although the tourists did not.

These few pluses have been achieved at considerable cost. China's economy was damaged by the loss of foreign currency, although it is true that it was already in crisis because of the far more important domestic problems of inflation. Those whom the regime must rely on if it is to drag the country into a semblance of prosperity have been severely disaffected. The intellectuals are now unwilling to co-operate with the regime, especially as a very public witch-hunt sought the ring-leaders of the demonstrations. A large number of activists were caught, many more were cowed, and some symbolic executions took place in public before it became too embarrassing to continue. The urban workers were driven into a sullen, and dispirited, acquiescence. Students and their teachers have been totally alienated and radicalized.

For all these swift reactions, and despite the depth of the economic crisis, the purge of top officials was tiny. Zhao Ziyang and his fellow Politburo member Hu Quili were removed from their highest posts at the 4th Plenum of the 13th Central Committee on 24 June. Yet none of the fallen leaders were put on trial, as the Gang of Four had been following Mao's death. Despite much talk in the Western press of dissension within the PLA, there were no purges of top military officials. At a plenary session of the Party in November 1989, Deng Xiaoping gave up his last official position, the Chairmanship of the Party's Central Military Commission, although he was expected to remain the power behind the throne for as long as he was able. His successor, Jiang Zemin, had been given Zhao's office of Party General Secretary at the June Plenum. The other new members of the Politburo 'elected' in June were the more moderate mayor of Tianjin, Li Ruihuan, and the more conservative Song Ping. The appointment of these three suggested that a complex compromise had been arranged. Jiang was previously in charge of the Party in Shanghai where unrest was dealt with firmly, but without bloodshed. Little is known for certain about his political orientation, but he seems to be an interim appointment while far stronger forces continue to jockey for power. To the extent that it is important, Jiang, like Deng, seems to be a supporter of continued economic reform while refusing any serious political reform.

Both as a result of the march of events during the past year and signs that Deng Xiaoping's health is deteriorating, speculation about the successor to ultimate power has increased. While Prime Minister Li Peng and President Yang Shangkun have been seen as conservatives whose power was strengthened during the course of the crisis, it is far from clear that either will be able to seize power after Deng. The limited nature of the purge and the appointment of Jiang Zemin suggest that a challenge is still being mounted by those, such as Qiao Shi (in charge of security) or Li Ruihuan, who favour Deng-like limits on political reform while pursuing economic reform and an open door to the outside world.

As always in China, these struggles must be seen primarily in terms of personality, although given the gravity of the economic crisis, they have major implications for the way the Chinese people will live. The Party plenum in November seemed to have agreed on the need for economic retrenchment, while disagreeing about when and how to restart the reforms. No serious political reforms were on the agenda, although the notion of greater professionalism and a separation of Party and State were still paid some lip service. Early economic indicators suggested that inflation was falling back to single figures and overall growth rates for the year were projected to be in the more reasonable 5–8% range. Nevertheless, the leadership debate continues.

The Role of the PLA

Any professional armed force knows that its basic duties include the preservation of law and order. By definition, when a relatively united political leadership calls on the PLA to intervene in politics, a professional PLA will do so. At the same time, no professional army will want to fire on its own people, and therefore it is not surprising that soldiers were reluctant to shoot to kill. The reluctance to shed blood, however, should not be confused with the basis for civil war between elements in the army and political hardliners, although many in the West hoped their favoured moderates would benefit from such a clash.

Civil war was never likely in the period between May and June. Yet Deng's determination to organize a special 'war front' of armies from around the country suggested that both the Party and PLA needed to be convinced that firm action by the military was necessary to maintain governmental authority. The open letter on 22 May calling for the troops to return to their barracks, signed by a number of leaders of the military, was a clear statement of opposition to bloodshed, but it was never meant to be a blanket opposition to the future use of such force.

Although not an exact parallel, because the action was against Tibetans and not Han Chinese, in early March the Party leaders and the PLA had demonstrated that they were prepared to resort to force if law and order were seriously challenged. Large-scale rioting had broken out in Lhasa; after three days Beijing declared martial law and on 5 March troops fired on unarmed civilians, killing up to 50 people and injuring hundreds. It must have been more difficult to convince the PLA that this kind of action was necessary in Beijing, but the fact that no major military men were purged after June suggests that the newly professionalized PLA did its duty without major opposition.

This is not to say that the PLA remains happy with what happened. Unofficially at least, some soldiers have described the events of May–June as a tragedy. As the use of the PLA in the Cultural Revolution and in the post-Mao arrest of the Gang of Four suggests, the PLA can intervene in support of 'moderates' so long as they are providing stability and have support from the majority of the Party. As the debates over economic issues continue, the PLA has been making clear, especially at the November Plenum, that it wants to focus on military modernization and not be bothered by the political education campaigns so beloved of Political Commissars. Indeed, there is evidence that the supposedly conservative President Yang Shangkun, himself a former General, shares this concern over PLA professionalism. The PLA will be a major factor in the succession struggle, but, like the rest of the country, it will be watching closely what happens in the Party's Politburo debates.

Relative Calm in Foreign Relations

The outside world had an effect on China's domestic crisis more because it was on the scene and observing, than through what it actively did at the time. The presence of the media (and through them the rest of the world), and the Gorbachev entourage, provided an opportunity for the Chinese people to play high-risk politics. But for the most part, the foreigners merely watched and reacted.

The reactions to the brutal *dénouement* varied widely. The people most affected were the normally politically apathetic inhabitants of Hong Kong, who came out on the streets as never before in support of the democratic movement, and then watched in horror as those who after 1997 will be their rulers used massive force against political dissidents. Confidence, that ever-so-volatile commodity in Hong Kong, took a beating, and while the stock-market plunged by one-quarter, queues for foreign passports turned into a near stampede.

Predictably, China blamed the UK for trying to 'internationalize' the problem of Hong Kong. The UK government refused calls from its colony, including the Governor, for the right of abode in the UK for all those with British passports. Proponents argued that this measure would provide insurance against worst-case outcomes after 1997, and thus militate against a mass exodus of key personnel in the intervening years. However, a package of measures announced in December looked likely to mean that up to 225,000 additional Hong Kong residents (50,000 key personnel and their families) would be granted full British citizenship. As the Foreign Office began discreet enquiries with fellow members of the developed world and the Commonwealth about the possibility of sharing the burden of refugees from Hong Kong, China claimed the UK was trying to undermine the agreement reached in 1984. In October relations deteriorated to such an extent that China briefly refused to accept the return of those Chinese who continued to flee to Hong Kong, making it plain that it would not tolerate the people of Hong Kong telling China how to run what Beijing considered were its own affairs.

From China's point of view, its goal of the convergence of Hong Kong with the mainland required most of the change to come from the former British colony. When East European communism collapsed with the push given by demonstrating masses, China became even more sensitive about demonstrations in Hong Kong. Beijing made it clear that its formula of 'one country-two systems' did not mean that the residents of Hong Kong would be allowed to call for a change in the system on the mainland. In the discussions of the Basic Law, which is to govern Hong Kong, China refused to accept that any more than a third of Hong Kong's Legislative Council would be directly elected before 1997.

No other territory, apart from Taiwan, was as immediately affected by the unrest in China. Japan went along with the limited Western economic sanctions, including suspension of new loans to China, but like other East Asians, Japan was not prepared to isolate China. Taiwanese urged Westerners to take a firm line, while resisting any attempt to sever their own trade contacts with the mainland. Indonesia paused in the process of restoring diplomatic relations with China, but by the autumn, talks had resumed.

China's neighbours were worried that a paranoid China would become more dangerous. There were signs that China was unwilling to make significant compromises over a settlement in Cambodia, especially if some Western countries wanted it. South Korea for its part saw the danger that the new-found economic advantage of its new relationship with China might be lost and was unwilling to be pushed into sanctions by the same Western countries that were complaining about South Korean trade surpluses. Above all, it was Japan which argued that it had not sold weapons to China or made irrational investments in joint ventures, and should therefore not pay the price for the excessive optimism in some Western countries about trade with China.

It was in the more distant US and Western Europe that the most vociferous attacks on China were mounted, even while some business continued as usual. President Bush, who had served as head of what later became the American embassy in China, and who had made a presidential visit to the country in late February 1989, quickly responded with a suspension of all high-level and military contacts and supported suspension of economic aid on the day after the massacre. As China's foreign debt was already growing, and the economy was in dire straits, the American-led action had more than a merely symbolic effect. Other Western countries, most notably in the European Community, adopted similar measures. On 26 June the World Bank deferred consideration of seven new development loans worth $780m.

There was more emotion than strategy to this reaction and soon those with business interests moved back to China. New business was likely to be much slower in coming, in large part due to the belated recognition in the West that the Chinese reforms were in trouble. It was more that the West learned lessons about China, than the Chinese were taught how to behave by the West. Indeed, Chinese were soon readmitted to the Grumman plant in the US as part of the agreement to refurbish Chinese military aircraft with American high technology. President Bush sent his National Security Adviser, Brent Scowcroft, to China twice in 1989, the first time in July. Clearly, despite intense public pressure in the US, the President was determined to keep contacts with China open, while maintaining an ostensibly critical official line. Italian and UK firms continued their sales of non-lethal military equipment. West Germany, by far the largest EC trader with China made no attempt to withdraw the majority of its business personnel in the immediate aftermath of the military suppression of the student movement.

Such evidence of raw pragmatism is not to suggest that all was completely 'business as usual'. France and the US were both host to dissident leaders, and thousands of Chinese were being supported with government loans or with a lenient policy on immigration and visas. The dissident academic, Fang Lizhi, continued to be sheltered in the US embassy in Beijing despite Chinese insistence that he be surrendered to their authority. China found it harder to get loans on preferential terms and its application to join the GATT was delayed. When East Europeans showed there was a much more pleasant way to cope with demands for democracy, China was held up as the symbol of all that was nasty about communism. If it were not for the fact that most analysts, in and out of government, felt that there would soon be a change of leadership in China and that there was some hope for a 'reversal of verdicts', the reaction might have been harsher. For the time being, academic and even official contacts with China were being restored in the hope of building bridges to those who might soon take over. China also derived leverage from its nuisance value by renewing the sale of ballistic missiles in the Third World, notably the Middle East. China was too important to be isolated, and the Chinese knew it.

Perhaps the most important long-term reaction was in the Soviet Union and Eastern Europe. It was in part a matter of political convergence that had brought the Soviet Union and China to the summit in Beijing in May. The more tolerant China grew of Soviet-style socialism under Gorbachev, however, the more, without trying, the Soviet Union became a factor in China's domestic politics. The choice that China's Communist Party faced in June 1989 – to use naked force in defending its leading role or not – was one that Soviet and East European communists recognized as their own fundamental option.

The distinctive political culture of East Asia made it easier for China to pick the authoritarian route of fighting to keep power. The Soviet, and most East European, reaction was to recoil in horror. Not only was Gorbachev's most sparkling foreign-policy achievement ruined by the chaos on the streets of Beijing and Shanghai, but the Soviet Union was put in the uncomfortable position of having to comment on Chinese domestic politics, just when it had built a *détente* based on non-interference in domestic affairs. Worst of all, the slaughter in Beijing damaged the reputation of communist reformers around the world. It suggested to those cynical of the Soviet reforms that they too would eventually have to resort to the tactics of Tiananmen. For the Soviet leadership, nothing was as vital as the fate of the reforms.

Thus, despite the officially cordial relations between China and the USSR and the still booming trade along the frontier, the Soviet Union made it unofficially plain that it was strongly opposed to the Chinese actions. Despite continuing negotiations on troop withdrawals and confidence-building measures along the frontier, Gorbachev has put rapid improvement in relations with China to one side. In any case, his attention, like that of the rest of the world, was focused on the shrivelling of communist power in Central Europe.

The option of using the tactics of Tiananmen was apparently considered by nearly every East European Communist Party in October–November, and each time the Soviet response was sought, it was to abjure reliance on force. Only in Romania in December were they tried, with bloody, but unsuccessful, results. The impact of events in China was far-reaching if only because it made plain the costs of fighting for communist power. Western sanctions and criticisms of China might be said to have had little effect on China, but they, along with the Soviet reaction, certainly made it far more likely that Eastern Europe would go down the road of political pluralism. At a time when China is in so much turmoil and uncertainty, it is perhaps the 'China lesson' that will be the most far-reaching and enduring impact of the events in Tiananmen Square. What remains to be seen is what, if anything, China has learned from the fate of Ceauşescu.

POLITICAL TREMORS IN JAPAN

Japan's sustained economic success over the last three decades has been closely associated with the continuous grip on power by the Liberal Democratic Party (LDP). Despite electoral ups and downs during the 1970s and 1980s, the LDP has managed to control the *Diet* throughout those years as well as earlier. In 1989, however, the LDP faced the most serious crisis of confidence in its leadership since the violent ideological clashes over the US–Japan Security Treaty in 1960; it lost its overall majority in the Upper House for the first time and it faced the prospect of losing its more crucial Lower House majority in elections scheduled for mid-February 1990.

The succession of financial and sex scandals which resulted in the fall of two prime ministers in as many months, inevitably made the Japanese government more inward-looking and preoccupied with domestic political tribulations. As a result, Japanese diplomacy, which had been curtailed by the lengthy illness of Emperor Hirohito, displayed even more passivity and hesitancy than usual. This was unfortunate at a time when a number of international developments, such as the suppression of the democratic movement in China and the dramatic changes in Eastern Europe, as well as increasing difficulties in the US–Japan relationship, called for a greater degree of Japanese engagement.

Political Setbacks

Prime Minister Noboru Takeshita spent much of the spring of 1989 trying to weather the ever-widening Recruit Cosmos share-dealing scandal, but ministerial resignations earlier in the year did not stem the tide of fresh revelations of corruption (see *Strategic Survey 1988–1989*, pp. 125–6). The former chairman of the Recruit company was arrested in mid-February on bribery charges, as were two former senior civil servants on similar charges in March; and the list of senior LDP politicians implicated grew to include former prime minister, Yasuhiro Nakasone. The LDP's morale and popular support continued to fall; in March the LDP withdrew from contesting a prefectural election for fear of certain defeat and by early April public opinion polls showed the government's support as having dropped to a mere 9%. The opposition parties, though themselves not all totally clear of involvement in the Recruit affair, nevertheless continued to boycott the *Diet*, refusing to pass the budget until Nakasone clarified his role in the affair. On 11 April Takeshita admitted that during 1985–7 he had received ¥151m in political donations from Recruit (despite his denial in October 1988 of any such receipt), although he argued that these funds had been handled in accordance with existing political funding laws.

Takeshita's admissions, which he had hoped would quiet the furor, only made things worse. Young LDP politicians were now in almost open revolt, calling for political reform, and Takeshita's fate was sealed when a prominent business leader called for a new prime minister. On 25 April, Takeshita announced his resignation, to take effect once a successor had been found and the budget passed. Numerous names were then canvassed, including one elderly ex-prime minister, before Sosuke Uno, Foreign Minister in the Takeshita cabinet and generally thought of as a 'clean' if lightweight politician, was selected. By the time he took office, in early June, the Recruit scandal was beginning to die down. Nakasone had resigned from the LDP though not the *Diet*, two leading politicians (one LDP and one *Komeito*) had been arrested, LDP politicians involved in the Recruit affair had given up their party posts and the public prosecutors had declared their investigations at an end.

Despite Uno's pledge to reform the political system and limit the flow of funds into the hands of individual politicians, his lack of a real power base (he was the first LDP prime minister not to have run his own faction beforehand) and his suspected lack of zeal for fundamental change did not augur well. He never had a chance to make a real impact, however, for his difficulties were made insurmountable by the revelations of a *geisha* girl that during the months of their intimate relationship he had not made adequate financial arrangements for her. His personal reputation never recovered; in the weeks leading up to the 23 July Upper House elections, the LDP campaign managers were forced to cancel plans for Uno to go on national electioneering tours, for fear that he would repel more voters than he would attract.

The field was thus left clear for Miss Takako Doi, the leader of the Japan Socialist Party (JSP), who forcefully appealed to the female voters upset by the consumption tax introduced in April and Uno's extra-marital affairs. Indeed, the JSP successfully adopted what came to be called the 'Madonna strategy' of running more female candidates than ever before to play on this awakened political consciousness.

The results of the elections (for only half of the 252 Upper House seats) were a decided blow to the LDP, which saw its representation cut by half while that of the JSP more than doubled. Taken in conjunction with the remaining seats which were not contested, the LDP nevertheless emerged from the elections still the largest party, with 109 seats, but for the first time since its formation in 1955, no longer with a majority in the Upper House. The JSP significantly enhanced its position as the leading opposition party, with 67 seats, while the other opposition parties faltered slightly, with the exception of a good initial showing for *Rengo*, a trade union-based organization.

A combination of factors led to this unprecedented setback for the LDP. One element in the LDP's political longevity had been its success in incorporating into its 'grand coalition' new groups or sectoral interests. Yet during 1988–9, the LDP not only alienated some of these newer supporters, such as the middle-class female consumers, by its badly-designed consumption tax, but also upset some of its more traditional supporters, such as the farmers, who resented the measures adopted under US pressure to open up the agricultural market, and the small business operators, who felt unprotected from the damaging effects of the economic restructuring wrought by the rising yen. The LDP, naturally, also suffered from the exposure of the widespread corruption and influence-peddling that emerged from the Recruit scandal and the sensationalism of Uno's meanness in his financial dealings with his concubine. The popular distaste for the LDP's 'money politics' was a reflection of the way in which the LDP's elderly leaders had become arrogant and rather out of touch with the changes taking place in Japanese society. Finally, Doi skilfully managed to camouflage the JSP's lack of unity or coherent policies and the continued existence of its wildly radical wing by mercilessly exploiting the LDP's misfortunes. In the end, however, the Japanese voters wanted, above all, to jolt the LDP out of its complacency, to give it the kind of shock that would put substance into the rhetoric of political reform without totally destabilizing the country's booming economic system.

Uno immediately resigned to take responsibility for the election setback and two weeks later Toshiki Kaifu, a relatively obscure politician from the LDP's smallest faction (*Komoto*), but with the advantages of being young, 'clean' and an eloquent speaker, became prime minister. Despite widespread disillusionment with the LDP's 'money politics' and initial scepticism over his own leadership abilities, Kaifu has not only survived, but has slowly and quietly restored some of the LDP's fortunes. Although his chief cabinet secretary resigned after only two weeks (over payments to a bar hostess), Kaifu cleverly appeased female opinion by appointing Mayumi Moriyama as Environment Minister, the first woman ever to hold this crucial post. Kaifu also played the role of international statesman by making visits to North America in September 1989 and Western and Eastern Europe in January 1990, as well as hosting the International Democratic Union Conference in September 1989. However, he made less progress over the revision of the consumption tax than he wished, for the LDP's proposals outlined in December 1989 owed more to the Takeshita faction's reluctance to countenance drastic change than to his own more radical ideas for transforming it into a 'social welfare tax'. Nevertheless, he managed to avoid a major controversy. The major scandal of the autumn, over the illegal use of *pachinko* (a variety of pinball games) profits for party donations, actually hit the JSP far harder than the LDP.

Indeed, the opposition parties found it difficult to maintain the momentum and euphoria of the summer. Although they occasionally flexed their muscles, by passing, for example, a symbolic, but nonbinding, resolution in the Upper House for the abolition of the consumption tax, the various parties involved in the convoluted discussions about a hypothetical post-election coalition government only managed to highlight their policy and personality differences. Within the JSP itself, Doi found herself heavily constrained by past ideological baggage and factional in-fighting; able for the first time for decades to consider themselves as a potential ruling party, the JSP leaders showed uncertainty about how far to compromise their deeply-imbedded policies in order to secure greater electoral appeal. As a result, by the end of 1989, the LDP had once again overtaken the JSP in the public opinion polls.

Despite some losses, the LDP won a convincing victory in the February 1990 Lower House elections. Nevertheless, although the LDP retained a Lower House majority, it will still have to live with an Upper House controlled by the opposition for at least three and, quite probably, six years. Complex post-election manoeuvring to create a loose or partial coalition between the LDP and one of the opposition parties seemed increasingly likely.

US–Japan Economic Tensions

Although the domestic political scene was often in a state of near paralysis, the economy continued to flourish, with 1989 GNP growth around the 5% mark for the third year in succession. Indeed, adopting the dynastic name of the new Emperor, Japanese economists began to talk about the '*Heisei* boom'. Like earlier booms in 1958–61 and 1965–70, the '*Heisei* boom' has come at a period of significant restructuring of the Japanese economy. Japan has weathered the storms of the 'high yen' and, in 1989, continued to rely on rising domestic demand, rather than exports, to fuel growth. The overall trade surplus declined from $95bn in 1988 to $85bn and the current account surplus from $79bn to $61bn.

Nevertheless, declines in Japan's overall surpluses did little to reduce friction with the US, which continued to be preoccupied with its own persistently large bilateral deficit with Japan; even though this declined slightly during 1989, at $40bn it still accounted for about one-third of the total US trade deficit. The temperature in the economic relationship definitely rose during the year. US concern focused not just on trade deficits and market-opening measures, but also on a wave of large-scale and high prestige Japanese investments (of which Sony's acquisition of Columbia Pictures and Mitsubishi's buying into the Rockefeller Center were the most controversial) and on signs of Japan gaining the edge in several vital areas of high technology. As the US continued its agonized debate on Japan, fuelled by a sudden burst of 'revisionist' literature on the 'Japan problem', the 'Japan-bashing' mood in Congress strengthened. One US public opinion poll even showed that, in an era of East–West neo-détente, Americans felt that Japan's economic strength was more of a threat to the US than Soviet military power. On the Japanese side, a controversial book co-authored by an LDP politician, Shintaro Ishihara (whose views are couched in extreme language), and the chairman of Sony, Akio Morita (whose criticisms are more moderate and constructive), expressed much of the frustration with the US attitude that was felt by an increasing number of Japanese. The rising tensions between the two sides were played out in the manoeuvring prior to the US introduction of anti-unfair trading provisions and the rethinking over the FS-X (Fighter, Support-Experimental) aircraft collaborative development agreement in the spring and summer of 1989, and the tortuous structural impediment initiative (SII) talks which began in the autumn.

Despite intensive Japanese lobbying and evidence of a split amongst US officials, Japan was listed in late May as one of the three countries deemed to have engaged in unfair trading practices harmful to US exports. Under the 'super 301' provisions of the 1988 Omnibus Trade and Competitiveness Act, the US was to enter into negotiations to eliminate these practices over a three-year period; unsuccessful negotiations would lead to unilateral US retaliation. Japan was cited for unfair trading practices, especially in super-computers, satellite and forest products and for rigidities in its internal investment structure. Japanese government and business leaders reacted angrily to being singled out in this manner, and only agreed to bilateral talks on the understanding that they were not under the aegis of the 'super 301' legislation.

The dispute over the development of the FS-X, a new advanced Japanese fighter aircraft based on the F-16, reflected a US fear that Japan, having achieved dominance in a number of other sectors, was now about to focus on the civil aviation industry. Although a company-level agreement on co-development had been signed in November 1988, a number of US Congressmen and the new Bush Administration's Secretary of Commerce, Robert Mosbacher, criticized the technology transfer provisions. President Bush decided in mid-March 1989 to support the deal, but asked for 'clarifications' about the US technology inputs and production shares. Not until the end of April was a solution reached, when Takeshita, keen to break the lengthy deadlock before he stepped down, agreed to a larger US share of production and more limited Japanese access to the software source codes. Even then, critical resolutions in the US Senate were only just defeated in May and September, and disagreements over the cost of transferring the Japanese technology to US companies and the use of this technology in other US military aircraft delayed the start of work beyond the end of the year. The second thoughts over this deal expressed by the US side amplified feelings of economic nationalism and provoked intra-administration conflicts in both countries. What had first been thought of as a model for future joint efforts by the two countries has instead served to sour any future considerations of similar deals.

The atmosphere created by the 'super 301' listing and the FS-X row did not augur well for the SII talks which began in the autumn as a result of a suggestion by Bush in May. Conceived as yet another way to try to reduce the trade imbalance, the US cited a number of structural problems hampering Japanese imports: excessive consumer saving, high land prices, exclusive business practices, the complicated distribution system, transactions within business groups and abnormal pricing mechanisms. The Japanese countered by arguing that the declining international competitiveness of US firms was largely responsible for the trade imbalance. Despite serious exchanges of opinion, little progress was made; indeed, Kaifu himself told Bush in September that the US should not expect an immediate improvement in the trade gap. However, faced with a slow-down in its own economy and with mid-term Congressional elections due later in 1990, the US is likely to exert even greater pressure on Japan to increase imports and carry out structural changes. Failure to make some progress by the time the SII interim report is due in spring 1990 will lead almost inevitably to Japan being listed in May for the second successive year under the 'super 301' provisions.

Regional and Global Security Partnership

The Japan–US relationship, of course, revolves as much around defence and security arrangements as it does around economic interdependence. However, a spillover effect from the heightened US–Japan trade friction, electoral successes for the JSP and the changes in global East–West relations all made the Japanese government more concerned about the relevance and popularity of their continued military build-up and the US–Japan security treaty.

As the FS-X dispute showed, Japan's weapons acquisition programme remains a sensitive subject; it was no doubt symptomatic of Japanese disillusionment with US attitudes that, in summer 1989, the Air Self-Defense Forces placed their first order for non-US aircraft (the British BAe 125, a navigational and calibration aircraft) and began serious discussions over the purchase of the British *Harrier* VTOL fighter. Some US Congressmen raised more demands that the Japanese increase their share of the costs of maintaining US troops in Japan from the current 40% to 100%, but the Japanese resisted these demands. Any moves towards a supplementary agreement on the costs (which the Japanese government began to hint about in late 1989) would require an amendment to the US–Japan Status of Forces Agreement. There was also US pressure on Japan to consider using Japanese troops in international peace-keeping forces, or in anti-terrorist operations, but the government only agreed to 'study' the question.

The JSP had traditionally been critical of the existence of both the Self-Defense Forces (SDF) and the US–Japan Security Treaty. In the aftermath of its electoral gains in the Upper House elections, however, the JSP began to appreciate that its stances on these issues were not only out of line with majority opinion in Japan, and therefore likely to impede further electoral growth, but also a major handicap in forging an effective coalition with other opposition parties such as the *Komeito* and the Democratic Socialist Party. Despite controversy within the party itself, the JSP began to edge away from its more extreme positions. Doi's policy statement in September thus advocated preserving the SDF (with the defence budget kept strictly below the psychologically important level of 1% of GNP) and maintaining the Security Treaty, though with a strict application of Japan's non-nuclear principles, a ban on joint military exercises and a phasing out of US military bases from Japan. Such conditions, in practice, would nullify much of the Treaty's effectiveness. This was still not enough to satisfy all the other opposition parties, however, and the JSP agonized over how much further to move.

The easing of US–Soviet tensions and the dramatic changes in Eastern Europe had a lesser impact on Japan than in most areas, because of the Japanese government's preoccupation with East Asian developments. Indeed, the impasse in Soviet–Japanese relations, the set-backs to reform in China and the absence of East European-style reform elsewhere in socialist East Asia, left the Japanese rather out of tune with the West European and American enthusiasms for the changes sweeping the socialist world. The defence White Paper (*Defense of Japan*), published in September 1989, was grudging in its analysis of the merits of the new Soviet diplomacy and warned that Soviet forces were still intensifying military tension in East Asia.

In fact, Soviet–Japanese relations showed few signs of a thaw; the sticking-point, as always, lay with the territorial dispute over the four islands north of Hokkaido. Four rounds of negotiations on a bilateral peace treaty were held during 1989, but they were mainly limited to each side reiterating its historical and legal claims to the islands. The Japanese made it clear that they were prepared to consider including items such as economic co-operation in a peace treaty only if the return of the islands was guaranteed. Soviet academics and commentators flew several kites during the year about compromise solutions, but a brief flurry of interest in a comment by a visiting senior Soviet Politburo member, Aleksandr Yakovlev, in November 1989 about a 'third way' to resolve this issue, was subsequently dampened by his explanation that he merely meant a 'constructive dialogue' towards a peace treaty. Mikhail Gorbachev did, at least, agree to visit Japan, but by setting the date for 1991 he suggested that there was no immediate prospect of a compromise over the thorny territorial dispute.

Whereas the Japanese have deliberately linked politics with economics in their relationship with the Soviet Union, their assiduous attempts to separate the two in their dealings with China were sorely tried by the repression in Tiananmen Square in June 1989. Premier Li Peng's visit to Japan in April 1989 had reflected the general improvement in Sino-Japanese relations and the Japanese government had given a cautious welcome to the Sino-Soviet *rapprochement* of May. However, the international reaction to the events in Tiananmen Square left the Japanese government caught between its understandable reluctance (given past Japanese atrocities in China) to comment on Chinese domestic actions and its potential isolation from its Western allies. Japanese official comments slowly became more critical of the Chinese actions, moving from an initial 'regrettable' to 'intolerable'; all planned aid loans and projects were suspended, and high-level visits postponed, but Japan was reluctant to carry out all the sanctions called for by the European and American governments. Japanese businessmen soon resumed quiet activity in China, but, despite urging from the business community, it was not until the Scowcroft mission in December 1989 and the lifting of martial law in January 1990 that Japan felt free to open up its contacts again and plan for reviving negotiations on the third massive yen loan package (for 1990–95) in the spring of 1990. While it had been reluctant to move ahead of them in resuming contacts, the Japanese government had consistently tried to persuade its Western allies of the dangers of leaving China too isolated; this concern was, ironically, heightened by the dramatic changes in Eastern Europe which the Japanese government otherwise welcomed.

Kaifu did try to pick up on the idea of 'global partnership' with the United States (and extend it to include Western Europe) which had first been raised by US Secretary of State James Baker in June 1989. As in previous years, Japan argued that its overseas development aid contributed to this sharing of responsibilities; it also saw its active involvement in US Treasury Secretary Nicholas Brady's Third World debt reduction plan, with its particular emphasis on Mexico and the Philippines, in a similar light. The Japanese government continued to be on target in its fourth medium-term aid expansion programme, and, indeed, in dollar terms, should overtake the US during FY 1989–90 to become the world's largest aid donor. The Kaifu cabinet's budget proposals in December 1989 envisaged an increase of 8.2% in the ODA expenditure for FY 1990–91, partly due to increased emphasis on environmental protection aid. This aid budget will also be supplemented by the commitments of $1.95bn announced to Eastern Europe during Kaifu's January 1990 European tour.

The 1990–91 budget proposals further showed a 6.1% planned increase in the defence budget, to ¥4,159bn, the highest rate of growth for five years. This rise stems mainly from higher appropriations to improve working conditions for military personnel rather than armament acquisition. In fact, in relation to GNP, the budgeted amount would actually fall below the symbolic level of 1% for the first time in four years. Nevertheless, the Defense Agency faces a critical period of reassessment of military needs before it submits to the *Diet* in mid-1990 its plans for following up the current Mid-Term Defense Build-up Program, due to end during 1990. It seems likely that the emphasis of the new programme will be on consolidation rather than continued build-up; on changes in command and logistical structures and force flexibility to meet changing conditions.

Although the Japanese government has broadened the range of its consultations with the Americans and the Europeans, to cover issues such as regional security, Third World debt, the environment, drugs and terrorism, many Japanese felt in 1989 that the internal political crisis and lack of leadership was leaving Japan rather marginalized from the dramatic changes in global politics. To counter this image of inaction and indifference, the Japanese government seized on the opportunity opened by the changes in Eastern Europe. Premier Kaifu's offer of nearly $2bn in aid to Poland and Hungary is meant to demonstrate Japan's willingness to play a positive global role.

Despite this, and the LDP's recovery in the Lower House election of mid-February (the LDP lost fewer seats than expected and managed to maintain a 20-seat majority), the LDP is still faced with a majority opposition in the Upper House and the knowledge that it held on to its ruling position more because of opposition weakness than because of its own popularity. In these circumstances, for the immediate future it cannot be expected to take many new initiatives with regard to trade, structural economic problems or in international politics.

THE KOREAN PENINSULA

Since the National Assembly elections in April 1988, when the combined opposition parties took a majority of the seats, the power of President Roh Tae Woo and the Democratic Justice Party (DJP) has been considerably reduced. There was a truce between government and opposition to ensure the success of the Olympic Games in Seoul in September 1988, but after that and for most of 1989, political relationships were dominated by the opposition's determination both to expose the misdeeds of ex-president Chun Doo Hwan, the long-time friend and former military and political superior of President Roh, and to restrain the power of the government. In response, the President struggled to escape from the past by distancing himself and his government from any former association with the Chun regime.

In these fluid and pluralistic conditions the press became relatively more independent and critical, student protest continued and became more violent, labour unions more numerous, active and demanding of economic benefits for their members, and Korean politics became increasingly nationalistic. These factors made it difficult for the government to handle political and economic problems throughout 1989, but in a dramatic development in January 1990, President Roh announced that the DJP was merging with the main opposition parties of Kim Young Sam and Kim Jong Pil. The newly formed Democratic Liberal Party (DLP) currently controls 215 National Assembly seats, some 75% of the total. President Roh described the merger as a development that will 'establish a new political order that will achieve democratic development and solve the Nation's economic crisis' and will 'put a full stop to politics that bring confrontations and splits over partisan interests'.

Towards a New Form of Democracy in South Korea?

The record of Chun Doo Hwan's Administration, and its links to both President Roh and the DJP, were both a cause of conflict and a basis for co-operation between the government and opposition. In March 1989 Kim Dae Jong released President Roh from his campaign pledge to hold a mid-term referendum on his record in office in return for a commitment to allow a more intensive public examination of the regime of Chun Doo Hwan. Despite very violent student demonstrations in May, demanding that Chun be brought to trial, the government did not resort to the usual tactic of alleging that the demonstrations were instigated by the opposition parties. In December all three opposition leaders, Kim Dae Jung, Kim Young Sam and Kim Jong Pil, keen to promote an image of responsibility and aware of public anger at the failure of politicians to address pressing economic and political problems, entered a pact with President Roh to end the legislative deadlock that had held up more than 100 bills, including the 1990 budget. Their reward was an agreement to allow a parliamentary review of the National Security laws, the removal of officials tainted by involvement in the Chun regime who were still in the government, and most importantly an assurance that Chun Doo Hwan would appear before a National Assembly hearing on 31 December 1989.

Although Chun's appearance was heavily stage-managed and left many important questions unanswered, it has laid the issue of the record of the Fifth Republic to rest and enabled Roh Tae Woo to construct a new political identity for himself and his supporters. The creation of the DLP can be expected to lessen public confrontations and splits by introducing a form of politics similar to that in Japan. There the ruling Liberal Democratic Party maintains a public front of unity to ensure electoral success, while settling political differences among the party factions privately behind the security of a large parliamentary majority, and rotating senior political posts among faction leaders. The political deadlock of the old four-party system in Korea, and the relative decline of its economy, were powerful motivations for creating a 'new politics' which all the leaders of the new party claimed would promote democracy and help alleviate industrial strife. The two Kims, in particular, dismissed assertions that they had joined the new party for personal or partisan advantage and insisted that they had joined for patriotic reasons. They argued that a powerful and united government had to be created to negotiate unification with Pyongyang and to undermine its claim that President Roh lacked popular support.

It is not necessary to doubt these claims of patriotism to recognize that it is likely that the DLP's leaders have reached a tacit agreement about their future roles in the party. Kim Young Sam and Kim Jong Pil are members of the new DLP's five-member ruling council, and the new party is likely to campaign for a constitutional revision long favoured by the two Kims that will introduce a cabinet system of government just before the April 1992 National Assembly elections. Kim Young Sam will almost certainly become the first prime minister in the new system after President Roh leaves office on 25 February 1993.

Kim Dae Jung has not joined the DLP; he clearly found it difficult to be allied to a party which describes itself as 'a grand coalition of moderate democratic forces', operates as a unified conservative bloc and is not committed to many of the reforms championed by his Party for Peace and Democracy (PPD). He is reluctant to abandon his role as the leader of 'progressive' forces in South Korea, but if the DLP alliance holds, it removes any hope of his ever achieving power. He and the senior leaders of the PPD are conducting a major review of their options, which are being kept as open as possible by challenging the constitutionality of the DLP. Kim has described it as 'a kind of *coup d'État* against democracy' in which political corruption may easily take root, and he has called repeatedly for immediate national elections.

Other Major Issues

In early 1989 extra-parliamentary forces focused on three main issues: the demand for further democratization; the record of the government;

and its links with ex-president Chun and the United States. Student protest became markedly more violent than in 1988; for example, on 3 May, seven riot policemen died as a result of an attempt to rescue five colleagues held hostage by student protesters in Pusan's Dongui University. Anti-government protest also flared in the south-western city of Kwangju in mid-May following the discovery of the body of Lee Chol Kyu, a student wanted by the police for publishing an article critical of the government and claiming that the US was responsible for instigating the Korean War. President Roh had warned that he would invoke 'emergency measures' after the Dongui University deaths, but this became unnecessary as the Kwangju protests culminated in a peaceful demonstration on 18 May by an estimated 100,000 people honouring those killed in the anti-Chun rebellion of May 1980.

Trade union protest and the economy were also major issues in early 1989. On 30 March more than 10,000 riot police staged an air, sea and land assault to end an unofficial strike in the Hyundai Heavy Industries shipyard in Ulsan; 697 workers demanding improved working conditions and higher pay during the 109-day occupation were arrested. The government's renewed ability to take action against labour unrest was a result of popular concern over the apparent decline of Korea's export 'miracle'. The export of cars was particularly badly hit with American sales of Hyundai cars falling to 183,216 units in 1989, some 30% less than in 1988. In September the government was forced to provide a 17-year, $225-m loan to Daewoo shipbuilding, a subsidiary of one of South Korea's four flagship companies, to keep it in operation.

As early as June the government, with the support of the opposition, had introduced a range of 'economic crisis' policies designed to control wages and prices, boost export industries and limit the appreciation of the won against the dollar to 3%. This was to prevent the kind of damage that was done to export industries in 1988 when industrial wages rose by over 15% and the won appreciated against the dollar by no less than 16%. In January 1990 the Labour Ministry introduced new regulations to control those strikes deemed to be political. By then, however, employees and unions had already moderated their demands in response to the widespread sense of crisis about the future of the nation's economy. Korea's trade surplus fell from $11.5bn in 1988 to $4.5bn in 1989, and in January 1990 a monthly trade deficit of $600m was recorded, a record figure for many years. The recent depreciation of the won against several major currencies, and fewer trade union disputes, suggest that the 1989 growth rate of 6.5% of GNP will be repeated in 1990, but even this has been insufficient to dispel fears that the economy was under siege, a feeling accentuated by the contrast with growth in both 1987 and 1988 of approximately 12%.

Reunification became a major issue for extra-parliamentary groups in the second half of 1989, in part because of President Roh's own election enthusiasm for, and expectations of, the northern policy. The immediate aim of the policy is to speed the process of 'cross recognition': full diplomatic recognition of North Korea by the US and Japan, and Seoul's full diplomatic recognition by the USSR and China. The longer-term aim is to reduce tension and finally achieve unification. The key element of the northern policy is to approach Pyongyang indirectly through Seoul's improving links with communist states. In this manner Seoul hopes both to encourage North Korea to end its self-imposed iso-lation and to play-down the propaganda confrontations that typify the bilateral relations between the Koreas. The importance of the unification issue in the South was also enhanced by Pyongyang which encouraged South Koreans to visit the North, especially for the World Youth Festival in July 1989. Concerned about the popular response to the call, the Seoul government arrested no fewer than 750 Hanyang University students in early July. There were, however, several cel-ebrated examples of 'illegal' visitors to the North.

The reunification issue not only allows dissident groups to criticize the government, but also enables them to focus criticism on the US. A widely held view is that the US presence on the peninsula is responsible for the nation's division and is the major impediment to reunification. Dissident groups claim that the US has propped up right-wing govern-ments in Seoul which are hostile to reunification and that the Ameri-can commander of the US–ROK Combined Forces Command gave approval for the release of the Korean armed forces used for the violent repression of the rebellion in Kwangju in May 1980. These radical views blend with a more widespread, if less trenchant form of anti-Americanism, that reflects political and public resentment of the high-profile US military presence in major Korean cities, notably in the capital itself; concern over US attempts to open the Korean market to US goods and services and to force up the value of the won; and hos-tility to US efforts to make Korea carry a bigger defence burden.

South Korean Diplomatic Progress

Continuity is the keynote of President Roh's diplomacy, although the international arena in which South Korea operates changed dramati-cally in 1989. The improvement in superpower relations and the increasing significance of the non-military aspects of security have reduced the strategic importance of North Korea to the USSR and China, as well as increasing the importance that Seoul attaches to its continued diplomatic and economic success in the world.

South Korean–US relations have been marked by a subtle shift away from the primacy of military affairs towards the promotion of a healthier US–ROK economic partnership. Indeed, the two issues are closely intertwined. US Defense Secretary Dick Cheney announced during his February 1990 visit to Seoul that 5,000 non-combatant US troops would be withdrawn from Korea by 1993. The US FY 1991 mili-tary budget contained provisions to shut down US Air Force oper-ations at three bases in South Korea with the withdrawal of 2,000 per-sonnel. A report on the 'feasibility and desirability' of US troop withdrawals from East Asia will be presented to Congress by the Pentagon on 1 April and it is expected to confirm US troop cuts in Korea and to recommend that Seoul assume even more responsibility for its own security in the 1990s. The report is also likely to recommend the transfer of several military missions and commands from the US to the Korean armed forces. The Roh government has accepted these changes with relative good grace, having calculated that it cannot prevent a partial US withdrawal at a time when Congress is preoccupied by the need to cut the US deficit, is angered by anti-Americanism in South Korea, and is concerned by Seoul's trade practices.

Seoul was also forced to make politically unpopular economic concessions to the US. The most notable were the last minute, but substantial, opening of its domestic market and the relaxation of import restrictions agreed in May 1989 to avoid Korea being placed on America's 'super 301' list of states which are deemed to trade unfairly. It became increasingly difficult for President Roh to meet the demands of the US on trade and defence burden-sharing issues and yet contain anti-American criticisms. Pressure from the US for additional concessions, especially those designed to increase South Korea's payments to off-set the cost of stationed US troops, made it less easy for the government to counter charges that the US plays an unacceptably dominant role in Korean affairs. Towards the end of 1989, demands from the US for additional economic concessions began to meet with tougher resistance from the Roh government, which became fearful that its credibility would be undermined and that serious political and economic instability would follow.

Elsewhere, President Roh's diplomacy has been remarkably successful. Formal diplomatic relations were opened with Hungary, Poland and Yugoslavia in February, November and December 1989 respectively, and in February 1990 Seoul and Moscow exchanged consular offices, providing South Korea with its first diplomatic representation in the USSR. Seoul expects to open full diplomatic relations with Czechoslovakia and Bulgaria and to 'normalize' relations with Romania by the end of 1990. Although South Korea believes that recognition by Beijing will come more slowly than from Moscow, it nevertheless hopes that full diplomatic ties with the USSR and China will be established before President Roh leaves office in February 1993.

South Korea's trade diplomacy with communist states has been even more successful and economic ties have been widely extended. Moreover, despite the Chinese repression of dissidents and Jiang Zemin's announcement in October that the liberalization of the Chinese economy would be suspended for at least three years, Sino-South Korean economic ties have continued to flourish. In 1989 more than 4,000 South Korean businessmen visited China and trade exceeded $3bn. Seoul is continuing its development of west coast ports in anticipation of increased trade with China, and Beijing has kept open its east coast special economic zones of Shandong and the Liaodong peninsula. It is expected that some 20 Sino-South Korean joint ventures will come on stream in 1990. South Korean trade with the Soviet Union has also expanded rapidly, with Korean businesses entering into a number of joint venture negotiations in the Soviet Union.

North Korea: Moderation or Retrenchment in Isolation?

The increasing isolation of the Democratic People's Republic of Korea (DPRK) during the 1980s, and the more recent rapid disintegration of communist regimes in Eastern Europe, has clearly had a deep effect upon Kim Il Sung. He recalled 30 ambassadors to Pyongyang to discuss the events, and ordered the return of a reported 1,700 students from universities in the USSR and Eastern Europe to protect them from the revisionist virus. Yet some observers believe that even Kim Il Sung will soon recognize the necessity of reaching an accommodation with the South, and they discern signs of moderation in Pyongyang's policies towards Seoul.

There are developments in North Korean policy that lend some credence to these views. The government recently invited to Pyongyang a number of prominent US scholars, journalists and churchmen. Officials have informed these visitors that North Korea no longer seeks to communise the South, nor poses any military threat to Seoul. In addition, the North has engaged in a series of negotiations with the South, ranging from the formation of a single Korean sports team for the 1990 Beijing Asian Games, to the reuniting of families separated by the war. It has also publicly acknowledged the economic achievements of the South and makes much of its desire to begin domestic economic reform and establish economic links with the West.

Pyongyang's third Seven Year Plan (1987–93) seemed to move in the direction of reform by emphasizing the development of foreign trade, an increase in consumer goods production, and investment in science and technology. But in all three fields it has been woefully unsuccessful. An estimated foreign debt of $4.5bn, which Pyongyang often fails to service, and a lack of hard currency, have prevented the promotion of any substantial economic development programmes and makes impossible the purchase of advanced technology from abroad. Beyond a few small-scale joint ventures foreign investment in North Korea is negligible. Even trade and economic links with the South, such as the proposed joint development of Diamond Mountain in the North as a tourist centre, which Seoul would have financed for political reasons, have fallen victim to Pyongyang's antipathy to doing business with governments in the South.

In a broader diplomatic context, Kim Il Sung seems to have at least accepted the dramatic changes in Eastern Europe. Kim's statement in February praising the concept of *perestroika* was in keeping with the North's recognition of the National Salvation Front in Romania and his letter of congratulation to Vaclav Havel in Czechoslovakia. All this has been done in the context of the North's declared policy of non-interference in other countries' affairs and as part of a policy in which Pyongyang has both reported and sent greetings to the leaders of the new non-communist governments in Eastern Europe.

These vague hints of change, however, are contradicted by a range of actions that are more consistent with Pyongyang's traditional behaviour and attitude to the South. In its negotiations with the South it consistently sets forth demands, such as the immediate withdrawal of American troops, that it must know are unacceptable to Seoul, yet these are constantly set as the price of progress. Responsibility for the failure of negotiations is attributed to Southern obduracy and this view is broadcast internationally in the most vitriolic terms. Kim Il Sung's government has encouraged opposition leaders and dissident students from the South to visit the North where it solicits statements damaging to Seoul. Its recognition of the economic strength and other achievements of the South are also conditioned by its internal and external propaganda broadcasts which portray South Korea as a land of repression and poverty in which a mass and united opposition struggles to unseat a 'fascist clique' supported by 'US imperialism'.

Military preparations in the North also belie the claim that it no longer represents a threat to the South. Current assessments of military strength show that the North continues to increase its armed forces. CIA estimates place the total number in excess of one million men, with the land army numbering 930,000; current work on partial census material recently sent by North Korea to the UN suggests even higher figures – a total armed force in excess of 1.2 million. In addition, the North stations approximately 60% of its land army close to the Demilitarized Zone (DMZ), with a particularly heavy concentration just north of Seoul, and has sufficient forward deployed munitions and other logistic materials to sustain a high intensity war for four months without resupply.

There are also reports that the North holds stocks of chemical weapons and is acquiring a capacity and materials to produce a nuclear weapon: it is alleged to be building unsafeguarded nuclear power and reprocessing facilities. Concern is heightened by the continued absence of a full-scope safeguards agreement between the IAEA and North Korea, five years after Pyongyang signed the Nuclear Non-Proliferation Treaty. North Korea's nuclear ambitions have raised sufficient concern for it to have been one of the issues discussed at the Baker–Shevardnadze meeting in Wyoming in September 1989. These developments cause even more alarm in the South when taken in conjunction with reports that the DPRK has reverse-engineered the Soviet *Scud*-B ballistic missile and developed its own production capability, thus adding to an already formidable armoury recently updated by the acquisition of SA-5 missiles and Su-25 and MiG-29 aircraft from the USSR.

On 3 March 1990 a fourth infiltration tunnel from the North to an area south of the military demarcation line was discovered in the eastern sector of the DMZ. It was almost certainly dug some time ago, but the tunnel was left open and appeared to be in an operational condition.

The South described the tunnel as 'an intolerable act of aggression' and regard it as proof that DPRK armed forces continue to be structured for a 'short decisive war'.

The suggestions that the North has become reconciled to more pluralistic forms of communism elsewhere and is likely to moderate its own style of government seem groundless. Indeed, North Korea is probably the world's most hermetically sealed society. Even while sending messages of congratulation to new Eastern European governments, it has vilified their attempts to make contact with the South. In October, at the height of the protests in East Germany and Hungary, the party newspaper *Rodong Shimum* warned against the 'dangers of bourgeois culture' and in November Kim Il Sung called upon the USSR, the GDR and Bulgaria 'to fight together for the victory of socialist-communism and against imperialism'. North Korea was one of the few states to support the repression of protest in China in June 1989.

The domestic politics of the North show little moderation in the style of government. Journalists reporting the World Youth Festival were not allowed to retain their own multi-band radio receivers and they noted that North Korean radios receive only government broadcasts. Several were warned against writing adverse reports on North Korea. Other reports suggest that several senior politicians (including former Vice Premier Hong Song Young and former Party Secretary Yu Chang Sik) are in prison for challenging the intended succession of Kim Jong Il to the presidency of North Korea. More recently there have been reports of demotions and the purging of senior members of the KWP for demanding more open government. Most disturbing of all are the allegations of the Washington-based Asia Watch that there are as many as 152,000 political prisoners in North Korea, some 0.7% of the population.

The North Korean Dilemma

In 1972, Kim Il Sung shifted power from the party to the state when he became President of the Republic and his son took control of the KWP. In recent years the younger Kim has moved into a position of greater prominence in North Korean politics by launching and, some argue, devising major policy initiatives. He is closely associated with the effort to increase production of consumer goods and some analysts see this as a sign of his recognition that ideological appeals have been unsuccessful in stimulating economic production and that he favours the pragmatic approach of material incentives. There is also some slight evidence that an increasing number of 'technocrats', such as Kang Song San and Li Jong Ok, are gravitating towards the state administration and that this has promoted some flexibility in government. Yet, however much either Kim Jong Il or the technocrats might wish to adjust, it is clear that it is neither party nor state bureaucracy that continues to suppress 'new thinking' but the dead weight of the cult of Kim Il Sung. Until he is removed there is little that anyone else can do.

The hostility of the North to the South, a key component of Kim's rule, remains undiminished and has become the major justification of the bureaucratic treatment and repression of the North Korean population. Its removal would undoubtedly expose the system to the pressures for change which appear to lie just below the surface. North Korea's armed might and the near manic commitment to its version of communism are fast wasting assets in the eyes of the USSR and China, and increasingly irrelevant to the emerging configuration of power in North-east Asia. The ultimate dilemma for Pyongyang is that an almost complete isolation from the effects of a rapidly changing international environment is necessary to preserve its hard-line domestic politics, but the regeneration of its crippled economy and society can only be achieved by integrating North Korea into the processes of dynamic change in the region. These contradictions will take on new salience as preparations proceed for the handover of power from Kim Il Sung to Kim Jong Il. While a transfer of power to Kim Jong Il soon, as seems increasingly likely, could well go smoothly, the long-term sucession, which will be fought out after the 78-year-old Kim Il Sung dies, may well prove to be far more traumatic.

INDOCHINA: THE STALEMATE RESTORED

Hopes of a diplomatic solution to the fighting in Cambodia were dashed in August 1989 when the failure of an international conference in Paris exposed the entrenched obstacles to a peaceful resolution of the 12-year conflict. There had been an expectation that the improving tone and substance of global relationships would have some attendant regional effect. In the event, the basic structure of the Cambodian conflict, informed as it always has been by the continuing Sino-Vietnamese antagonism, was not transformed by the changes in the international scene. Limited military confrontation between opposition and Cambodian government forces revived while the Paris conference was under way when it became clear that Vietnam fully intended to withdraw all its forces from Cambodia. After the failure of diplomacy, the opposition forces attained limited military gains in the north and west of the country. An Australian diplomatic initiative for a UN role in a settlement encouraged an interest by the permanent members of the Security Council but failed to gain positive support at regional talks in Indonesia in February 1990. The stalling of this initiative took place concurrently with reports of a return of Vietnamese troops in a battle role and the recovery of lost ground by government forces.

The Promise of Diplomacy

Optimism about the prospect of a political settlement in Cambodia had been encouraged by the improvements in the relationship between the Soviet Union and China who have been the principal patrons of the belligerent parties. In December 1988 the Chinese Foreign Minister Qian Qichen visited Moscow, the first time a Chinese official at this level had done so in over 30 years. Since the second half of 1986 China had insisted that Soviet policy towards Cambodia was the prime obstacle to an improvement in Sino-Soviet relations; Qian Qichen's discussions with Eduard Shevardnadze and Mikhail Gorbachev demonstrated that the question of Cambodia no longer stood in the way of a Sino-Soviet summit which was set for the first half of 1989.

Vietnam, whose invasion and occupation of Cambodia in December 1978 had been supported diplomatically and materially by the USSR and opposed vigorously by China, was particularly disturbed by the rapidly maturing Sino-Soviet *rapprochement*. Suffering as it was from economic distress, Vietnam employed a progressive withdrawal of forces from Cambodia in an effort to contain mixed Soviet and Chinese pressures and to retain essential Soviet economic and diplomatic support. The announcement, just before Qian Qichen left for Moscow, that a promised withdrawal of 50,000 troops from Cambodia would take place before the end of the year, was a boon to Soviet diplomacy in managing Moscow's relations with China.

The next Vietnamese move set in train a series of diplomatic initiatives which reinforced expectations that peace might be at hand. On 6 January 1989, Vietnam's Foreign Minister Nguyen Co Thach announced that all remaining 'volunteer troops' would be withdrawn from Cambodia by the end of September if there were a political settlement which provided for the curtailment of external military assistance to all sides in the conflict. Three days later, Air Chief Marshal Sitthi Savetsila made the first visit to Vietnam by a Thai Foreign Minister since 1976. His visit reflected the softening of domestic Thai policy since Chatichai Chunhavan had become Prime Minister in August 1988 and announced his intention of turning Indochina from a battlefield into a market place. The tone of the meeting between Sitthi and Nguyen Co Thach was promising, even if they failed to reach any accord on Cambodia. Of greater significance was the visit to Beijing on 14 January of Dinh Nho Liem, Vietnam's First Vice Foreign Minister, for talks with his Chinese counterpart, Liu Shuqing. Despite the lustre with which this meeting was imbued – it was the first ministerial contact between the two governments since the end of 1979 – it too failed to produce an agreement on Cambodia or other divisive issues.

More dramatic was the visit to Bangkok on 25 January of Hun Sen, Chairman of the Council of Ministers of the People's Republic of Kampuchea (PRK), who came ostensibly as the private guest of Prime Minister Chatichai on an informal basis without political recognition. The visit violated a long-standing consensus among the ASEAN governments not to deal with representatives of an administration established by a Vietnamese act of force. It also humiliated the Association whose foreign ministers (including Thailand's) had agreed only two days previously in Brunei to participate in a second round of informal talks on Cambodia on the basis of reaffirmed support for the Coalition Government of Democratic Kampuchea (CGDK), which consisted of the *Khmer Rouge*, the forces of Sonn Sann and Prince Norodom Sihanouk's supporters, and was headed by Sihanouk.

Thailand's invitation to Hun Sen stood in marked contrast to its rejectionist policy of the previous decade. Vietnam's initial invasion and occupation of Cambodia had violated Thailand's view of its own sphere of influence and had prompted Thailand to embark on a tacit alliance relationship with China. Now, Hun Sen's presence in Bangkok indicated that Thailand, influenced by Vietnam's economic distress and its own contrasting economic progress, had undertaken a fundamental reassessment of the external threat.

This series of promising diplomatic developments provided a backdrop for the visit to Beijing in early February by Soviet Foreign Minister Shevardnadze. On 5 February, he and Qian Qichen issued a joint statement on Cambodia. They claimed to be in general accord on a political settlement to be based in part on Vietnam's withdrawal of forces, but they were unable to translate their common support for national reconciliation within Cambodia into an agreed formula for power-sharing among the warring factions. At issue was the status of the existing administration in Phnom Penh which China regarded as the political legacy of Vietnam's invasion, and which it insisted should be replaced by a four-party interim government, consisting not only of the Sihanouk, Son Sann and Hun Sen forces, but also the *Khmer Rouge*, all under the leadership of Prince Sihanouk. Despite the high priority it gave to *rapprochement* with China, Moscow was not prepared to abdicate support for Vietnam to the extent of repudiating the PRK Administration.

Although such differences which touched the very heart of the Cambodian conflict remained, they were not permitted to stand in the way of improved Sino-Soviet relations. A firm date was set for Gorbachev to meet Deng Xiaoping in Beijing in mid-May, demonstrating that the issue of Cambodia had been relegated to the margins of mutual differences through an agreement to disagree. The effect of decoupling this regional conflict from Sino-Soviet relations, however, was not powerful enough to facilitate a political settlement for Cambodia. The two patrons were able to reconcile *rapprochement* between themselves with sustained diplomatic and material support for their contending clients, and this continued to fuel their confrontation. The promise of diplomacy was an illusion.

From Jakarta to Paris

The second round of regional talks on Cambodia convened in Jakarta on 19 February 1989 with participation from all ASEAN and Indochina states and all Cambodian factions. A prior meeting in Beijing of the CDGK had reiterated the demand that the administration in Phnom Penh be dismantled in favour of an interim four-party government which would conduct elections under the auspices of the UN to determine Cambodia's future. The inflexibility of this position was pointed up by Prince Sihanouk's conspicuous presence in Beijing for the duration of the Jakarta meeting, a meeting that was a complete failure. Once again the Cambodian parties, sustained by external support, were unable to reach agreement either on a system of power-sharing or on international supervision of Vietnam's withdrawal of troops and of the peace process. The diplomatic deadlock in Jakarta also obstructed any hope of progress in a Sino-Vietnamese *détente*. As a result, China refused to receive Vietnam's Foreign Minister.

Vietnam made yet another attempt to revive the momentum of diplomacy by announcing on 5 April that all its troops would be withdrawn from Cambodia by the end of September 1989, whether or not a political settlement had been reached. The statement incorporated the qualification that if foreign countries continued to arm rebel forces after the September deadline, the PRK reserved 'its legitimate right to call on other countries to give assistance'. The commitment to accelerate withdrawal represented a calculated risk in an attempt to reconcile security and economic priorities, and may well have drawn inspiration from the experience of Afghanistan. The statement, however, was dismissed out of hand by Prince Sihanouk, who had been at the centre of diplomatic attentions since December 1987 when his first meeting with Hun Sen in France raised expectations of a political settlement through a bilateral deal which would exclude the *Khmer Rouge*.

Two further bilateral meetings in 1988, however, made no progress. Despite personal acrimony, a fourth meeting was arranged in Jakarta early in May. Although there had been no real meeting of minds, the tone of the meeting was conciliatory and an arrangement was made to meet again in Paris in July with the prospect of an international conference to follow. On 8 May, Dinh Nho Liem, Vietnam's First Vice Foreign Minister visited Beijing for a second time but without any visible improvement in Sino-Vietnamese relations. During Gorbachev's visit to China for the Sino-Soviet summit (15–18 May) Cambodia was discussed in some detail in meetings with Deng Xiaoping, but the two leaders only reaffirmed the terms of the joint statement issued by their foreign ministers in February.

The Paris Conference

The first international conference on Cambodia, held in New York in July 1981 under UN auspices, had been boycotted by Vietnam and the USSR because the ousted government of Democratic Kampuchea held the UN Cambodian seat. The second conference, called at French initiative, attracted participation from all competing interests. The participation of foreign ministers from all five members of the UN Security Council had generated some optimism at the beginning, and this mood was encouraged by signs of flexibility from the US and China. US Secretary of State Baker, speaking in Brunei at the ASEAN post-ministerial meeting in early July, had indicated a preference for an interim Cambodian government which excluded the *Khmer Rouge*. He also gave the impression, however, of being sympathetic to Sihanouk's insistence that they be included in order to prevent civil war. Such ambivalence reflected a US view that a solution could be found which denied power to any communist grouping. In Paris, Baker argued that 'there is an alternative to the teeth of the *Khmer Rouge* or the jaws of foreign military domination', but in the end he lent his government's support to the ASEAN formula backing Sihanouk.

The US stance in Paris suited China. The significance of the conference was that it provided China with an opportunity to prove that it had not been made an international pariah because of the June bloodshed. An apparent public distancing from the *Khmer Rouge* was not translated into compromise over the terms of a settlement. The revised pattern of global relationships had given China a freedom of political manoeuvre over Cambodia which enabled it to hold tenaciously to its policy of eliminating any residual Vietnamese influence.

The conference on Cambodia convened on 30 July with 23 delegations (including four Cambodian) in the presence of the UN Secretary-General and devolved into working committees. The first was charged with drawing up cease-fire terms and defining the mandate of an international control mechanism to oversee a settlement. The second was required to construct guarantees for independence. The third was asked to work out arrangements for repatriating refugees from the Thai border. And an *ad hoc* committee consisting of France, Indonesia and the four Cambodian factions was set up to address the internal aspects of the conflict and to work out a power-sharing system prior to internationally supervised elections.

The committees concluded their deliberations on 28 August without constructive outcome, primarily because of the failure of the Cambodian parties to reach an accord. At issue was the status and composition of an interim authority, the role of the UN in the control mechanism, the validity of the term 'genocide' and the matter of Vietnamese settlers in Cambodia. Sihanouk closed ranks with the *Khmer Rouge* and enjoyed support from the international alignment which had challenged Vietnam's occupation from the outset. Vietnam and the government in Phnom Penh attracted support from the USSR. The result was to reinstate a deadlock. In the circumstances, the foreign ministers of the UK, China, the USSR and the US did not attend the final session, at which the conference proceedings were suspended with a recommendation that fresh consultations begin in six months.

The conference proved to be a major setback for Vietnam which had anticipated a partial settlement making provision for monitoring and endorsing its withdrawal of troops. There was an expectation that such a provision would pave the way for ending a costly economic isolation as well as indirectly ensuring a measure of legitimacy for the Phnom Penh government. ASEAN's call for a comprehensive political solution was intended to deny a partial settlement to Vietnam's advantage. Any possibility of Vietnam securing international confirmation of its troop withdrawal, however, was prevented by its refusal to accept a UN monitoring role for the UN unless the Cambodian UN seat was declared vacant. The obsessive concern of the Central Committee of Vietnam's Communist Party – which convened concurrently with the Paris conference – with the surge of political pluralism in Eastern Europe may have stiffened attitudes in Hanoi.

The Paris conference also exposed the diplomatic marginality of ASEAN. The Association had earlier played a notable role in mobilizing opposition to Vietnam's occupation of Cambodia, especially within the UN, but Thailand's blatant disregard of ASEAN's long-standing policies had thrown the Association into disarray. In Brunei in July, in the absence of an alternative policy on which all governments could agree, the foreign ministers closed ranks around a jaded formula. In the meantime, Vietnam's commitment to withdraw from Cambodia, which gave an immediacy to the prospect of a *Khmer Rouge* resumption of power, also rendered ASEAN's position redundant. Given the failure of diplomacy and the resumption of fighting within Cambodia, ASEAN's lack of direct impact was evident. Thailand was in a position to affect the balance of forces by sealing off its border with Cambodia. But denying access to the insurgent factions and, more importantly, cutting off their military resupply was not contemplated while China insisted on confrontation and was not challenged by the US.

Vietnam's Withdrawal and Strategic Priorities

Vietnam's invasion of Cambodia asserted by force the strategic interdependence of the three Indochinese states. The Political Report of the Sixth Congress of Vietnam's Communist Party meeting in December 1986 affirmed that consolidating and developing Vietnam's special alliance relationship with Laos and Cambodia was 'a sacred international duty and a task of strategic importance to the vital interests of independence, freedom and socialism in our own country and on the Indochinese peninsula as a whole'. Vietnam's willingness to withdraw its forces from Cambodia while leaving the administration it had installed in Phnom Penh without substantial international recognition and prey to insurgent challenge may have suggested to some that Vietnam was revising its strategic priorities in the same way that the Soviet Union was tolerating political change in Eastern Europe. But there was little or no evidence of this. Vietnam's Communist Party General Secretary Nguyen Van Linh had described Cambodia as a fraternal socialist country in his national day speech at the beginning of September 1989. He also gave a strong impression of reaffirming Vietnam's strategic position in Indochina in a statement which did not suggest an abdication of a long-held strategic perspective incorporating Cambodia in a greater Indochina.

Vietnam announced that its remaining 26,000 troops had been withdrawn from Cambodia between 21 and 26 September. On 1 September, a Defence Ministry spokesman disclosed that about 23,000 Vietnamese servicemen had been killed in Cambodia since 1979 and another 55,000 wounded. The withdrawal did not make an immediate contribution to conflict resolution; nor did it ease the problems which had been visited on Vietnam following its invasion of Cambodia. On 6 September, Cambodia's President Heng Samrin led a delegation to Vietnam. A joint communique stipulated 'that the complete withdrawal of Vietnamese army volunteers must be linked to the prevention of the genocidal Pol Pot's regime's return to Cambodia, the cessation of military aid to the Cambodian factions and foreign interference in Cambodia's internal affairs . . .'. Vietnam's withdrawal was not acknowledged in the eleventh annual resolution on Cambodia which was endorsed by the UN General Assembly in November by a record 124 votes to 17. It reaffirmed support for the insurgent CGDK and its preferred solution.

A flurry of minor diplomatic activity began from mid-December 1989 when the Australian government took up an initiative by US Congressman Solarz. The plan called for an interim UN administration for Cambodia which would conduct elections. The objective was to overcome the deadlock over power-sharing by requiring each side to make a substantial concession. To this end, key preconditions were the dismantling of the incumbent administration in Phnom Penh, and declaring vacant the Cambodian seat in the UN. The Australian proposal was discussed at a meeting of senior officials from the five permanent members of the Security Council in Paris in mid-January 1990. The meeting endorsed 'an enhanced role' for the UN in the settlement of the Cambodian problem but made no provision for administration by the organization. A second meeting in New York early in February also failed to advance matters.

The proposal was discussed again at another informal meeting in Jakarta in mid-February attended by all Cambodian factions, governments of ASEAN and Indochina, with representation also from Australia and France. Some optimism had been generated by a prior meeting in Bangkok between Prince Sihanouk and Prime Minister Hun Sen at which they signed an agreement stating that 'the UN presence at appropriate levels in Cambodia is essential and should be encouraged', but the Jakarta talks ended on an inconclusive note. They served only to rehearse entrenched adverse positions, and it became apparent that the contending sides were interested in a UN role simply as a means to promote an exclusive solution to the conflict.

The Military Balance

The failure of diplomacy throughout the year and the apparent withdrawal of Vietnam's troops has restored the possibility of a military reckoning. Intermittent fighting had been taking place at the same time as the diplomatic process. In the months before their withdrawal, Vietnamese troops, along with Cambodian regular forces, had conducted softening up operations with heavy artillery against *Khmer Rouge* positions designed partly to prevent movement into the interior of refugees under *Khmer Rouge* control. The Vietnamese estimates of insurgent strength in September corresponded roughly with Western assessments: *Khmer Rouge* strength was put at 23,000 fighting men, while adherents of Prince Sihanouk and the Khmer People's National Liberation Front (KPNLF) numbered 12,000 and 10,000 respectively. The government in Phnom Penh is believed to command an army of around 30–40,000, raised partly by conscription and backed by regional militias of some 100,000 men. Its military record has been mixed – some successes, but also accounts of desertions.

After the collapse of the Paris talks in July, the *Khmer Rouge* and the KPNLF, in particular, stepped up military operations which initially had only limited success in three provinces in western and northern Cambodia bordering Thailand. Seizure of a few district capitals, including the gem-mining town of Pailin, served as a prelude to an inconclusive *Khmer Rouge* attack on the major provincial town of Battambang in early January. This attempt by the *Khmer Rouge* to demonstrate their military prowess and political entitlement was combined with a penetration of the interior with the object of dominating the countryside in the vicinity of Phnom Penh. Although the threat to the capital had not materialized, fears of the *Khmer Rouge* were so widespread that the government reinstated a curfew there on 20 October. By the end of February 1990, however, the balance had begun to shift back in favour of the government forces. At the same time, there were reports that Vietnamese troops had returned in a combat role; Vietnamese ambassador to the UN, Ngo Dien, however, would only admit that advisers had gone back to Cambodia in October 1989 after the fall of Pailin.

International interest in the Cambodian conflict has diminished considerably, but still at issue is the balance of power in Indochina defined with reference to the geopolitical advantage or disadvantage of Vietnam. Its prime adversary, China, has given up representing Vietnam as an agent of the Soviet Union, with whom it has repaired relations and which has been reducing both its support to Vietnam and its presence there (in January 1990 it began to withdraw the offensive naval and air forces it had been maintaining at Cam Ranh Bay). With no significant opposition from either the USSR or the US to deter it, Beijing has sustained its rigorous interest in restricting Vietnam's regional role. China remains resolutely opposed to the political legacy of Vietnam's invasion of Cambodia. The continuing insistence of Vietnam on incorporating Cambodia within its sphere of influence and China's adamant opposition to such incorporation means that they continue to support their rival clients inside the country, and it seems all too possible that the only solution will be through *force majeure*.

South and South-west Asia

AFGHANISTAN: THE REGIME SURVIVES

When the last Soviet soldier crossed the Amudar'ya mountains back into the USSR on 15 February 1989, the common expectation was that the fall of the Kabul regime, headed by President Najibullah, would soon follow. Yet, more than one year later, the regime is still in power. It would appear that most observers seriously underestimated the sharp divisions within the *Mujaheddin* forces; their general unreadiness (and lack of appetite) for set-piece warfare; the continued heavy support by the USSR for the ruling People's Democratic Party of Afghanistan (PDPA) and the resilience of Najibullah, as well as the inadequacy of the joint US–Pakistan strategy for pursuing the conflict. The consequence of these factors has been a military stalemate which in turn offers the prospect of a negotiated political settlement to the civil war. Yet that settlement will not be reached without a change of attitude by all the major actors in the drama. The alternative – a reversion to a loosely-linked agglomeration of semi-feudal fiefdoms, with no writ running countrywide – appears no less possible and might be as durable.

Resistance Unity Dissolves

As soon as it was clear that the Soviet troops were indeed withdrawing from Afghanistan, the ideological dimension to the war began to fade; with it went the *jihad* (Holy War) spirit, the element that had united the *Mujaheddin* warriors into a common force. Once the foreign troops were out of sight and the existing Afghan government had implemented a 'national reconciliation policy', presenting itself as a nationalist and Muslim force, the traditional divisions within the resistance resurfaced, preventing it from acting as an effective force. These divisions were aggravated by the growing divergence of aims between the 'inside' *Mujaheddin* field commanders and the 'outside' bureaucracy based in Peshawar, and between the *Mujaheddin* under Pakistan/Saudi/US patronage and those groups sponsored by Tehran.

Violent clashes between Gulbuddin Hekmatyar's fundamentalist *Hezb-i-Islami* party and other *Mujaheddin* groups broke out. In July 1989, seven of Ahmad Shah Massoud's local commanders were assassinated by the *Hezb-i-Islami* forces in Takhar Province in north-east Afghanistan. Massoud retaliated by executing four of the killers in December. In Mayden, a strategic market town south of Kabul, the *Hezb-i-Islami* fighters launched an offensive in October in an effort to disarm all the other parties in the area. Sharp differences between Persian speakers, including the Shi'as, and Pashtuns, fuelled by the competition between Iran and Saudi Arabia, increased.

The failure of the *Mujaheddin* over the past year was more political than military. They did not expect to have to move from guerrilla war to a classical military confrontation in order to topple the PDPA. They expected that under continued and effective military pressure, the Afghanistan army could be induced to desert in droves, and the Kabul regime would subsequently collapse from its own internal contradictions. In fact, the 'inside' *Mujaheddin* have been conspicuous by their lack of military activity since the Soviet withdrawal. They have allowed the Pakistani military to devise both the military strategy and the political alternatives. The large-scale battle against Jalalabad beginning in February 1989 was neither planned nor waged by major *Mujaheddin* field commanders, but by those based in Pakistan. Nor did PDPA successes in the major frontal battles of the last year undermine the military strength of the *Mujaheddin* inside Afghanistan. On the contrary, the government had vacated hundreds of small outposts after the Soviet withdrawal so as to concentrate its troops around the most significant endangered areas (Kabul, Khost and Jalalabad). The *Mujaheddin* were thus able to gain new territories and improve their lines of communication at no cost. It was the political decision by Pakistan to play the Peshawar-based parties off against the field commanders, and to support Gulbuddin Hekmatyar against the other leaders, that undermined the *Mujaheddin* military strength.

Thus, by early 1990, although the *Mujaheddin* continued to control the bulk of the countryside, most of them had in effect ceased being *Mujaheddin*, in the sense that they were no longer fighting against the central government, but were instead attempting to work out compromises with Kabul which would ensure their local power, particularly against their former fellow comrades in arms. Most local commanders had reverted to the traditional relationship between local powers and a weak central state that has shaped Afghan history since the eighteenth century. The central state is seen less as an enemy than as a referee which can help to promote the interests of the local group. This development was expected to play a decisive role after the collapse of the Najibullah regime, not before. That it has come into play so soon is a result of the unexpected adroitness of the regime, aided by the ineffectiveness of US–Pakistan policies.

The Resilience of the Kabul Regime

In February 1989, the Kabul regime, with its back to the wall, closed ranks by including representatives of the different feuding factions in the Cabinet. Atrocities committed by the *Mujaheddin* and Arab volunteers against their opponents in Jalalabad convinced much of the army that they had little choice but to fight on to the death. The inhabitants of the large cities, puzzled by the lack of political perspective on the part of the *Mujaheddin* and alienated by waves of indiscriminate rocket attacks, remained conspicuously neutral. Meanwhile, Moscow, eager to gain a decent interval between the withdrawal of its own forces and the expected collapse of the regime, launched an airlift of food and weapons to Kabul; the sophisticated weapons that it managed to bring in, such as additional modern combat aircraft and *Scud* surface-to-surface missiles, had a negative impact on the *Mujaheddin*.

In the political realm, the PDPA stressed its commitment to multi-party elections, a political settlement, patriotism and Islam. It renounced everything that could possibly identify it with communism. This policy of 'national reconciliation' had had no credibility as long as Soviet troops remained in Afghanistan. Now, however, it began to have an effect in the countryside among demoralized *Mujaheddin* minor commanders, who were prepared to make deals with the regime. Thus, the government apparatus was replaced by local traditional leaders and militia in many areas. This may not have improved law and order in those areas, but it gave the government the breathing space which it so desperately needed. The hard core of the army could now be concentrated in the major cities and it acquitted itself well in the ensuing battles. The morale, fighting spirit and professionalism of Kabul's army have greatly improved as a result. Although heavy battles were fought in Jalalabad (from February to May) and in Khost (August and September) the army was able to resist effectively, and this was enough to provide the regime with a political victory, given the high expectations which had been raised both within the *Mujaheddin* and among their supporters.

The Failure of the Joint US–Pakistan Policy

At the end of 1988 Washington and Islamabad developed a two-pronged policy: to form in Peshawar a so-called Afghan Interim Government (AIG), which would provide a political alternative to the Kabul regime; and to launch a major military offensive against the town of Jalalabad, whose fall, it was thought, would trigger the collapse of the regime. The Pakistani military intelligence organization, the Directorate of Inter-service Intelligence (ISI), was placed in charge of both operations. In February 1989, a council (or *Shura*) was convened in Rawalpindi to elect the AIG. In fact, the delegates were carefully screened by the ISI and came almost exclusively from the Seven Party Alliance based in Peshawar, thus excluding not only the Shi'a and royalists, but also all the field commanders. The AIG largely represented the Ghilzay Pashtun ethnic group. Pakistan blocked any possibility of the Durrani Pashtun group, from which the previous monarchy stemmed, playing a role in the AIG, as it has barred them from any role in the Seven Party Alliance. Judicious use of Saudi Arabian money ensured that Abdul-ur-Rabb-ur-Rasul Sayyaf, a member of the Wahhabi sect of Islam, was chosen as Prime Minister, despite the fact that the Wahhabi in Afghanistan are a small minority cordially disliked by the other groups. As could be expected of a *Shura* controlled and directed by Pakistan, fundamentalists were also given a significant role.

From its conception, the AIG was weakened by its alienation of important segments of the Afghan resistance. Riven by the same ethnic and religious divisions as the Seven Party Alliance, it has been unable to exert influence over commanders who control liberated territories, or to co-ordinate the war effort effectively. It soon lost all credibility.

The military offensive against Jalalabad was a failure because the ISI ignored the realities of the situation, failed to involve the experienced and popular field commanders, used poorly trained troops from the refugee camps and did not provide them with a real central command. These were hardly inadvertent mistakes, for the ISI's priority has seemed to be less the collapse of the Kabul regime than the control of the *Mujaheddin* movement. The main danger, in the view of the ISI, would have been a victory for the *Mujaheddin* field commanders over whom Islamabad has no control. Such a victory might have been a step towards a strong and independent Afghanistan that could revive the old Pashtunistan issue. To divide and control the Afghan resistance, the ISI has always played the Pashtuns off against the Persian speakers, Ghilzay Pashtuns against Durrani Pashtuns, Peshawar against the *Mujaheddin* field commanders, and *Hezb-i-Islami* against the others. This strategy has been supported by Saudi Arabia and the Arab Muslim Brothers active in Peshawar, who saw in Hekmatyar the best bulwark against any Iranian influence in Afghanistan. The determination of the ISI to install at any cost the most pro-Pakistani government possible in Kabul has undermined the *Mujaheddin* movement. If the ISI cannot bring about a pro-Pakistan government, it has often appeared to prefer a besieged Najibullah to a true *Mujaheddin* victory.

The inability of the *Mujaheddin* to achieve any significant success in Afghanistan has been partially due to the incoherence of American policy since the signing of the Geneva Agreements in April 1988. The first mistake was to advocate the concept of 'positive symmetry', that is the continuation of military supplies by both Moscow and Washington to their respective allies, thus allowing the USSR to supply economic and military support worth billions of dollars to the Kabul regime. This was compounded by the US practice of 'negative symmetry': having backed the ISI which encouraged the *Mujaheddin* to launch the ill-fated assault on Jalalabad, Washington then cut off most of its supplies to the rebel forces. This tipped the military balance between the *Mujaheddin* and the Kabul regime in favour of the latter.

The second major error was to agree to Pakistani policies when the Soviet withdrawal should have argued for a change in priorities in the area. Hekmatyar, the most anti-Western and extremist leader in Peshawar, thus became the main beneficiary of American aid. A third flaw was to undermine the strength of the *Mujaheddin* field commanders, precisely when they could have made a difference on the field of battle, by backing the AIG, which was doomed to failure from the start but which received the bulk of both military and humanitarian aid until August 1989. In the critical early months of 1989, the field commanders found that both their financial and military supplies were being curtailed. The US Administration even put pressure on private voluntary organizations and UN agencies to stop providing direct help inside Afghanistan, and advised them instead to work through the AIG. In this way, it established an inefficient bureaucracy in Peshawar and a show-case administration in the non-strategic Kunar valley: there USAID built a bridge and a road which are used mainly by timber smugglers, thus accelerating the deforestation of one of the last tree-covered areas in Afghanistan. At the same time, the USSR was spending over $300m per month to enable the Kabul regime to provide both cash and economic incentives to a war-weary population.

By summer 1989, Washington was becoming aware of both the ineffectiveness of this policy and the danger represented by Hekmatyar, who was adopting an increasingly anti-Western stance. A decision was taken to give help directly to the *Mujaheddin* field commanders and to broaden the base of the AIG, from which Hekmatyar had half-withdrawn in August. The aim was to strengthen the *Mujaheddin*'s hand in working towards a political settlement. But Washington lacked the means of enforcing a real shift in ISI policy.

The decision to channel aid directly to the field commanders, in order to decrease the influence of *Hezb-i-Islami*, had the opposite effect: because of inadequate American monitoring, the Pakistani military were able to channel the bulk of the weapons provided to field commanders under the control of Hekmatyar. In addition, the Saudi government had agreed to provide more than $400m in aid, but given the close links between Saudi Arabia and Hekmatyar, most of this can be expected to end up with him or his supporters. Thus it is probable that the US boycott of Hekmatyar will have little effect. The attempt to broaden the AIG met with the same fate; negotiations with Tehran to merge the AIG and the Tehran-based Shi'ite Eight Party Alliance was unsuccessful, mainly due to opposition from Saudi Arabia.

The US also pinned some of its hopes on the prospects of a coup in Kabul, engineered by nationalist elements of the communist *Khalq* faction and some *Mujaheddin* who had infiltrated into Kabul. Attempts were made in August and December, and perhaps, most significantly in early March 1990, with a coup mounted by the Defence Minister Gen Tana'y – and supported by Hekmatyar – but all failed. In any event, given the ethnic links between the *Khalqi* and Hekmatyar, such a coup might well have resulted in a coalition between these two groups and not a *Mujaheddin* victory in Kabul.

Drugs and Destabilization

The fading of the ideological issues which sustained the East–West dimension of the war has unleashed new and uncontrolled forces. Besides ethnic and tribal rivalries, the most worrying trend is the spread of drug cultivation and trade. The 'tribal belt' – the area on both sides of the Afghan–Pakistan border – has turned into an 'Islamic drug cartel'. As in Colombia, poppies are cultivated by peasants and marketed by private networks which benefit from collusion with local and state administrations. In Afghanistan there are two kinds of drug dealers: *Mujaheddin* and private businessmen. The *Mujaheddin* drug dealers are concentrated in the eastern and southern tribal belt. Elsewhere, drug dealers whose expansion had originally been thwarted by the *Mujaheddin* became richer than the local *Mujaheddin* commanders when the US cut off direct support to the field commanders. The result has been that peasants and traders work for those dealers or make deals with the local government, or even join it in order to ensure a safer business. Drug cultivation and trade is now beyond the control of all the regionally interested governments, not only of Kabul and Islamabad, but also of Tehran and Moscow.

A Military Stalemate

By the early months of 1990 it was obvious that the *Mujaheddin* were unable to take Kabul by force. The major field commanders like Massoud, who may have both the organization and strategic perspective to pull off such an action, are victims of a blockade organized by the ISI. On the other hand, Najibullah's position remains shaky: it relies more on the goodwill of traditional local leaders than on the extension of a strong central state apparatus. Although the government's army looks able to hold some key cities, it cannot be expected to be strong enough to counter-attack and regain ground.

A decisive factor is probably that of foreign aid. It has cost the Soviet Union an enormous amount to ensure Najibullah's survival; yet it looks probable that the US Congress will not continue to vote for high levels of military aid (at present $300m per year) to the *Mujaheddin*. Thus, a true 'negative symmetry' might come into effect, which will induce either a general political settlement or the extension of local truces. In any case, the intensity of the battles around Jalalabad should not hide the fact that the fighting within Afghanistan has generally diminished. A remarkably stable balance of power both between the government and the *Mujaheddin* and between the political parties in the resistance has been established. The predominance of local and well-entrenched forces is striking, although it must be noted that the power they wield does not result in the clear demarcation of territorial entities, with strict borders between distinct groups. Power rests more on a combination of political, personal, tribal and ethnic affiliations.

Towards Negotiation?

Owing to the military stalemate, the superpowers, Pakistan and Iran, might find considerable merit in a political settlement based on a coalition government in Kabul. The stumbling block is Najibullah. The US, Pakistan and the *Mujaheddin* still insist on his removal before any settlement can be reached, although the US no longer insists that he must be removed even before negotiations can begin. The Soviet Union, along with Iran, does not want to commit itself to any change in

Kabul until a settlement is reached. The evolution of the situation over the past year has lent some weight to the Soviet position.

The Soviet Union has surprised the US by not simply giving up in Afghanistan after the withdrawal of its troops, continuing instead its extremely costly support for Najibullah. The reason is fairly obvious: Afghanistan borders the Soviet Union and Moscow thus has a clear strategic interest in its stability. Yet, though the USSR refuses to countenance the American suggestion that Najibullah be replaced before a political settlement can be reached, it is still committed to one.

During the visit of Iranian President Rafsanjani to Moscow in June 1989, Iran and the USSR apparently came to an agreement on Afghanistan. Iran, which worries about a strong Sunni *Mujaheddin* government in Kabul supported by Saudi Arabia, prefers a coalition government which would contain both the PDPA and *Mujaheddin*. This is also Moscow's position. Given that the US is unlikely to continue support for the *Mujaheddin* after 1990 if the military stalemate still exists, the ISI would be isolated (or at best supported only by Saudi Arabia) in its policies. Thus a political settlement, which will lead to a coalition government in Kabul, is likely. But this will not prevent an internal reshuffling of alliances, which might result in pockets of power based on ethnic lines, particularly since the permanence of a stalemate would dissociate the local *Mujaheddin* from the external negotiations, in which case they would have no credible political representation. The failed coup against Najibullah in March 1990 showed that ethnic affiliations are now playing a bigger role than ideological commitment. The ISI was still pursuing its goal of controlling the next government in Kabul through the Ghilzay Pashtuns, whatever their political affiliations, at the expense of a political settlement which seemed to be favoured early in 1990 by Gen Beg, the Pakistani Chief of Staff.

Ironically, Pakistan's hard-line policies have back-fired. Because there is no stability in Afghanistan, the Afghan refugees will not return home soon. As a result, Benazir Bhutto's weak regime has become endangered by the continued presence of a large refugee population in the North-West Frontier Province which is becoming more difficult to contain. Pakistan's policies have alienated the strongest of the *Mujaheddin* field commanders, while at the same time creating a political entity in Peshawar which will probably oppose a coalition government in Kabul and remain well entrenched in Peshawar, thus presenting a threat to Pakistan's own internal stability.

PAKISTAN: BHUTTO BELEAGUERED

Prime Minister Benazir Bhutto's weak regime drifted without direction in 1989 and early 1990, floundering in perennial domestic problems and facing renewed international problems. The Combined Opposition Party demonstrated its challenge to the Pakistan People's Party (PPP) by presenting a motion of no-confidence on 1 November 1989, which Bhutto just survived by the narrow margin of 12 votes. Managing policy towards Afghanistan and India was made more than usually difficult by the gravity of the Afghan refugee problem, and a resurgence of Muslim dissent in the Indian province of Kashmir.

While this first full year of democratic rule resulted in few new domestic or foreign policies, there were some new emphases. A new socioeconomic welfare agenda was developed, and political liberalization intensified: political prisoners were freed, and press censorship and the ban on trade unions were lifted. Yet the regime offered no solutions to Pakistan's principal domestic crises, and it demonstrated little skill in confronting Pakistan's old dilemmas and power structures.

Domestic Power Structures
Bhutto's powers continued to be sharply limited by the terms under which she had agreed to take and share power, especially by Gen Zia's constitutional legacy which had shifted the balance of power from the prime minister and a parliamentary form of government to the president. In her first year of rule Bhutto quarrelled with President Ghulam Ishaq Khan over military and judicial appointments, though she later took important steps to improve her relationship with him. As Pakistan entered the 1990s, it still possessed four, often competing, sources of political power: Bhutto; the President, who represented the establishment and the still powerful remnants of the Zia forces; the *Islami Jamhoori Ittehad* (IJI) under Mian Nawaz Sharif, who controlled Punjab Province where 62% of Pakistanis live; and the army.

The single most important decision for Pakistan in 1989 was that taken by the army under its Chief of Staff, Gen Aslam Beg, to continue to stand aside from politics and to allow democratization a chance to succeed. Beg also directed the army towards a new spirit of openness in civil-military relations: the army's largest-ever manoeuvres, *Zarb-e-Momin*, were conducted in December 1989 amidst extensive publicity, and military leaders regularly invited the press to discussions of military programmes. Although the army is no longer in the foreground of power, the public continues to view it as a central source of political strength. It therefore remains a pivotal element, and the divisive behaviour of Pakistan's politicians and the growing reliance of the regime on the army to keep the peace in Sind could test its patience.

Domestic Conflict
Pakistan's domestic problems were exacerbated in 1989–90 by, among other things, the political consequences of the electoral results. The divided vote in the late 1988 general election had resulted in a weak PPP central government and a strong IJI provincial opposition. The parties feuded at the centre (where the PPP narrowly dominates) and in the Punjab (which the IJI governs). The bitterness of their dispute threatens democracy and has created economic difficulties. For example, the PPP

tried to dislodge the Punjabi Chief Minister, Nawaz Sharif, in February 1989, while the latter complicated the implementation of the PPP's People's Work Programme (PWP), and inaugurated an independent Bank of Punjab (termed by the PPP as 'unconstitutional'). Thus, the PWP, launched in February 1989, became the first major economic victim of the political squabbles between the central and provincial leadership.

During her first year in office, Bhutto's relations with other political parties deteriorated in every province. Baluchistan's leadership accused the PPP of interference in provincial affairs and of stalling development projects; it also quarrelled with the centre over the implementation of the PWP, and threatened to withhold gas revenues. In the North-West Frontier Province (NWFP), the PPP was abandoned by its coalition partner, the Awami National Party, and in Sind, where the PPP commands a majority, its alliance partner, the *Muhajir Qaumi Movement* (MQM) which represents the *muhajirs* or migrants from India, broke with the PPP in October 1989. By the end of 1989, politicians in all four provinces were calling for greater provincial autonomy.

It was once believed that because of Bhutto's roots in Sind, the PPP regime was well suited to resolve that province's dire ethnic and economic problems. Yet the PPP has had little success in attenuating conflict between rural groups in Sind. Trapped between its powerful Sindhi (and often anti-*muhajir*) constituency and the practical need to co-operate with the MQM, the PPP has not successfully promoted any major initiatives to achieve peace in Sind. A joint PPP–MQM accord to resolve Sind's problems collapsed in October 1989 when the MQM, insisting that the PPP had failed to live up to its responsibilities under the accord, signed a secret agreement with the opposition IJI.

During the year the IJI, which had started with 65 seats in the lower house as opposed to the PPP's 106 (10 short of a majority), had formed the COP and enticed all the minor parties and independents under this banner. The PPP had been governing on the basis of a majority formed with the eight members of the Federally Administered Tribal Areas and the 14 members of the MQM. When the MQM joined forces with it in November the COP felt that the stage. was set for a motion of no-confidence. Bhutto managed with some difficulty (there were charges and counter-charges of bribery and intimidation from both sides) to hold on to a small majority of 12, but the essential fragility of her position was exposed.

Not only has Bhutto's weakness made it difficult to deal with economic and social problems, but the country has continued to be rent by ethnic violence, Sindhi–*muhajir* rivalry, and banditry exacerbated by the spread of sophisticated weaponry and drugs from the Afghan War. Today, parts of Karachi, Pakistan's main urban-industrial centre, are under daily curfew. In the absence of an adequate police force, Bhutto has had to rely increasingly on the army to enforce civil peace. At the end of February 1990, she forced the Sindhi Chief Minister to resign, but there was no sign that his successor would do better in curbing the growing violence.

The principal issue separating Sindhi nationalists and the *muhajirs* is the introduction of Biharis into Sind. While MQM supporters insist that the Biharis (who fought alongside the Pakistan Army in the 1971 Bangladesh conflict and remain in Bangladesh in squalid camps) are 'stranded Pakistanis' who must be repatriated to Sind, many Sindhi leaders vehemently insist that if the Biharis are to be repatriated any-where, they should be sent back to Bihar, in India. They argue that Sind has been inundated by migrants from other provinces, including Afghans and the *muhajirs* themselves, and that the Sindhis are fast becoming a minority in their own province. The IJI's offer to shelter the Biharis in the Punjab if Sind and Baluchistan refuse entry to them has only complicated inter-provincial relations.

The Economy

The new economic rights promised to Pakistan's poor have also not yet materialized. When Bhutto became Prime Minister the frail underpinnings of the economy, despite years of good harvests and large infusions of foreign economic aid in the 1980s, had begun to be revealed: the tax base was narrow; the savings rate at less than 5% was too low to achieve an investment rate that could either sustain growth or repay Pakistani debts; remittances from migrant workers in the Middle East were falling; and the foreign debt stood at $16.4bn. The PPP mani-festo promoted a shift from traditional spending patterns to an empha-sis on socio-economic welfare, but in 1989–90 the PPP regime proved unable to make good its promises.

Like Zia, Bhutto has used foreign policy as a tool of domestic econ-omic management, travelling and lobbying extensively for foreign economic support. She based her requests for aid not on geopolitical imperatives, but rather on the need to support Pakistan's fledgling democracy. Results were quickly evident. Western donors promised $3.1bn to Pakistan in April 1989 and the IMF eased the harsh restric-tions it had placed on a three-year, nearly $1-bn line of credit to Pakis-tan. If implemented as originally construed, the IMF requirements could have had adverse political consequences for the regime.

Still, infusions of foreign aid alone cannot remedy Pakistan's struc-tural economic problems. The 1989 budget revealed the economic and political realities which prevent the PPP from embarking on a new course in domestic economic policy. To reorder its spending priorities towards socio-economic welfare, the PPP would have to take politically dangerous stands either on agricultural taxes or on defence expendi-tures. It is prepared to do neither. New agricultural reforms and taxes seem unlikely because of the political power of landowners in both the PPP and the opposition, while a reduction in military expenditures is also unlikely at a time when the new civilian regime must reassure the army of its concern for the nation's security.

In the 1990s Pakistan will also face new sources of potential economic concern. As the pace of development in the Middle East oil king-
doms has slowed and competition from other labour-exporting states
has risen, the Pakistani migrants who spent much of the 1980s working
there are returning permanently. Their remittances, upon which the
Pakistani exchequer was heavily dependent, were not properly chan-
nelled or spent during the 1980s; instead, they were largely frittered
away on current consumption, luxury goods and unproductive investments. In the 1990s Pakistan will have to cope not only with the
decline of remittances, but also with the potential costs of the economic,
political and social reintegration of returning migrants.

The scourge of the Afghan War – the trade in guns and drugs – has
added to Pakistan's vast store of bureaucratic and political financial
corruption, hindering economic reform. The profits of the drug trade
alone have been estimated at between $4 and $7bn a year. Although the
PPP has promised a war on drugs (with US help), and is making efforts
to reduce poppy and heroin production, few expect a dramatic
reduction in drug trafficking soon. In fact, there is concern that if and
when the Afghan refugees do return to Afghanistan, poppy, being easy
to produce and lucrative, will be the first crop they plant.

Foreign Policy

The return of these Afghan refugees continues to be Pakistan's main
goal. In an effort to settle the war, Bhutto has continued Zia's policies,
co-operating with the United States and the Pakistan Army. The US
remains Pakistan's principal ally, supplying it with a six-year $4.02bn
package of military and economic aid, which is the financial and military backbone of the Afghan *Mujaheddin's* war efforts. Still, as a new
US–Soviet agreement on a strategy to end the Afghan civil conflict
grows more likely, Bhutto cannot count on sustaining the high level of
American interest in Pakistan which existed during the 1980s. These
years marked an era of unique US-Pakistani co-operation based upon a
mutual perception of threat from the USSR. In the 1990s the main
issues governing US–Pakistani relations are likely to be the pace of
Pakistan's democratization and of its nuclear weapons programme.

While Bhutto has travelled extensively, brought Pakistan back into
the Commonwealth, and received substantial economic aid from Japan,
Pakistan's principal foreign-policy preoccupations are regional:
Afghanistan and, increasingly, India. Until the some 3.5 million Afghan
refugees return home, Pakistan will remain hostage to the continuing
Afghan civil war. The departure of Soviet troops did not end the flow of
refugees: in 1989 over 70,000 more arrived. At the same time, international donors have reduced their commitments, resulting in
insufficient current aid to support growing refugee needs. Pakistani
officials are increasingly worried that the number of registered and
unregistered refugees is rising, while food stocks are falling. Of the 3.58
million registered refugees in 1990, the World Food Programme is now

able to feed only 2.7 m. The shortfall is being met through Pakistan's own grain stocks.

While bearing the future economic burden of the Afghan refugees will be difficult, so too will managing relations with India, whose own domestic instability only serves to increase tensions with Pakistan. On assuming power, Bhutto quickly sought a wide-ranging reconciliation with India, promoting many useful if modest agreements in the areas of travel, trade, cultural exchange, information transfers, drug trafficking, rail traffic, double taxation, border security and smuggling. Early on, too, Bhutto promised non-interference in the domestic affairs of India, especially in Punjab. Her own domestic weakness, however, may hamper her efforts to improve Indo-Pakistani relations. (The same is true of her counterpart V.P. Singh.) The attacks of her opponents, and the opinions of the army and the President, who, in 1989 accused India of having 'hegemonistic' designs in South Asia, forced Bhutto near the end of the year to rein in her enthusiasm for *rapprochement*.

Any gains made were put at risk by the resurgence of conflict in Kashmir, over which India and Pakistan have already fought two major wars. The rapid rise of anti-Indian secessionist and pro-Pakistani agitation in Kashmir – and the domestic pressures in both countries for a tough position on this politically sensitive dispute – could destroy hopes for improvement in Indo-Pakistani relations. In this predominantly Muslim Indian state, where renewed protests began two years ago, the clashes between Indian troops and pro-independence supporters in late 1989 left more than 70 persons dead by late January 1990. The Indian government has accused Pakistan of training and financing terrorists both in Punjab and in Kashmir, thereby implying that Bhutto's early pledges of non-interference have not been kept.

While Bhutto, like all Pakistan's leaders, strongly supports a plebiscite under UN supervision so that Kashmir can determine its own future (agreed to by India and Pakistan in 1949, but later rejected by India), the Pakistani government has denied any involvement. Despite their heated rhetoric, both leaderships still stress the need for a peaceful resolution, and troops have not been mobilized along the border. The Kashmiri crisis has its own momentum, however, and it is not yet certain whether India or Pakistan will be able to restrain inflamed popular passions in support of a seceding Kashmir.

It is impossible to be sanguine about the prospects for maintaining democracy in Pakistan. The agreements which Benazir Bhutto made in order to rule as prime minister have guaranteed a weak central government, beset by continuing challenges from provincial leaders, mounting ethnic strife exacerbated by the presence of Afghan refugees, a stumbling, debt-ridden economy, and new troubles on the frontier with India. In these circumstances, it may not be long before the army finds it difficult to adhere to its pledge of neutrality in the political arena, despite its awareness that it, too, would be hard-pressed to find any better answers to the Pakistani dilemma.

INDIA: THE END OF A DYNASTY?

Indian politics in 1989–90 were dominated by the general election of 22–26 November that resulted in the country's first minority government, and by elections in eight states on 27 February 1990 which made more likely an early end to the Nehru family's pivotal political role. An upsurge in communalism, which affected both these elections, and foreign-policy crises with neighbouring states, made for a complicated domestic and external security environment.

The general election in 1989 echoed the post-Emergency Indira Gandhi–*Janata Dal* contest of 1977 and, like it, illustrated the enduring importance of personalities in Indian elections. The opposition sought to turn it into a referendum on Rajiv Gandhi's political style and popular image and were able to add high-level corruption to their catalogue of charges when further revelations on the Bofor's arms deal appeared. While these may not have directly implicated him, they failed to completely exonerate him. Gandhi was criticized for taking India back to the old politics of manipulation for partisan and personal reasons, which created increased authoritarianism, a deterioration in centre-state relations, and too frequent imposition of the president's rule on the states. Added to this were charges of policy incoherence and a lack of vision in foreign policy.

The opposition National Front leader, former Finance and Defence Minister V.P. Singh, cultivated his reputation for incorruptibility and made honesty in government an election issue. But the opposition had its own image problem. The National Front was united for electoral purposes, but this disguised underlying intense political division. While Singh appeared to be the most electorally attractive opposition leader, his position as a prospective prime minister was by no means assured; if he clearly stated this ambition it would have seriously disturbed his colleagues both within *Janata Dal* and the National Front as a whole. Consequently, on many occasions he equivocated on the question of his own ambitions so as to preserve opposition unity. Without conclusively dispelling doubts about the Front's ability to provide coherent government, Singh adopted the high moral ground of the anti-corruption crusader. Observers who interpreted this as a lack of political ruthlessness were proved wrong once the election result was declared.

The other issue which dominated this election was the upsurge of Hindi–Muslim communalism, centred on the revival of the controversy over the Basri-Masjid mosque which had been built in the sixteenth century on the supposed site of the birth of the Hindu God Ram. This issue was especially significant in the electorally important 'Hindu belt' of North India states and served as a test of the adherence by political parties to the secularism enshrined in the Constitution. Tensions were exacerbated when the Hindu fundamentalist party *Vishwa Hindu Parishad* (VHP) launched a campaign to 'liberate' the site in Ayodhya alleged to be the birthplace of Ram. Their objective was to demolish the mosque and erect a temple on 9 November 1989. In late September, therefore, they ceremonially inaugurated a collection of 'holy' bricks, provoking riots in which over 100 people were killed. The dispute embarrassed both the government and the opposition; the former's decision to acquiesce in the building of the temple alienated its traditional Muslim constituency, whilst the latter was compromised through its association in the broad anti-Gandhi coalition with the avowedly Hindu chauvinist *Bharatya Janata* Party (BJP), which in turn refused to disassociate itself from the VHP.

The election was marred by violence and malpractice; the south stood firmly behind the Congress (I), while the Hindi belt of North India voted overwhelmingly for the opposition. Congress (I) suffered a drastic reduction of its 1984 tally and the loss of a working majority, but with 192 seats was still the single largest party in the 545-member *Lok Sabha.* As a result of *Janata Dal's* triumph in the north, the National Front secured a total of 144 seat; the combined Left Front won 51 seats, and the resurgence of communalism was translated into a spectacular, if disturbing, BJP victory in 86 constituencies. Overall, the electorate had registered disapproval of the *status quo* by electing in almost all cases candidates from parties opposed to the ruling state governments. It rejected Rajiv Gandhi, but without fatally humiliating him, and immediately after the election he was unanimously re-elected leader of the Congress (I). The desire for change at the centre had not been an unequivocal vote of confidence in the opposition.

On 2 December, in a dramatic and adroit manoeuvre, Singh outflanked his main rival, Chandra Shekar, to win leadership of the *Janata Dal* in the *Lok Sabha* and accordingly, premiership of the subsequent minority government. His choice of ministers, the majority of whom owe their allegiance to him, has alleviated fears regarding indecisive and disunited government.

Challenges for the Minority Government

V.P. Singh was bequeathed a series of challenges on the domestic and regional fronts and was forced to operate within the constraints of a minority government dependent on both Marxist and Hindu chauvinist support for its survival. Soon after the election Singh established his mastery of independent political manoeuvre on the domestic scene, and by indulging in a modest peace offensive he departed from the previous policy of aggressive assertiveness in regional affairs.

Two early events indicated that, in contrast to those of his predecessor, the methods Singh planned to use to counter the persistent centrifugal pressures would be imaginative and shrewd. His visit to Punjab (ostensibly for religious reasons) with cabinet colleagues soon after they had been sworn in, considerably enhanced goodwill for the new administration and auspiciously coincided with the emergence of the moderate Simrajit Singh Mann as the new president of *Akali Dal*, the Sikh political party in Punjab. The choice of the Kashmiri Mufti

Mohammed Sayeed as India's first Muslim Home Minister also allayed fears about the extent of BJP influence.

Centrifugal tensions have a dynamic of their own, however, which can easily jeopardize the best intentions and continue to bedevil regional relations. This was quickly illustrated by the kidnapping of Sayeed's daughter by Jammu and Kashmir Liberation Front (JKLF) separatists, her release in exchange for five of their colleagues on 13 December, and the recourse on 18 January to presidential rule and military power in Kashmir to suppress the popular uprising in support of secession. In the current context of communalism, the ingenuity and survival of the minority government will be severely tested.

Seething Kashmir

Kashmir, with its Muslim majority, lies symbolically at the heart of the Indo-Pakistani antagonism, encapsulating the *raison d'être* of the two states – the Indian commitment to secularism against the Pakistani claim to be the guardian, if no longer the home, of the subcontinent's Muslims. Although the roots of the problem can be traced to the partition of India, the causes of the present discontent are located in the corrupt and inefficient state government of Farooq Abdullah (1987 to January 1990), and its economic stagnation; together they have fuelled a widespread demand for secession. At issue is the legitimacy of the permanent incorporation of Kashmir into the Indian Union – the militants either advocating union with Pakistan or national self-determination, and the BJP committed to full integration within India and abolition of Article 370 of the Constitution which gives Kashmir special status. Tensions have been inflamed by the emotive rhetoric emanating from the Pakistani *Azad*, or 'Free Kashmir', leadership, and the influx of its supporters across the 1948 cease-fire line contributed to a death toll of over 100 in the first two months of 1990. New Delhi's insistence that Pakistan is sustaining the rebellion, and the pressure of Islamic fundamentalists and nationalists on the Bhutto government, has badly affected the improvement in relations nurtured by Gandhi and Bhutto. A meeting of the foreign ministers of the two governments on 22 January failed to improve the situation. Pakistan's threats to internationalize the issue infuriated India, which maintains that the 1972 Simla Accord pledging the two states to settle differences through bilateral negotiations also applies to Kashmir and supersedes any other framework, including the 1949 UN plebiscite proposal.

Despite mutual recriminations and limited border skirmishes between Indian and Pakistani troops, the Indian decision on 19 February to dissolve the state legislature implies a recognition of some responsibility for the impasse and a desire to resolve the conflict domestically. Given the extent of Kashmiri resentment, however, it is doubtful that fresh elections will be enough to resolve the conflict.

As both Prime Minister and Defence Minister V.P. Singh cannot afford to be seen as weak on this explosive issue without risking a

nationalist backlash against his minority government. This is a dilemma he shares with Benazir Bhutto. Neither of them can renounce another war over Kashmir as a policy option, even though both would rather avoid one – Singh because of its potentially debilitating effect on his development priorities, and Bhutto because of the delicate civil–military equation in Pakistani politics. While Hindu militants had appeared somewhat more accommodating when they agreed on 9 February 1990 to suspend further efforts at construction in Ayodhya for four months, the BJP is bound to be more intransigent on Kashmir.

The results of the elections held on 27 February 1990 in the eight states controlled by Congress (I), involving approximately half the national electorate, will encourage the BJP to exert greater influence on the minority government and dictate Singh's options on Kashmir. Congress (I)'s otherwise disastrous performance was only relieved by victories in Arunachal Pradesh and Maharashtra. In Madhya Pradesh and Himachal Pradesh (neighbouring Kashmir) the BJP won outright, whilst in Bihar, Gujarat and Rajasthan it made substantial gains, pointing to a coalition with the *Janata Dal*, which secured power only in Orissa. One possible release from this dilemma is for Singh to call a fresh general election in hopes that a majority government would give him greater freedom of manoeuvre on Kashmir.

Although these state elections show that the *Janata Dal* has yet to prove that it is a major political force, the party has gained members from Congress (I) who are displeased with Rajiv Gandhi's leadership. Over time, a confirmed and lasting realignment of secular forces in India under Singh is a distinct possibility. Most voters support secular, rather than religious, tendencies and secularism could therefore triumph over fundamentalism in the long term. The formidable allure of nationalism, however, will militate against a peaceful and enduring solution to the Kashmir question.

Nepal

One regional dispute which Singh inherited proved to be less contentious as reconciliation had already been initiated by the Gandhi government. The cause of the conflict with the landlocked Himalayan kingdom of Nepal, with which India has a Treaty of Peace and Friendship dating back to 1950, was the expiry on 23 March 1989 of trade and transit agreements between the two neighbours. The agreements lapsed in 1988 and had been extended twice for periods of six months, but this time India closed 13 of the 15 border points. Although New Delhi insisted that this would not affect essential supplies, the resulting fuel shortages have meant severe austerity in Nepal.

The true cause of India's closure of the points was an arms deal which Nepal had signed with China in August 1988. India, which had been Nepal's sole arms supplier, viewed this as an encroachment on its strategic preponderance in the area. In addition, New Delhi cited actions by Kathmandu concerning the employment rights of Indian workers and increased tariffs on Indian goods which it claimed violated the 1950 agreement. New Delhi's desire for a more subservient Nepalese foreign-policy orientation clearly motivated its actions.

Talks between the two states at foreign minister level in March were deadlocked, but by the time of the Non-Aligned Summit in September, communication had been restored. A joint statement on 20 February 1990, after further talks, indicated that the Singh government's commitment for a more amicable regional policy will be expressed in mutually accommodating arrangements. Separate agreements on trade and transit (which Nepal had previously pressed for and India had refused) as well as cross-border smuggling are expected to form the basis of a new accord. Nepal will no doubt also need to show that it is more sensitive to Indian security concerns for a new agreement to work.

SRI LANKA: ESCAPING INDIA'S CONTROL

India's dispute with Sri Lanka assumed crisis proportions on 1 June 1989 when Sri Lankan President R. Premadasa demanded the total withdrawal of the Indian Peacekeeping Force (IPKF) deployed in the north-east of the island by 29 July, the second anniversary of their introduction under the 1987 Indo-Sri Lankan Accord. The Gandhi government refused this demand, and in the face of Sri Lankan threats to confine the troops to barracks, or even to eject them, dared Premadasa to do his worst. What was at stake were the authority of the Sri Lankan President, and the nature of the obligations which India, theoretically on behalf of the Tamils, had accepted under the Accord. At a more fundamental level was the question of the virtual Indian veto on Sri Lankan foreign policy that then-President Jayawardene had conceded to Gandhi in the exchange of letters accompanying the Accord.

Premadasa, besieged by the anti-Indian, chauvinist Sinhala *Janatha Vimukti Peramuna* (JVP) insurgency in the south, desperately needed to confirm his nationalist credentials and Sri Lanka's sovereign right to conclude its tortuous nation-building process without external intervention. This earned him the support of the principal Tamil militant group, the Liberation Tigers of Tamil Eelam (LTTE) who had opposed the IPKF and moved in to control areas the IPKF had evacuated in previous phased withdrawals throughout 1989. By agreeing in April to talks with the Sri Lankan government, the LTTE threw its weight behind the president's efforts to obtain the IPKF withdrawal. On 28 June it strengthened his hand further by announcing a permanent ceasefire with the Sri Lankan Security Forces.

The JVP, however, were not impressed and unleashed a series of crippling nationwide strikes to augment their armed insurrection. By September, however, a reconsideration by India of its position led it to agree to end offensive operations against the LTTE by the end of the month and to complete an IPKF withdrawal by 31 December 1989. India, however, qualified this by linking it to progress on the effective devolution of power to the pro-Indian Eelam People's Revolutionary Liberation Front (EPRLF) provincial government of the merged north-east province, headed by Varatharaja Perumal.

The Singh government affirmed its commitment to respect the 31 December deadline, but was only able to complete its withdrawal by the end of March 1990. Nevertheless, Singh, in warmly welcoming a Sri Lankan draft of a treaty with India on 12 January 1990, has affirmed the commitment to a more suitable framework for governing relations between sovereign states, enabling Premadasa to deliver on his electoral promises.

India and the Tamils

India's relationships with Sri Lankan Tamil groups that it has cultivated since 1987 are in flux. New Delhi's policy of strategic denial in Sri Lanka that led to the deployment of the IPKF enlarged India's commitment of support for the ERPLF and its Tamil National Army (TNA). By mid-December, when the LTTE defeated the TNA to take control of Batticaloa in Perumal's eastern province stronghold, it had become apparent that the last Indian offensive against the LTTE had failed and that further attempts to prevent it from capturing power, or to project Perumal as a credible alternative, would either imperil India's political objectives, or incur unacceptable costs. By the end of the year New Delhi acknowledged what Premadasa had earlier realized: there could be no settlement of the Tamil problem in Sri Lanka without the consent of the LTTE and a recognition of its central role.

Nevertheless, if removing Indian troops is to end in LTTE control of north-east Sri Lanka, Indian prestige requires that the political formula enshrined in the Accord (replacing secession with provincial autonomy) is implemented. This was made clear by accounts not only of the Premadasa–LTTE talks but also of the meetings between Indian and LTTE representatives at the end of 1989 and in mid-February 1990. Earlier indications included the formation by the LTTE on 20 December of a political party, the People's Front of Liberation Tigers (PFLT) which conspicuously omits Eelam from its title, and a willingness by the LTTE to attend the September All-Party Conference convened by Premadasa to discuss the national crisis.

Although Perumal has indicated a reluctance to accept LTTE hegemony, the Singh government's desire to express regional goodwill by withdrawing from Sri Lanka and India's continuing opposition to secession will mean that Perumal cannot gain Indian support. Thus the absorption of the EPRLF and its residual eastern province base into a LTTE-dominated arrangement seems assured. Premadasa's ability to make the appropriate territorial adjustment depends on his command over politics in the majority Sinhalese south of the island and in particular, an ending of the JVP insurgency.

Sinhalese Politics and the Future of Sri Lanka

In December 1988 the United National Party (UNP) under its leader President Premadasa won a narrow victory in the presidential election over the Sri Lanka Freedom Party (SLFP) under a former president Mrs Banadaranaike. The UNP followed this up by a comfortable majority in the general elections of February 1989, winning 125 seats and a majority of 25 in parliament. Having settled the intra-establishment contest through these two elections the Premadasa government now faced the fundamental challenge of inducing the JVP to give up its armed struggle and to enter the political mainstream.

All attempts to do so foundered on JVP insistence that the Premadasa government was illegitimate. Underpinning the Sri Lankan crisis is the potent argument that the 11-year monopoly of state power by the UNP has provided the impetus for revolutionary extra-parliamentary opposition in the form of the JVP and institutionalized violence as the ultimate arbiter of political debate on the island. And the JVP was prepared to continue its terrorist campaign without cease, despite the high toll of casualites on each side. There is some sign that the government may have begun to get the upper hand: on 13 November the JVP leader Rohana Wijeweera and his deputy Gamanayake were killed near the JVP Kandy headquarters. The backbone of the rebellion may thus have been severely damaged, but it has by no means been broken.

The nation- and state-building challenge has to be met on two fronts. First, the government's counter-terrorist apparatus has to be disbanded to dispel the psychosis of fear that has engulfed the island, and second, political and economic reconciliation with the JVP constituency has to be implemented swiftly if faith is to be restored in a democratic polity. The regulation empowering the security forces to dispose of bodies without an inquest was dropped on 15 February and a complete repeal of the Emergency Act was promised, but the real test of calling the para-military forces to account has yet to be satisfied. There are still extensive extra-judicial killings in Sri Lanka. In the absence of an undisputed military leader an army coup can be discounted, but the security forces will continue to be influential, especially since the JVP in August chose to threaten government families.

The government must target the most deprived areas of the south for a concerted development programme if it is to address properly the socio-economic grievances of the JVP constituency. In October Sri Lanka's international donors pledged $785m to the country's war-torn economy, but not unconditionally. They were mindful that the second tranche of a standby loan negotiated in 1987 had been suspended in March 1989 for six months because the government failed to live up to the loan's conditions. They thus imposed an IMF-designed Policy Framework Plan (PFP) on Sri Lanka to curb populist extravagance and to extend liberalization. As a result the country's economic programme is being radically altered with World Bank assistance to meet more modest objectives. The enduring commitment to social welfare in the PFP and potential savings from the military budget provide grounds for cautious optimism. The road to a restoration of human rights and democratic freedom in Sri Lanka is strewn with enormous obstacles, but they are not insuperable.

Latin America

The pattern of events in Latin America provided a sobering counter-point to the optimism engendered elsewhere by the crumbling of communist regimes, the withdrawal of Soviet military power and the widespread espousal of liberal democratic political and economic values. States that in 1989 began the first stages in the process of democratic transition might well ponder the lessons of recent Latin American experience. Despite progress in several countries, seven years after the breakdown of authoritarian rule in the region the prospects of restoring economic stability and of creating legitimate and effective political systems seemed, in many cases, as remote as ever, and professions of international support for fragile democracies have only sporadically been translated into effective action.

Optimists in the West could take some comfort from the fact that the momentous events in Eastern Europe were to some extent echoed in Latin America. The defeat of the *Sandinista* government in the Nicaraguan elections of 25 February and President Ortega's willingness to accept the result provided the best example of an allegedly totalitarian system opening up to the forces of pluralist democracy. The US invasion of Panama on 20 December (see pp. 34–5) did allow the Bush Administration to claim that the number of countries under democratic rule had been extended in 1989, although the means raised many questions and some protests, not least from within Latin America itself.

Cuba was becoming increasingly isolated by Castro's insistence on the maintenance of a purely one-party, communist state while other communist parties around the world, led by the Soviet Union, moved to multi-party elections. More serious for Castro were the clear signals of Soviet displeasure with his continued criticism, and growing reluctance by the Soviet Union to continue the massive economic subsidies which have maintained his regime. Despite his bluster, questions were multiplying about Castro's ability to stay in power in the face of changing circumstances.

If democratic consolidation is measured by the ability to hold regular elections with peaceful transfers of power, there were a number of encouraging events during 1989. In February Michael Manley was returned to power in Jamaica. On 1 May the Paraguayan presidential election was won by Gen Andrés Rodríguez of the *Colorado* Party who had first taken power in the coup of February 1989. In Argentina the presidential elections on 14 May resulted in the victory of the Peronist Carlos Saul Menem over Eduardo Angeloz of the ruling radical party, the UCR. On 27 May the final results of the Bolivian elections were announced with the victory of Gonzalo Sánchez of the ruling National Revolutionary Movement (MNR). Beneath these encouraging signs, however, were a host of social, political and economic problems throughout Latin America which required a tempering of optimism.

SOUTH AMERICA: STILL STRUGGLING

At the end of 1989 the long process of political transition from military authoritarianism to democratic norms in Chile and Brazil was completed. In Chile this was accomplished with the presidential elections on 14 December. These elections – the first since the military coup in 1973 – resulted in the victory of the Christian Democratic candidate, Patricio Aylwin, who headed a coalition of 17 centre and centre-left parties. He defeated Gen Pinochet's candidate Hernán Büchi by 53.8% to 28.7%, and assumed office in March 1990. His task will be made more difficult by the frequent attempts made by Pinochet in 1989 to structure the country's constitution and political system so that the new president's freedom of action would be severely restricted, for example, in terms of control of the Central Bank and of the armed forces.

Although the transition to civilian rule in Brazil occurred in March 1985 and although several series of elections have taken place since then, the two-round elections of November and December 1989 were the first in which the country had voted directly for a president since 1960. The second round on 17 December was won by the centre-right candidate, Fernando Collor de Mello who defeated Luis Inacio da Silva (Lula) of the Workers' Party. There was thus much evidence that electoral systems could continue to function efficiently even in conditions of stringent economic austerity and political instability.

Western optimists could also take comfort from the significant shift during 1989 away from the state-led import substitution industrialization, for so long dominant in the region, towards the adoption of liberal economic policies. A prominent example could be found in Mexico; more surprisingly, in Argentina Carlos Menem initially jettisoned many of the shibboleths of Peronist tradition by adopting radical free-market economic policies, appointing leading industrialists to head his economics team and distancing himself from the powerful trade union movement. In Brazil, too, Collor's victory was achieved in part by the success of his attack on the bloated and inefficient federal bureaucracy and state sector. Moreover, since his election and during his world tour in February 1990, he reinforced his commitment to privatization and trade liberalization.

Yet, whilst formal democratic structures continued to function (a not inconsiderable achievement), the underlying political, social and economic situation showed little improvement. At the end of the decade average per capita product in the region was more than 8% below its 1980 level. In 1989 significant growth occurred only in Costa Rica, Paraguay and Chile whilst inflation soared to new heights in Brazil and Argentina. Despite the Brady Plan of March 1989, which accepted for the first time the principle of debt reduction, the size of the external debt did not shrink, but stabilized at around $US416bn. Net export of capital dropped from the 1988 total of $29bn to around $25bn, bringing the cumulative net transfer of resources out of the region in the period

1982–9 to just over $203bn, a level still far too high to allow stable growth. The one encouraging sign was the continued expansion of exports which rose to $110bn in 1989, compared to $101bn in 1988 and $87bn in 1987. Yet even this increase masked a long-term decline in Latin America's overall share of world exports: 3.7% in 1989 compared to 5.1% in 1985 and 12.5% in the mid-1950s. The abiding difficulty of promoting structural economic reform within the constraints of unstable political systems could be seen in the two largest countries of South America. In Brazil the so-called Summer Plan (an austerity pro- gramme named after the then minister of finance) announced in early 1989 failed, and for most of the year there was little effective economic management. This was partially a result of political pressures caused by electioneering in the lead-up to the November and December presiden- tial elections. But it also reflected the political weakness of the outgo- ing president, José Sarney, whose overall support fell still further and whose administration was beset by resignations and financial scandals. By the end of the year it was hoped that the newly-elected president, Collor, who took office in March 1990, would be able to develop the authority to take swift and effective action. Events in 1989, however, had already served to underline the difficulties he would face.

First, Collor's victory was above all a protest against the failures of the existing political class (especially the largest party, the Brazilian Democratic Movement Party) that had dominated politics since the transition to civilian rule in 1985. Collor conducted a personalist and populist campaign with no significant party backing; his television per- formance and promotion played a major role. Yet he will have to work within the 1988 constitution which gives Congress significant power over economic policy. Second, although it was defeated, the presidential elections signalled an important shift on the left. The best organized left-wing party, the Workers' Party, emerged as the major opposition force, ahead of both the veteran socialist Leonel Brizola's Democratic Workers' Party and the Social Democratic Party of Brazil. Moreover, having come so close to victory in December, with 47% of the vote, and with the prospect of yet more elections (this time for Congress in November 1990) the left will see little reason to co-operate with a Collor government. Finally, there is the seriousness of the inherited economic situation. Although the economy grew by 3% in 1989, financial insta- bility reached new heights. Inflation rose from 933% at the end of 1988 to nearly 1,500% in the 12 months to November 1989. Moreover, Brazil's trade surplus fell from $19bn to $16bn which, together with the substantial increase in accumulated interest arrears, will significantly reduce the incoming government's room for manoeuvre.

Argentina was another example of the difficulties of trying to implement radical economic restructuring at the same time as seeking to maintain financial stability. Menem's abandonment of wage, price and exchange controls and promise of wide-ranging privatization failed to stem either the dramatic loss of public confidence in the currency or the soaring inflationary spiral; prices rose an estimated 5,000% in 1989, and over 100% in February 1990 alone. Since the resignation of his second economics minister in December 1989 (the sixth since the start of 1989), Menem has been engaged in a fruitless attempt to draw the opposition Radical Party into a government of national unity and to win the co-operation of the powerful trade union movement.

In Peru and Colombia the internal security situation continued to cause alarm and reinforced the belief that future threats to regional security will come far more from the breakdown of social and political order within states than from inter-state conflict. In Peru in May 1989 there was a significant escalation of violence by the Maoist *Sendero Luminoso* guerrilla group marked the ninth anniversary of the start of military action with a three-day 'armed strike' and the killing of 73 people on 17 May. In October the government extended the state of emergency to Lima as a result of an increase in attacks in the capital. Drug-related violence escalated in Colombia during the first half of 1989 with an increase in the murders of judges and officials, and there was widespread rioting in Bogota in March following the murder of two prominent politicians and the wounding of a third. The growing seriousness of the situation was symbolized in August 1989 by the murder of the prominent Liberal Party politician, Luis Carlos Galán, prompting President Barcos to implement wide-ranging emergency measures against the drug cartels.

International Developments

There has been considerable debate over the ways in which the tremendous changes in the character of the international system that occurred in 1989 will affect Latin America. There were many who argued that Latin America stood to gain from these changes: the much-discussed decline in US hegemony would create more space for regional actors and enhance prospects for regional co-operation; a more pluralist world order would create new opportunities for Latin American foreign policy; and the reduction of Soviet influence in the area would reduce international confrontation and polarization.

Yet, whilst these arguments are not completely without substance, the broader pattern of world events looked less than wholly reassuring, for several adverse trends that will shape the region's international behaviour emerged during 1989. Notwithstanding Canada's joining the Organization of American States (OAS), Latin America's problems slipped down the foreign-policy agendas of most major states. For example, in the early 1980s Europe could develop an increased role in Latin America safe in the knowledge that its fundamental foreign-policy interests and alignments were secure. Events in Eastern Europe and the disputes over the process of further integration overturned this assumption and led to a marked decline in the interest of even those states (such as Italy and the FRG) that had led the growth of European involvement in the region through the 1980s. Most immediately, the promises of economic assistance to Eastern Europe (above all by the FRG) will leave few resources available for debt relief or environmental assistance in Latin America. On a more positive note, the UK and Argentina improved their relations significantly with the formal ending of hostilities in October 1989 and the restoration of diplomatic relations in February 1990.

Japan remained the 'new partner' most likely to develop a significant future presence in the region. Indeed, the steady increase in Japan's role in the international financial system during 1989, and its willingness to assist the implementation of the Brady Plan, amply demonstrated that potential. Yet, political uncertainty within Japan, the caution of the banking and business community given the depth of the present economic crisis in Latin America, and events in Eastern Europe, all served to hold back the growth of Japanese involvement.

Second, these trends were partially underpinned by a significant decline in the levels of economic interdependence between Latin America and its partners. No longer forced to lend 'involuntarily' and thus able to adopt a far more detached view of events in the region, Western banks continued to make very substantial provisions against bad loans in Latin America. The seven-month process of completing the Mexican debt package, the first in the region under the aegis of the Brady Plan, provided evidence of this shift. In addition, changes in the pattern of industrialization and the increasing importance of high-technology manufacturing processes contributed to a long-term decline in the interest of multinational companies in investing in the region. There were therefore worrying signs that favourable investment policies may not be enough to stimulate the return of significant foreign investment on which the region's economic recovery depends. It is true that alternative forms of interdependence, above all in terms of the fight against drug traffic and the protection of the environment, were strengthened in 1989. But there were clear signs in both areas of the difficulties of effective international action and of the extent to which these issues can become sources of friction. The scale of US drug-related assistance to the region increased significantly in 1989. In August the Administration announced a $65-m emergency aid package to Colombia, and in September 1989 it unveiled a $2-bn five-year aid programme to Peru, Colombia and Bolivia and decided to send up to 100 US military advisers to train the Colombian armed forces in the fight against drug producers and traffickers. Yet, although Western commitment to the drugs problem was widely welcomed in Latin America, there was also a significant feeling that the region was being made the scapegoat for the failure to tackle the problem at the level of consumption. Latin American governments also protested at the gap between the anti-drug rhetoric and the scale of assistance. Thus Colombia protested at the US decision to reject renewal of the International Coffee Agreement (costing Colombia around $400m a year) and to instigate trade action against Colombian exports of cut flowers.

A similar pattern was visible over environmental issues and, in particular, over the problem of Amazonian deforestation. International pressure on Brazil at the inter-governmental level did achieve some results and in April 1989 President Sarney announced the 'Our Nature' programme which strengthened the government's forest protection agency, following the earlier abolition of tax incentives for forest clearance. Yet the difficulties of actually implementing such policies were graphically illustrated by the refusal of the Brazilian army in the autumn to remove gold-miners from the Yanomani Indian reserve near the Venezuelan border. International criticism of Brazil also created a nationalist uproar at external intervention and gave rise to claims of 'ecological imperialism'. This backlash declined, however, as the Brazilian government began to formulate a series of more reasoned complaints that are likely to remain prominent features of the ecology debate. The absence of any significant environmental assistance, the failure to appreciate the extent of the region's other environmental problems, and the unwillingness to consider broader measures of debt relief that would help tackle the underlying pressures on the rain-forest were raised. Brazil's position gained regional support at the meeting of the Amazon Pact in May 1989.

Third, it is not at all clear that Latin America will stand to gain from the withdrawal of Soviet power and influence that gathered pace in 1989. After all, the existence of a balance of power has been an important factor underpinning the autonomy of Third World states throughout the post-war period. Although there was much talk in 1989 of a significant increase in economic ties between the USSR and the major Latin American economies (especially following Sarney's visit to Moscow in October 1988), little concrete progress was made.

Finally, the events of 1989 had a significant impact on US–Latin American relations. On the one hand, the disparity of power between the two halves of the hemisphere remained immense and the invasion of Panama demonstrated very clearly that older unilateralist, or Monroe-ist, tendencies were far from dead. Indeed, with a relaxation of the East–West rivalry the justifications for US policy were now being framed in terms that echoed an earlier era, namely the need to bring order and democracy to the region. On the other hand, during 1989 it became clearer than ever that the US no longer has the resources to solve the region's problems. As the limited character of the Brady Plan showed budgetary difficulties restricted the scope of US policy. Moreover, as in the case of the EC, the dramatic expansion in 1989 of the list of new democracies claiming American assistance will further limit US freedom of manoeuvre. The difficulties of securing adequate funding for the reconstruction fund for Panama and Nicaragua – both countries of particular political sensitivity for any US Administration – attest to what will remain an abiding problem.

PROMISE AND CHALLENGE IN CENTRAL AMERICA

After a full decade of conflicts Central America faced the 1990s with both continued grounds for pessimism, after some of the worst fighting for years in El Salvador, and some grounds for hope, as the democratic elections in Nicaragua on 25 February 1990 brought unexpected defeat for the *Sandinista* National Liberation Front (FSLN). The *Sandinista* leadership's acceptance of the result was in sharp contrast to the behaviour and fate of Gen Manuel Noriega in nearby Panama. Taken together, however, the two changes in government have brought about a notable shift in the political and strategic profile in the region. They heighten the promise, created by changes in Soviet policy and in relations with the United States, of some reduction in international tensions in this sensitive zone.

The Nicaraguan elections also mark a significant change for the prospects and the pattern of the Central American peace process. In the past 12 months it, too, has had remarkable ups and downs. Hopes for peace were maintained and given new form in the Tela agreements in August, brought to the verge of collapse by continued fighting, and then salvaged at an extraordinary summit meeting in December. With the transition in Nicaragua under way, but an unresolved war in El Salvador and a volatile situation in Guatemala, the peace process now faces different, but equally daunting, challenges.

The turmoil in El Salvador had an impact in neighbouring Guatemala, making the interrelation of the problems in these two, particularly closely-linked countries all the more apparent. A notable deterioration had already occurred in the situation in Guatemala, with another coup attempt on 9 May 1989; a resurgence in guerrilla activity by the Guatemalan National Revolutionary Union (URNG); and further increases in violence, both criminal and political, and human-rights abuses. Attempts to improve the institutional system to protect human rights had little effect; in mid-October the OAS Human Rights Commission concluded that there was still a need for the security forces to submit themselves to the judicial authorities. Although there had begun to be some *rapprochement* between the US and Guatemalan armed forces, US concern was voiced at the end of the year by the new Ambassador, and further emphasized by his temporary withdrawal at the beginning of March 1990.

Tension within the country had heightened because of the FMLN's November offensive, which came amid the rise in guerrilla activity; increased popular discontent in response to new economic measures; and extreme right-wing pressures against the decision to try the officers involved in the coup attempt and then against the sentences handed down by the Council of War on 30 November (which were sharply reduced by the Court of Appeal on 29 January 1990). The far right pressed for a tougher counter-insurgency strategy and the introduction of urban Civilian Defence Patrols. The violence at the end of the year included the killing of the 2nd Secretary of the Nicaraguan Embassy and the explosion of a bomb outside the residence of the Foreign Minister, who had been accused by the Secret Anti-Communist Army of favouring the *Sandinistas* and showing favour to the FMLN. Allegations by President Cerezo of a connection between Salvadorean extremists and Guatemalan death-squad activities were followed by the murders in Guatemala in January of the prominent moderate left-wing Salvadorean politician Hector Oqueli and a Guatemalan social democrat. Clearly there will be no end to the violence in Guatemala until the situation in El Salvador is brought under control.

Nicaragua: Another Failure for Communism

The overriding task for the *Sandinista* government in Nicaragua during 1989 was to deal with a economy which had run out of control. Inflation had reached some 33,000% in 1988, GDP per capita had fallen back to 1960 levels, and, by some assessments, the country had become the poorest in the Western hemisphere. The radical stabilization plan introduced at the beginning of 1989 required peace if it was to do more than merely increase austerity.

Faced with the deteriorating situation, the government announced in February 1989 that it had decided to bring forward to 25 February 1990 the general elections called for by the Arias regional peace plan. The FSLN took a decision to carry out the elections with sufficient internal and international credibility to secure domestic consensus and business confidence, the final demobilization of the *Contra* forces in the Nicaraguan Resistance (RN), and an end to the US economic embargo and a restoration of normal external relations.

Consensus was not easily reached even over the context for elections. Amendments that were made in April to the 1988 electoral law were criticized by the opposition as insufficient, while the government expelled eight US diplomats, including the Ambassador, allegedly for provoking destabilizing activities. Despite continued sparring over various provisions covering the election, a political agreement was reached by early August between the government and 21 recognized parties (who had joined in the National Opposition Union (UNO) created in June) which not only ensured opposition participation in the elections, but resulted in a joint declaration calling for demobilization of the *Contras*.

In early August the five Central American presidents involved in the regional peace process met in Tela, Honduras, and produced a joint plan for the voluntary demobilization and repatriation or relocation of the RN and their families. They agreed to create within 30 days an International Commission of Support and Verification (CIAV), made up of representatives of the Secretaries-General of the UN and the OAS, and urged the RN to begin demobilization within 90 days of the establishment of the CIAV. For its part, the FSLN would strengthen its 'national reconciliation' and democratization, which in turn would induce members of the RN to return.

The plan had, of course, been made possible by the national political agreement in Nicaragua, but President Ortega went further, accepting two other steps. He agreed to defer until 8 December 1989 Nicaragua's case against Honduras in the International Court of Justice (ICJ) in view of a Honduran agreement to request the UN Security Council to send an international peace force to help prevent use of Honduran territory by irregular forces. He also joined with the other presidents in calling on the rebel forces in El Salvador, the Farabundo Martí National Liberation Front (FMLN), to carry out a constructive dialogue with the government, which was in turn to provide full guarantees for the reincorporation of the members of the FMLN into peaceful life. Once an end to the armed struggle and reincorporation had been achieved, the same demobilization procedures as those that applied to the RN would come into effect.

By December the whole process was on the verge of collapse. The only element which had not either failed, or deteriorated almost to the point of failure, was the Nicaraguan electoral process. Between 1 and 22 October over 1.7 million Nicaraguans registered to vote, and the campaign officially opened on 4 December. There was considerable international co-operation, and massive international observation: teams from the UN, the OAS and the US were in place. Even a number of prominent leaders of the armed opposition had returned to Nicaragua to participate in the political struggle.

Unfortunately, other rebels also returned with different ideas in mind. Demobilization of the RN was as distant as ever. Some 2,000 *Contra* combatants entered Nicaragua after the Tela summit, leaving death, damage and civilian casualties in their wake. On 27 October, after 19 members of the army reserves were killed while going to register for the election, Ortega lifted the cease-fire which the *Sandinistas* had maintained since March 1988. Discussions were eventually held to try to settle the growing problems, but when the RN refused successive FSLN concessions, talks were broken off on 22 November.

At the same time, the disputes between Central American governments resurfaced. The government of El Salvador suspended relations with Nicaragua after a light aircraft, which had taken off from Nicaragua, crashed in the south-east of El Salvador on 25 November, revealing a cargo of 25 surface-to-air missiles and other munitions. The Nicaraguan government responded to the RN's refusal to demobilize by the 5 December deadline by concentrating forces on the border with Honduras and reactivating its case against Honduras in the ICJ. Nor were the new international bodies able to prevent any of this. The UN observer group (ONUCA) had been appointed by the Security Council on 7 November, but deployment of the 560 mixed military and civilian observers was slow, and the immediate effect was minimal. The CIAV could do little more than carry out inspections, and the US, which had allocated $67m to the RN humanitarian aid and only $3m to the CIAV, did little to encourage the RN to demobilize.

The peace process was salvaged at an extraordinary summit, held in San Isidro da Coronado, Costa Rica, on 10–12 December 1989, primarily due to Ortega's need for a period of quiet and his willingness to make a diplomatic sacrifice of the Salvadorean guerrillas, the FMLN. Prior to the summit Ortega had been strongly critical of the Salvadorean government's response to the November FMLN offensive (see below) and he brought an FMLN peace proposal with him to the summit. In the end, however, he signed a document which strongly condemned 'armed terrorist actions' by irregular forces in the region, firmly supported the Cristiani government and its efforts towards a peaceful and democratic solution, and called on the FMLN to cease hostilities immediately and to rejoin the Salvadorean dialogue.

In return Ortega received support from the summit for his proposal that the US funds that had been approved for the RN be given to the CIAV to help with the demobilization, and a call on the RN to cease immediately all actions directed against the electoral process and the civilian population of Nicaragua. Since he had little doubt that he would win the election, Ortega also gained implicit support from the other presidents through their explicit support for Cristiani which was for the 'invariable policy of backing governments which are the product of democratic, pluralist and participative processes'.

The inter-governmental disputes were patched up: El Salvador and Nicaragua were urged to continue relations, and the ICJ case against Honduras was deferred to 11 June 1990. The summit also proposed a wider role for outside actors with a request to the UN Secretary-General that he try to involve more directly states with a direct interest in the region, not only by accelerating ONUCA's activities to prevent supplies of arms from reaching the RN and the FMLN, but also by broadening its mandate to include verification of the cease-fires and demobilizations.

The Stunning Upset

The Nicaraguan election was considered by all international observers to have been sufficiently equitable and honest to make whichever party that won the legitimate government. Such irregularities as were noted, and the degree of violence and intimidation which were observed, were no higher than in many other Latin American elections; they had tended to decrease during the campaigning; and they were certainly not sufficient to invalidate the result. The outcome itself, however, belied the opinion polls and overturned the expectations of the FSLN, of almost all observers, and even of the US government which had clearly begun to prepare itself for a new era in which it would have had to deal with an elected, and thus legitimate, *Sandinista* government. Daniel Ortega lost resoundingly.

It was a clear statement by the majority that they had had as much as they wanted of the *Sandinistas* and their programmes. Although inflation had been brought down to an estimated 1,689% in 1989 and the annual rate of decrease in GDP had improved from some −8% to around −2.9%, the government's radical economic measures were only increasing the immediate hardship felt by the electors. Whatever the relative importance of US hostility, international economic adversity, or FSLN mismanagement in creating this situation, no substantial improvement seemed possible without a definite end to the rupture with the United States, unlikely if the FSLN won. Moreover, the rest of the world news was dramatically shaking all assumptions about the permanence of regimes which had depended on the Soviet Union, or which had gone too far in angering Washington. For the uncommitted electors who did not just vote with their stomachs, any lingering hopes that might have tilted the balance in the *Sandinista's* favour seemed to have been outweighed by a belief that an alternative could not be any worse, and might conceivably be better.

Unless some unexpected upset occurred − and the election had only confirmed that in Central America the unexpected is always possible − on 25 April 1990 Violeta Barrios de Chamorro, the UNO candidate who had been a member of the ruling junta in the first nine months of the revolution, would be President of Nicaragua. Her running mate, Virgilio Godoy, leader of the Independent Liberals and labour minister in the *Sandinista* government until 1984, would be Vice-President. The transition, and then the political management of the country would not be easy, and might well involve clashes and even violence.

The UNO coalition was a heterogeneous and fragile grouping of parties ranging from the old-style conservatives to the orthodox communist, beset by internal frictions and only barely held together in support of the candidates, particularly Godoy, who has not enjoyed the confidence of, and was even denounced as a Marxist by, the right-wing and conservative business sector. Friction can also be expected between the returning *Contras* and the politicians who stayed. Moreover, Nicaragua's history has prevented the development of any stable party system, and even of any real parties, in the Western sense. The FSLN has been much more than a party and the others much less, their organizational weakness exacerbated by a permanent process of fragmentation within each nominal political tendency.

The defeat of Ortega as president only touched the tip of the pyramid of *Sandinista* power. The FSLN, who won over 40% of the vote, will still have a powerful voice as the country's largest single party. It will be a difficult and sensitive process to 'nationalize' the state apparatus, security forces and army. Their nature and role have been at the heart of the political conflict and will inevitably have to be part of negotiations for the transition and the final demobilization of the *Contras*.

The first and most pressing demand is to rebuild the economy. In that process the US will inevitably have a special role to play. In the eyes of many it has a special obligation now to repair the damage as well as a special opportunity to help build democracy and development constructively. US policy has certainly contributed strongly, and perhaps crucially, to the end of *Sandinista* rule. However, whether or not the regional peace process sought the removal of the FSLN (the other Central American governments essentially did), it is that process which can take much of the credit for the positive form in which the Nicaraguan conflict has finally ended: through a fully participative national election rather than the internal chaos of military intervention; and a promise to leave the nationalist left as a legitimate residual force within a democratic structure.

El Salvador: A More Difficult Case for Treatment

The presidential elections on 19 March brought outright first-round victory for businessman Alfredo Cristiani, candidate of the right-wing Nationalist Republican Alliance (ARENA). In war-torn El Salvador there was deep concern about the change of government on 1 June, and a further reduction of the prospects for talks with the FMLN, who were still determined and had at least 6–7,000 full-time combatants and many more part-time fighters and supporters.

On the economic front, the new government lived up to expectations. It rapidly adopted liberalization measures, including sharp and unpopular price rises for transport and electricity, and moved to reverse the nationalizations of foreign trade and the banking system, and to limit and individualize the agrarian reform. Detention of trade union personnel, students and other suspected left-wing organizations increased. There was also a further rise in political violence, including death-squad killings against the left and assassinations of figures on the right.

President Cristiani, however, did not accept the extreme right-wing's candidate, hardline Air Force Chief Gen Rafael Bustillo as Minister of Defence, and quickly named a national commission for contacts with the FMLN. The new president's attitude tended to increase belief amongst the population in the existence, if not necessarily the power, of moderate right-wing groups genuinely interested in a modern political structure and in peace talks. Indeed, Cristiani was seen by many moderate left-wing leaders and even some in the FMLN as a man with whom one could do business. Even those of the left who did not distinguish Cristiani from the traditional elite at least considered that ARENA was a more valid interlocutor as a representative of the real powers in the land.

The atmosphere for talks between the FMLN and the government was not improved in July and August by the attacks or threats against the left, or by the series of assassinations (including the Minister of the Presidency and the Attorney-General) and murder attempts (including the Vice-President of the Republic and the Presidents of the Supreme Court and Legislative Assembly). Nevertheless, the potential for talks was still there and, although both the government and the armed forces insisted that the Tela agreements did not imply any form of negotiations, a first round was finally held in Mexico City on 13–15 September, which produced an agreement on procedure. Another round was held in Costa Rica on 16–18 October, in the presence of representatives of the Salvadorean Church, the UN and the OAS.

The FMLN presented a proposal for a cease-fire to be verified by UN observers that was unpalatable to the government. It included geographical demarcation and, although demands for power-sharing had long been forgotten, it linked a definitive end to hostilities to a series of reforms, partly to be ensured by amendments to the 1983 Constitution. The government proposal called for an immediate end to hostilities, defined to mean all hostile acts by the FMLN and all offensive operations by the armed forces, and the demobilization of the FMLN by 15 January 1990 and its reincorporation into civic life. This was to be carried out by a Special Operative Commission and supervised by the CIAV.

The FMLN talked of 'irreconcilable differences' and complained that the government was still only proposing dialogue and not negotiation. By the end of the month, the process had been halted. On 30 October the FMLN carried out a bomb attack on the army headquarters resulting in civilian casualties; the next day a bomb at the headquarters of the National Federation of Salvadorean Workers killed ten and wounded 35. On 11 November, the heaviest fighting for years broke out as the FMLN occupied many areas in and around San Salvador, and mounted attacks on other cities. As FMLN units fought in the streets in the poorer section of the capital, the armed forces responded with devastating heavy air support. The FMLN retaliated by moving into the wealthier residential areas, temporarily occupying the Sheraton Hotel where US military personnel were staying. Exact casualty figures of the fighting are unknown, but by 30 December the FMLN had admitted to 401 deaths, while the armed forces indicated that 476 of their troops had been killed. Over 2,000 civilians were killed.

Any limited political space that had been opened by the conduct of talks between the two sides was therefore dramatically closed. A state of siege was declared on 12 November and a draconian new 'anti-terrorism' law, passed on 24 November, legally proscribed practically all forms of protest. A wave of repression and detention followed, even directed against churches and religious bodies, as well as foreign human-rights, church and aid workers. Even the UN withdrew its personnel when they received threats. Practically all left-of-centre unions and other organizations closed or went underground. Moderate left-wing leaders took refuge in embassies or fled the country. The abuses came to a head with the brutal murders on 16 November by members of the military of the Rector, Ignacio Ellacuría, and five other Jesuit priests at the University of Central America, along with their cook and her daughter. Ellacuría, a prominent intellectual and liberation theologian, had long been hated by the extreme right. He was a key figure in any political solution, capable of talking both to Cristiani, whom he had publicly considered sincere, if ingenuous, and to the FMLN, whom he had urged to end all dreams of insurrection.

Is There a Way Forward?

The immediate question now is whether the regional peace process can do anything to bring about a positive outcome in El Salvador, as it did in Nicaragua. The bloodshed of November made it clearer that peace in El Salvador can only be achieved by negotiation, and all the more unlikely that the warring parties can ever live together.

The stated objectives of the November offensive were multiple, and not entirely consistent. The FMLN's main argument was that, since the government did not take them seriously enough to negotiate with and apparently believed that they were militarily spent, the offensive would demonstrate their capability and thus strengthen their bargaining position. Other aims were to provoke a split in the military and a violent backlash that would discredit the government and break the bipartisan consensus in the US Congress for military aid, and to bring about ungovernability and even insurrection.

The success of the FMLN, the blunt military response and the wave of violent repression certainly cast serious doubt on the supposed achievement of democratic authority and military superiority. To all appearances, the President was not in control of the military and the military was not in control of the country. The armed forces had been under serious pressure for weeks. There had been a massive failure of intelligence, but they were also shown to have neither decent contingency plans nor training for urban warfare. There was criticism of not only the tactics employed, but also of the brutality shown by the Air Force which rocketed the same houses that they were bombarding with leaflets, calling on the people to kill all members of the FMLN and their international supporters.

There were indeed strong protests in the US against further military aid, and various proposals were made in Congress to restrict aid. But the Salvadorean government did not fall, and the bipartisan American consensus was not broken, although it was severely strained. The murder of the Jesuits was investigated and on 19 January 1990 a colonel, two lieutenants and six lower ranks were formally charged with murder. Gen Bustillo, the Air Force Chief, and others were removed from command. President Cristiani, during a visit to Washington at the end of January, insisted that his government was still committed to dialogue, and received complete support from President Bush.

The FMLN has shown that it is not, and probably cannot be, militarily eliminated. On the other hand, that is all it has shown. New recruitment, forced or otherwise, may make up for some of the heavy losses sustained, but the offensive has resulted in an exposure and loss of urban infrastructure. Furthermore, although the FMLN clearly did receive support from among the inhabitants of the poorer districts they occupied, at least at first, the country was clearly shown not to be on the verge of a popular uprising. At the same time, the FMLN's own image has suffered. The quick calls for insurrection during the offensive, and the attacks on Cristiani – who in the past has seemed willing to talk –

strengthened doubts about the FMLN's sincerity in wanting talks. Its continued receipt of arms from abroad was confirmed and its identification with Cuba – and thus with all that is most anti-American and anti-*perestroika* in the region – was strengthened.

For both sides there seems little rational alternative to talks. Even then, nothing can ensure that talks will produce agreement, and whatever the possibilities may be for an eventual understanding between Cristiani and the moderate political left, the distance between ARENA and the FMLN and its backers remains huge. Moreover, rationality is not the only or even the main element shaping behaviour in El Salvador. The degree of ideological confrontation, visceral hatred and fanaticism has always been higher in El Salvador than in Nicaragua, and the actors in the Salvadorean tragedy have consistently demonstrated a much greater resistance to external influence and change.

Given all that, there are a few grounds to hope that a strengthened regional process might be able to help facilitate a political solution in El Salvador. The regional process arose as an alternative to superpower involvement and East–West conflict, and as a means to deal with a regional crisis caused by the escalatory interaction of multiple conflicts within a small, easily crossed and closely interdependent sub-region. On the one hand, neither superpower any longer wants to be positively involved and the East–West stakes have been significantly reduced. On the other, the Nicaraguan elections have not only removed one of the conflicts, but promise to end another of the exacerbating factors which have made progress so difficult: the issue of local government support or tolerance of insurgencies, with the probable disbandment of the *Contras* and the end to all use of Nicaragua by the FMLN and other guerrilla forces. The electoral defeat of the *Sandinistas* can be expected to demoralize as well as weaken the FMLN. It deprives them of any remaining hope for material or diplomatic support from Nicaragua. Together with US action in Panama, it might also rationally be expected to deprive them of any remaining belief in the possibility of revolutionary victory. However, it is not likely to make the FMLN give up, while it may further weaken the willingness of the Salvadorean elite and the armed forces to contemplate anything less than the guerrillas' surrender. The challenge then is to provide the pressures and guarantees required to tilt the balance in favour of compromise, by capitalizing on the positive achievements of the regional process and following the conclusions of the December summit in favour of a stronger role for international organizations and interested parties.

Factors in Security

A VINTAGE YEAR FOR ARMS CONTROL

It has long been argued that negotiated arms control is needed most when agreements are difficult to achieve, and least when the political conditions would allow for rapid success. The events of 1989 have given this argument new force, particularly in Europe, where negotiators find it difficult to match the pace of political developments.

During 1989, however, the negotiators met the challenge, and when George Bush and Mikhail Gorbachev met in December off Malta it appeared that 1990 would be the year of arms-control agreements. Each committed himself to use the planned May 1990 summit in Washington to sign the verification protocols on nuclear testing and an agreement to reduce US and Soviet chemical-weapons stockpiles. The summit also became the target date for concurring on the principles of a Strategic Arms Reduction Talks (START) treaty. The US further accepted a Soviet proposal to aim for a multilateral summit in the autumn of 1990 to sign a treaty on Conventional Armed Forces in Europe (CFE). This ambitious schedule was boosted when US Secretary of State James Baker travelled to Moscow in February 1990 and progress was made in each of the four arms-control negotiations. The Malta schedule was reaffirmed and it appeared at least feasible that four agreements could be reached by the end of the year.

Even so, there is still likely to be room for arms control in the 1990s. The destabilizing trends in weapons development deferred in START will require further agreements, while CFE will probably not be the last negotiated step towards winding down 40 years of military confrontation. In the years ahead, the focus will perhaps be less on reducing the military capabilities of erstwhile alliances and more on ensuring long-term strategic stability, notably in Europe. In addition, the role for confidence-building and transparency measures among all European countries will undoubtedly increase. The threats posed by chemical weapons remain as pressing as before, particularly outside Europe. Efforts to reduce the number of chemical-weapons states and ultimately to eliminate these weapons completely should be intensified. In short, in a world in turmoil where massive armaments still exist, arms control can continue to play a useful role in equalizing capabilities at lower levels, easing tensions and reducing uncertainty, and make it legally and politically difficult to revert to former force levels and postures.

START – Nearing Fruition
At the 1986 Reykjavik and 1987 Washington summit meetings between President Reagan and General Secretary Gorbachev, the basic outline of a START treaty emerged, namely that each side would be allowed to

deploy 6,000 warheads on 1,600 land- and sea-based missiles and heavy strategic bombers. Of the 6,000 warheads, no more than 4,900 could be deployed on ballistic missiles. Each deployed ballistic missile warhead would be counted as one warhead under the 4,900 ceiling, while the entire complement of bombs and short-range missiles on a single bomber would count as only one warhead under the 6,000 limit. A separate ceiling of 1,540 warheads on 154 'heavy' land-based missiles had also been agreed, as had a reduction of 50% in Soviet ballistic missile throw-weight. Finally, it was determined that long-range nuclear sea-launched cruise missiles (SLCM) would be limited outside of the 6,000 warhead and 1,600 delivery vehicle ceilings.

Aside from detailed questions involving precise definitions and the drafting of treaty language, negotiations on strategic forces have since early 1988 focused on the resolution of four outstanding issues (see *Strategic Survey 1988–1989*, pp. 43–7): whether mobile land-based missiles should be banned and, if not, how their deployment should be limited and verified; how to count air-launched cruise missiles (ALCM) within the 6,000 warhead ceiling, how to distinguish between conventional and nuclear ALCM, and what range capability should be employed to define those ALCM to be limited under the treaty; whether restrictions should be placed on SLCM and, if so, how such restrictions would be verified; and what relationship should there be, if any, between reductions in strategic offensive arms and limitations on strategic defences.

During 1989 compromises were reached on each of these four issues. In September 1989 Secretary of State Baker announced that so long as Congress would fund the proposed deployment of MX and *Midgetman* missiles in a mobile mode, the US would no longer insist on a ban on mobile missiles. At the same time, Soviet Foreign Minister Shevardnadze accepted the US proposals to settle the issues of strategic defences and SLCM outside the text of a START agreement. During their meeting in February 1990, Baker and Shevardnadze agreed on how many ALCM to attribute to each side's strategic bombers. Despite continuing disagreements about various technical questions, by early 1990 both sides expressed optimism that an agreement in principle would be ready for the June 1990 summit, and that a formal signing of a START treaty could take place later that year.

On balance, the emerging START treaty will make a positive, albeit limited, contribution to international security and strategic stability. It will place strict quantitative restraints on ballistic missile warheads and launchers, force significant reductions in highly accurate land-based missiles and overall missile throw-weight, and provide for unprecedented verification and transparency measures. On the other hand, the contemplated reductions, to be implemented over a seven-year period, will be much less than the 50% cut first envisaged by Reagan and Gorbachev at the 1985 Geneva summit. Post-START arsenals will possess approximately the same number of warheads as when the negotiations began in 1982. Perhaps more importantly, the decision to defer difficult issues detracts from the overall contribution that a START agreement promises to make, and suggests that the negotiations for a follow-on agreement will be difficult, complex and time-consuming.

The Contributions

START will mandate deep cuts in US and Soviet ballistic missile inventories. The 4,900 ceiling on ballistic missile warheads will result in cuts of 51% in current Soviet and 37% in US holdings. In strategic nuclear delivery vehicles the US will eliminate over 350 launchers (a 19% cut) and the USSR almost 1,000 launchers and bombers (a reduction of 38%). In addition START would eliminate half of the Soviet SS-18 inventory of 308 ten-warhead missiles, long regarded as the most threatening element of Soviet nuclear forces. The two sides, however, still disagree over whether modernization of heavy missiles will be allowed under START. The US insists that development, testing and deployment of modernized heavy missiles should be banned, while the USSR argues that such a ban should apply only to new missiles. Acceptance of the US position would result in future US–Soviet equality by ensuring the eventual obsolescence of all heavy missiles. The Soviet position, on the other hand, could open a plethora of future compliance concerns not unlike those that plagued the discussions following SALT II regarding the distinction between a new missile and a modernized one.

Another positive element of the START treaty is that the deployment of mobile intercontinental ballistic missiles (ICBM) would be allowed. In view of the increased accuracy of modern ballistic missiles, silo-based ICBM have long been regarded as vulnerable to a pre-emptive attack. Given that as few as two warheads could theoretically destroy a silo-based missile carrying up to ten warheads, such vulnerability has generally been regarded as destabilizing. Mobility is one solution as it would take many more warheads to destroy mobile launchers that dispersed on warning. The two parties also agreed in February 1990 to limit non-deployed mobile missiles and their attributable warheads, thereby partly addressing the fear that allowing mobile missile deployments could provide either side with a substantial break-out capability.

The fear of break-out has also been addressed by the provision to reduce ballistic missile throw-weight to a level 50% below that held by the USSR, which would limit either's ability to deploy additional ballistic missiles with less than the maximum number of warheads. Although both have agreed to the limitation, the US argues for reductions to be based on the Soviet throw-weight level of 31 December 1986, whereas the USSR argues that the level should be fixed at the time of the treaty signature, when it is likely to be greater. There is also as yet no agreement on how to define missile throw-weight. The USSR has proposed the SALT II definition (the combined weight of re-entry and post-boost vehicles plus penetration aids), while the US has suggested the maximum pay-load a missile can carry over a specific range.

Perhaps the most significant contribution lies in START's verification and transparency measures. For the first time the two sides will exchange detailed data on their respective strategic arms inventories. As was the case in the Intermediate-range Nuclear Forces agreement of 1987, the data exchanges are to be verified through on-site inspections and updated periodically. They have also agreed to exchange declarations of deployments of SLCM (even though these will not actually be limited under the terms of START) and to pledge not to deploy more until the next declaration.

Although many specific verification details remain to be worked out, the general provisions have been established. These include: on-site observation of the elimination of treaty-limited items; permanent portal and perimeter monitoring of critical production sites; short-notice inspections at declared sites; challenge inspections at some non-declared sites; a ban on concealment; and measures to enhance verification by national technical means (NTM), including open display of treaty-limited items at missile and bomber bases and submarine ports. There are also many specific provisions to verify limits on mobile missile deployments, including restrictions on deployment at predetermined sites, restrictions on exit and entry from such sites, limits on the number of systems that can be deployed at a given location, and specific measures to enhance verification through NTM, such as the open display of road-mobile launchers outside their shelters.

Verification measures have been of particular interest to the Bush Administration, which appeared to believe that rigorous verification was required to ensure START's ratification by the US Senate. In June 1989 the Bush Administration proposed a number of specific verification measures and trials that could be undertaken even before an agreement had been finalized. These measures included: an exchange of detailed data on strategic nuclear forces; trial monitoring of SS-24 missile production facilities; direct inspections of warheads on ballistic missiles; a ban on the encryption of telemetry of missile flight tests; a demonstration of tagging for mobile missiles; a ban on the testing of sea-launched ballistic missiles (SLBM) in a depressed trajectory or short-time-of-flight mode; and notification provisions for strategic exercises.

During the course of the year considerable progress was made. At the Wyoming ministerial in September 1989 an agreement on verification and stability measures was signed which committed both sides to conduct trial inspections and experiments as proposed by the US. They also signed an agreement on notification of strategic exercises involving heavy bombers. In December 1989 the US and USSR exchanged information on missile tagging technologies. Two specific trial verification agreements were signed in December 1989 and January 1990: one involved provisions for inspecting the *Bear* and B-1B bombers to ensure that bombers carrying ALCM could be distinguished from those that do not; the other concerned the method and timing of the inspection of the number of warheads on various ballistic missiles. Unlike SALT II, in

which missiles were assumed to carry the maximum number of warheads with which they were actually tested, START allows each side to
declare the number of warheads that are deployed on different types of
missiles. In trial inspections to verify the attributed number, the US will
inspect warheads on the SS-N-23 and SS-18 missiles and the Soviet
Union will inspect those on the MX and D-5 missiles. At the February
1990 ministerial in Moscow the two sides also agreed how to ensure the
non-denial of telemetry data during flight tests of START-accountable
ballistic missiles. These provisions will be included in the START treaty
to take effect on the date a treaty is signed.

Although reductions in strategic forces and missile throw-weight are
not necessarily either desirable or stabilizing, START would force cuts
in the most destabilizing systems, such as heavy land-based missiles,
while affecting other systems, like bombers, to a lesser degree. The
transparency measures provide for enhanced predictability of present
and future developments in strategic forces. Intrusive verification provisions, including on-site inspections, not only enhance the ability of
each side to monitor compliance, but also help build overall confidence.

The Shortcomings

Although the START agreement will place restraints on all elements of
the US and Soviet strategic nuclear forces, it does so in a manner that
leaves both sides with very large and redundant forces. In fact, depending on the exact nature of each side's bomber force, both parties could
theoretically deploy under START nearly as many warheads as they
currently possess. In addition, there are a number of areas where
additional measures or limits would have been advantageous. Some of
these areas, including restrictions on multiple-warhead ICBM, were
addressed only indirectly. In others, such as SLCM and strategic
defences, it was agreed to defer negotiations.

The widely-publicized 50% reductions will only affect the USSR's
heavy ICBM, ballistic missile warheads, missile throw-weight, and
possibly its ICBM warheads. The latter depends on Moscow's willingness to agree to the US demand that ICBM warheads be limited to a
sub-ceiling of 3,000–3,300. The USSR has stated that it will only accept
such a limit if the US accepts a similar ceiling on SLBM warheads,
which would limit the US to roughly 50% of current levels. Hence, with
the possible exception of this last provision (which Washington is
unlikely to accept), none of the US force will be subject to a 50% cut.

The principal reason is that not all the weapons which can be carried
by bombers are actually accountable under START limits. Thus, under
the agreement worked out by Shevardnadze and Baker in February
1990, ten ALCM would be attributed to each US, and eight to each Soviet, ALCM-carrying bomber (the US assured the Soviet Union that its
bombers would be equipped to carry no more than 20 ALCM each and
the USSR said its bombers would not carry more than 12). It had earlier
been agreed that the entire weapons load on non-ALCM-carrying pen-

etrating bombers would count as one weapon. In addition, the US has proposed, and the USSR has in part agreed, that a certain number of strategic nuclear weapons should not be included in START limits. The two sides have agreed to declare their planned SLCM deployments, but neither to limit nor count them against the START ceiling. Washington has also proposed the exclusion of 72 SLBM launchers on the argument that at least three *Trident* submarines would at all times be in overhaul, and thus not available for nuclear strikes.

The fact that actual reductions under START will be far less than advertised need not necessarily be considered a drawback. Significant reductions will still be made in many of the more destabilizing elements of the strategic nuclear forces. START will also provide a major incentive to emphasize the more stabilizing bomber forces over ballistic missile deployments. In a number of other respects, however, it does not directly address, or deliberately defers addressing, the more potentially destabilizing force developments.

While START for the first time places specific constraints on warheads, the negotiations thus far have not directly confronted the issue of multiple-warhead missiles (MIRV). In fact, by limiting strategic nuclear delivery vehicles to 1,600 in addition to constraining warheads to 6,000, START encourages their deployment. It is generally agreed that the deployment of land-based MIRVed missiles was a particularly destabilizing factor in the strategic arms competition. If deployed in fixed sites, such missiles are inviting targets for pre-emption, yet when mobile they raise questions about a break-out potential.

Concerns about MIRVed ICBM were raised during the Bush Administration's strategic review of early 1989, resulting in suggestions that an additional ceiling be placed on multi-warhead silo-based missiles, or that mobile MIRVed missiles be banned. Neither option was pursued at Geneva but the possibility of banning mobile MIRVed missiles continued to attract attention. There seemed to be agreement that verifying limits on rail-mobile missiles, such as the SS-24 and MX, would be more difficult than verifying those on road-mobile systems, like the SS-25 and *Midgetman*. Because they resemble other rail carriages, rail-mobile missiles are more easily hidden than road mobiles. Perhaps more important, however, the covert deployment of a missile carrying up to ten warheads would pose a much greater threat than a concealed single-warhead missile. For these and other reasons, the President's national security adviser, Brent Scowcroft, with the not inconsequential backing of Sam Nunn, the influential chairman of the Senate Armed Services Committee, continued to press for a ban on multi-warhead mobile missiles. Because no agreement could be reached within the Administration, however, proposals to ban MIRVed land-based missiles were deferred to follow-on negotiations.

Sea-launched cruise missiles also raised concerns about stability. Unlike MIRVed ICBM, SLCM were discussed extensively during the negotiations, but in the end a decision was also deferred. Still to be settled is the issue of which cruise missiles would be covered by declaration; the USSR argues for the inclusion of both conventional and nuclear long-range SLCM, while the US insists that only nuclear SLCM should be covered. Such a declaratory approach would not be submitted for ratification and thus would only be politically binding.

The principal obstacle to the inclusion of SLCM limitations in START was the US belief that adequate verification would not be possible. While verification concerns had led the US to propose a ban on mobile ICBM, in the case of SLCM Washington took the opposite approach of insisting on no limits at all. Before it agreed to the declaratory approach, Moscow had argued that strict limits on SLCM were necessary in order to prevent circumvention of START limits on strategic nuclear arms. It had proposed a variety of verification measures, including production monitoring, tagging and on-board inspections. The USSR also suggested alternative approaches, such as a total ban on nuclear cruise missiles of all ranges. None of these proposals was acceptable to Washington. Although US officials agreed that nuclear SLCM limits could be verified if inspections aboard naval vessels were allowed, the US refused to contemplate such intrusive inspections, notably for fear that it would violate its policy neither to confirm nor deny the presence of nuclear weapons aboard its naval vessels.

However, while the declaratory approach should reduce present uncertainty, it does nothing to curtail future SLCM deployments. Moreover, while the present political climate makes comparisons with earlier times less persuasive than usual, it should be remembered that in the past those elements of the strategic force structure not explicitly limited by agreement became subject to rapid development. The case of MIRVed missiles, which were deliberately excluded from SALT I limitations, is instructive. Just as the deployment of these missiles was ultimately regarded as a destabilizing development, the exclusion of long-range nuclear SLCM from START may come to be regretted, not least in view of the US's geographical vulnerability to threats from the sea.

A final issue was that of strategic defences, which Washington had insisted throughout should not be linked to START. Moscow had argued that reductions in strategic offensive arms could only be contemplated along with constraints on strategic defences. In September 1989, however, Shevardnadze announced that Moscow would be willing to sign a START agreement without first settling the issues surrounding strategic defences if both sides signed an explicit understanding that a violation of the Anti-Ballistic Missile (ABM) Treaty would allow the other side to withdraw from START. During the February 1990 ministerial Shevardnadze announced that such a statement would no longer be a precondition. Strategic defences are still effectively linked to START, however, for a violation of the ABM Treaty could be considered grounds for invoking the supreme national interests clause which would enable withdrawal from a START treaty. Moscow is considering a unilateral statement indicating an intention to view any ABM Treaty breach in this light.

However, ambiguity regarding the ABM Treaty may prove unacceptable to the US Senate, which is likely to insist on binding obligations not to withdraw from the Treaty other than when supreme national interests are at stake. It will probably also insist on continuing restrictions on the development and testing of ABM components contained in the traditional 1972 interpretation of the Treaty.

The START II Agenda

The fact that so many issues remain to be settled suggests that the agenda for follow-on START negotiations will be a full one. It is likely that additional reductions in strategic forces will be included in the next round of talks. In particular, a less liberal approach to bomber weapons would appear to be an important consideration once it becomes clear that present START limits hardly affect the nuclear capability of bomber forces. A ban on MIRVed mobile missiles, or on all MIRVed land-based ICBM, would certainly be a prime candidate for discussion. Similarly, although the declaratory approach to the SLCM issue might prove to be workable in the near term, further reductions in ballistic missile warheads and bomber weapons are bound to raise questions about the advisability of leaving an increasingly substantial part of the nuclear force posture legally unconstrained. The role of strategic defences will also have to be more precisely defined. Not only will definitions and constraints on development and testing activity have to be negotiated, but the extent of permissible strategic defence deployment must also be decided. That many of these issues are complex and difficult to resolve is underscored by their deferral in the present round. The challenge will be to solve them in less than the over eight years it took to reach agreement on START I.

Conventional Forces in Europe

Even though optimism was already high when the CFE negotiations opened in Vienna in March 1989, events in May and the months thereafter provided a further boost, resulting in widespread agreement that a treaty could actually be signed by the end of 1990. And in early 1990 that optimism was further confirmed when NATO tabled a comprehensive set of proposals designed to meet Soviet positions on most of the major outstanding issues.

A first indication that the CFE negotiations were on the right track came in a meeting between Baker and Gorbachev on 11 May in Moscow when Gorbachev proposed specific limits on personnel, tanks, armoured combat vehicles, artillery, combat aircraft and helicopters. The proposed ground force ceilings in many respects mirrored those NATO had tabled at the opening of the Vienna negotiations. When the Warsaw Treaty Organization (WTO) proposals were formally presented on 23 May 1989, the Soviet delegation also indicated the Pact's willingness to accept two key provisions of the earlier NATO proposal, which would place numerical sub-ceilings on the forces of an individual country (the 'sufficiency rule') and on those deployed outside national territory (the 'stationing rule'). In addition the WTO presented proposals for specific troop and equipment levels in various geographical zones of the Atlantic-to-the-Urals (ATTU) region.

This movement by the WTO was followed by significant changes in NATO's position, based on proposals by Bush at the NATO summit of 29–30 May. Partly in response to the rapid succession of Soviet arms-control initiatives and CFE proposals, and partly in an effort to overcome the intra-NATO squabbles over short-range nuclear force (SNF) modernization and negotiations which were threatening to make NATO's fortieth anniversary summit its last, Bush put forward a four-point plan that both transformed the summit and overcame a number of long-standing differences that had divided the two sides in Vienna. Bush's four points, endorsed by the NATO heads of government, were:

– Endorsement of the ceilings accepted by the WTO for each side's tanks and armoured troop carriers;
– Acceptance of limits on aircraft and helicopters, with specific reductions to be approximately 15% below NATO levels;
– Placement of a limit of 275,000 each on US and Soviet troops stationed in foreign countries within the ATTU region; and
– Acceleration of the negotiating timetable, with agreement to be reached in six months to a year, and reductions to be completed by 1993.

Points two and three responded directly and positively to the WTO's demand that limits on aircraft, helicopters and personnel be included in CFE, while the fourth point was critical to solving the disagreement over SNF within the Alliance. West Germany had been insisting that SNF negotiations begin immediately, but now that NATO had formally pledged that it would seek the conclusion of a CFE agreement in 1990 it could accept the US position that such negotiations begin only after a CFE agreement had been signed and implementation was under way.

Further progress in the succeeding months led Shevardnadze to propose in late September that the 23 WTO and NATO nations meet in the autumn of 1990 to sign a CFE agreement. At the Malta summit Bush endorsed Shevardnadze's suggestion of late 1990 as the target date for completion of a treaty. This would appear to be realistic in view of the broad-scale agreement that exists on most of the issues in the negotiations. Although some differences remain, the fact that the revolution which swept Eastern Europe at the end of 1989 threatened to undermine the political basis of the CFE negotiations made it likely that, with the possible exception of airpower, which might be deferred to follow-on negotiations, such differences could be resolved by the year's end. Before this happens, however, further agreement is necessary on issues concerning equipment ceilings, definitions of matériel to be limited, and on verification and stabilization measures.

Ceilings and Sub-ceilings

The accompanying table sets out the NATO and WTO CFE proposals, including limits for alliance-wide force deployments, for forces possessed by a single country and for those stationed outside the national territory of a party to the treaty. There is agreement on the number of tanks and helicopters that each alliance can deploy (20,000 and 1,900 respectively), as well as on the number of US and Soviet troops that can be stationed in Europe (225,000 and 195,000 respectively). NATO and WTO proposals for ceilings of other forces to be limited are not too far apart, and are in most cases the result of differing definitions of equipment.

NATO and WTO CFE Proposals

	Max. no. for each alliance		Max. no. for single nation		Max. no. for foreign-stationed forces[1]	
	NATO	WTO	NATO	WTO	NATO	WTO
Tanks	20,000	20,000	12,000	14,000	3,200	4,500
Artillery	16,500	24,000	10,000	17,000	1,700	4,000
Armoured combat vehicles	30,000[2]	28,000	16,800	18,000	6,000	7,500
Aircraft	5,200[3]	4,700[3]	2,820	3,400	no limit	1,200
Helicopters	1,900	1,900	1,140	1,500	no limit	600
Troops	no limit	no limit	no limit	no limit	195,000[4,5]	

[1] NATO limits on foreign-stationed forces apply to weapons in active units only.
[2] With a sublimit of 14,000 on armoured infantry fighting vehicles.
[3] Includes a sublimit of 500 on aircraft designated as air defence interceptors.
[4] USSR in Central Europe only.
[5] US can deploy an additional 30,000 troops outside the Central European zone.

There are three significant differences in the proposed ceilings that need to be resolved. First, despite agreement on the definition of artillery, the Warsaw Pact still proposes a 45% higher total as the ceiling for both alliances. Second, NATO has rejected limits on foreign-stationed aircraft and helicopters. It argues that their inherent mobility would render verification impossible while further sub-ceilings would be essentially meaningless in view of the fact that such equipment can be rapidly reintroduced into any sub-zone. Of course, the same would be true for limits on aircraft and helicopters in the ATTU region itself. A final disagreement concerns NATO's distinction between equipment deployed with active units and equipment maintained in storage. NATO's proposals for ceilings on both foreign-stationed forces and geographical deployments apply only to forces in active units, whereas similar WTO ceilings apply to equipment both in active units and stored. The difference in the proposed ceilings is thus partly accounted for by whether to count stored equipment in other than alliance-wide totals.

None of these disagreements, however, detracts from the fact that the level of conventional force reductions that the WTO in particular must undertake will be truly significant. Using NATO proposals and data, the WTO would have to reduce its tanks, artillery and armoured combat vehicles by about 60%, while helicopters and aircraft would drop nearly 50%. Soviet troops in Eastern Europe would be cut by more than two-thirds. NATO reductions, however, would be under 15% for tanks and aircraft, and under 5% for artillery and armoured combat vehicles. Close to a third of the US manpower now stationed in Europe would have to be withdrawn as a result of CFE.

Definitions

A major difficulty is the lack of agreement on treaty-limited items: by March 1990 the two sides had only settled on the definition of one category of systems, namely artillery. In October both sides announced that only artillery with a 100mm or larger calibre would be counted. This represented a concession by the WTO, which had previously proposed inclusion of weapons with calibres between 50–100mm plus anti-tank guns and recoilless rifles.

With regard to tanks, the Warsaw Pact has provided only a broad definition which does not clearly differentiate among systems that would be covered by the proposed ceiling of 20,000 tanks. NATO, on the other hand, has now defined a tank as a self-propelled armoured combat vehicle weighing at least 20 metric tons if wheeled, or 13 tons if tracked, armed with a gun of at least 75mm calibre. Although agreement has yet to be reached on the weight threshhold for a wheeled tank, this definition, tabled in February 1990, resolved a long-standing dispute between NATO and the WTO on whether light tanks should be included under the 20,000 tank ceiling. NATO had previously insisted on their exclusion, but now most of its light tanks fall under the new definition. The remainder will be counted as part of an enlarged limit on armoured combat vehicles, which includes categories for Armoured Infantry Fighting Vehicles and Heavy Armed Combat Vehicles (defined as a self-propelled system of at least seven metric tons with direct fire guns of 75mm calibre or more).

The two sides also differ over helicopters. The WTO definition refers to helicopters armed to engage ground and air targets and specially equipped to carry out air reconnaissance or electronic warfare. While NATO originally defined helicopters as permanently land-based, combat-capable rotary aircraft employing air-to-air or air-to-surface ordnance, in February 1990 it widened the definition to include both attack and support helicopters, but argued that limitations should only apply to the former. Attack helicopters are considered to be systems that have anti-armour or air-to-air weapons aboard guided by an integrated fire-control and aim system.

Aircraft pose the most complex and controversial definitional issue. Following NATO's May 1989 reversal on inclusion of aircraft in CFE, it proposed in July a limit of 5,700 on each side. NATO defined aircraft broadly to include anything capable of delivering ordnance. While the WTO welcomed the decision to include aircraft, it disagreed with the definition. Instead, the Pact favoured making a distinction between the offensive and defensive missions of aircraft, and limiting only those fulfilling the former role. Although this meant that even reconnaissance aircraft were to be excluded, by late September the WTO proposed to include such aircraft as well as bombers, fighter-bombers and attack aircraft under a proposed ceiling of 4,700 systems.

These proposals, however, did not cover all the aircraft that NATO felt should be limited. The Pact still excluded some 6,000, including trainer aircraft, air defence interceptors, naval aviation and medium-range bombers. It argued that trainers were not combat aircraft, that naval aviation should be part of naval arms control, and that the role of interceptors was to defend against carrier-based aircraft, cruise missiles and strategic bombers, none of which were limited under CFE. The Soviet Union did indicate that it would be willing to agree to a separate ceiling on interceptors provided that the West did not expand the threat against which such aircraft are meant to defend.

In an effort to bridge the gap between the two sides, NATO tabled a new aircraft proposal on 8 February 1990. It set an alliance limit of 4,700 combat aircraft which would include permanently land-based naval aviation and medium bombers. In addition, each side could deploy 500 air defence interceptors, with each side deciding which types of aircraft to include in this category. Aircraft in this category above 500 would count against the 4,700 total. Primary trainers would not be included, but no armament could be added to existing trainers and no future primary trainers could be armed. The USSR has indicated that, while they will include medium bombers, they still wish to exclude naval aviation and what they describe as secondary trainers. They also want the air defence interceptor limit raised, possibly to 1,500.

Verification and Stabilization Measures

NATO tabled its proposal for verification and stabilization measures in September 1989 and the WTO responded the next month. The proposals are close in many aspects. It is clear that a CFE treaty would include highly intrusive inspections, constraints on sizable military activities, and other military transparency measures. Both proposals were more specific with regard to stabilization measures than verification provisions. The latter were the subject of intense intra-NATO discussion: the US generally favoured more intrusion, while Western Europe, particularly France and the UK, resisted such demands. France, Italy and the UK, for example, opposed a US-proposed provision for monitoring defence industries in Europe alone and also objected to permanent inspections of ports and airports to monitor the import and export of military equipment. As a result, in January 1990 the US dropped its demands for such inspection provisions.

Despite a lack of detail, the NATO and WTO proposals did include specific verification measures. Both agreed to exchange data on the size and structure of military forces, although the Pact would catalogue such information only down to the regiment/brigade level while NATO would go to battalion level. Both proposals subject all declared sites to short-notice inspections without a right of refusal. NATO also proposed challenge inspections of suspect sites but with an ultimate right of refusal. Both sides proposed aerial inspections, a topic now being developed separately in the 'Open Skies' concept (see below). Each side's storage sites, elimination facilities and low-strength units would also be subject to monitoring by the other. Bridging equipment would be limited at a yet to be specified level. To substantiate its claim that the offensive and defensive nature of aircraft can be readily distinguished, the WTO proposed specific and highly intrusive verification measures for aircraft. NATO has similarly proposed on-site inspections to distinguish between attack and support helicopters. Both sides have also proposed measures to restrict the number and size of military activities, as they have in greater detail in the separate talks on confidence- and security-building measures (CSBM) (see below).

Is CFE Still Relevant?

Even before a CFE agreement has been completed, questions have arisen about its continuing relevance. The rapid dissolution of the WTO as a meaningful military alliance has arguably wholly upset the calculations of parity and balance upon which the negotiations have essentially been based. By late 1989 such questions were often expressed in terms of demands within both NATO and the WTO to negotiate even deeper reductions, particularly in overall troop levels. The USSR has already agreed to demands from Czechoslovakia and Hungary that Soviet troops be removed from their soil by mid-1991. It is likely that similar pressures will arise in East Germany. In a dramatic demonstration of new-found confidence, Hungary proposed in January 1990 that there be a limit on foreign-stationed troops which would be 'much below' the 275,000 level first proposed by NATO in May. Bush responded on 31 January when he announced in his State of the Union address that NATO would propose a lower limit of 195,000 US and Soviet troops stationed in Central Europe.

Moscow also informally began to propose reduced limits on troops. In January 1990 the chief Soviet CFE negotiator, Oleg Grinevskiy, indicated in an interview with the *Washington Post* that the USSR would be willing to withdraw all its troops from Eastern Europe by 1995 as part of a second stage of the CFE negotiations, provided NATO agreed to remove all US and Allied foreign troops from Western Europe. This proposal raised the spectre of the total Soviet withdrawal in Eastern

Europe becoming linked to a US withdrawal from Western Europe. It was to counter this possibility that the Bush Administration in January 1990 proposed only a limit on troops deployed in the central region, leaving US deployments outside that region unaffected.

The initial Soviet reaction was positive regarding the proposed level, but negative towards asymmetrical reductions. Moscow thus suggested a limit on US and Soviet troops in all of Europe of either 195,000 or 225,000 troops. Within days, however, the USSR had altered its attitude towards the question of asymmetry. It agreed to a cap of 195,000 on US and Soviet troops in Central Europe, while the US would be allowed to deploy an additional 30,000 troops outside the central region. At the same time, the Kremlin also indicated its willingness to remove all Soviet troops from Hungary, Czechoslovakia and Poland even in the absence of a CFE agreement. Soviet troops in East Germany were, however, still regarded as 'a special issue', to be addressed within the framework of Soviet rights and obligations in Germany arising from the outcome of World War II.

The issue of further troop reductions clearly demonstrates that the volatile political climate in Europe threatens to leave the CFE process in the political dust. Some commentators have therefore raised questions about the continuing utility of a process whose political basis is increasingly being undermined. The CFE negotiations, some argue, may be not only increasingly irrelevant to the emerging political order in Europe but might actually become a definite obstacle to the further evolution of political change, notably by legitimizing levels of Soviet troop presence in Eastern Europe.

A different view argues that the inherent uncertainty and instability of the current situation demand both a continuation of the CFE process and its rapid conclusion. An agreement along the lines that is emerging would lock in important Soviet force reductions, thereby guaranteeing, even if the political climate should change, a drastically-reduced Soviet military presence in Eastern Europe. Without an explicit agreement, there could be no certainty of achieving either intrusive verification provisions or the actual destruction of withdrawn equipment. It is likely that this more cautious approach will in the end prevail over the euphoria of the moment.

Whatever approach is adopted, serious questions are likely to be raised about what will follow CFE I. Are further reductions to be negotiated on the basis of two distinct alliances, at least one of which may have lost a member (the GDR) and probably will not be able to generate common positions? Should the goal be, as US officials have begun to argue, to complete the process of eliminating a Soviet military presence beyond its own borders? What effect would that have on the US presence in Europe? How would further force cuts, limited to members of the two alliances affect regional imbalances, notably in south-eastern Europe? Finally, how can German reunification, with its attendant new security problems, be addressed by a structure that in the final analysis has been based on the assumption of a continued German division? It is increasingly apparent that questions such as these will come to dominate, if not actually overtake, the conventional arms control agenda in the months ahead.

Other Arms-Control Negotiations

During the year there were a number of other negotiations covering CSBM, the 'Open Skies' proposal, chemical weapons and nuclear testing. In many of these both Soviet and US willingness to compromise led to agreements that have long evaded both parties. In early 1990 there was considerable optimism that continued steady progress could be made and that the coming year would see yet more agreements.

Confidence- and Security-Building Measures

In addition to the CFE negotiations, a second set of negotiations was taking place in Vienna, involving all 35 nations in the Conference on Security and Co-operation in Europe (CSCE). They were considering the question of CSBM, attempting to improve the set of measures agreed in Stockholm in late 1986. Detailed proposals have been tabled by NATO, the WTO and by neutral and non-aligned delegations. Both NATO and the WTO also proposed CSBM at the CFE negotiations; in both cases the main aims were to create more transparency about military organization and activity, greater predictability about military exercises, and to improve contact and communications between participating states. To these ends the proposals dealt with the exchange of information, early notification of military activity, limitation both in size and frequency of military activity, invitation of observers to military activity, arrangements for the inspection of suspected activity, and the development of communications and risk-reduction centres.

In general, the NATO proposal for the limitation of military activity confined itself to those activities already limited by the Stockholm Document: i.e., ground force activities (but including air force participation), and amphibious landing and parachute assault activities. The neutral and non-aligned nations' proposal also was an expansion on the measures already agreed in the Stockholm Document. The WTO, however, expanded the areas under discussion by calling for limitations on purely air force activity and on naval activities.

One of the more restricting CSBM is that governing the size and prior notification of large-scale notifiable military activities (those involving more than 13,000 troops). The Stockholm Document stipulates that activities involving more than 40,000 troops will not be carried out unless notified in the annual calendar which must be submitted by 15 November the previous year. Those involving over 75,000 troops must be notified in the calendar submitted two years ahead.

The proposals made at the CSBM talks would take these restrictions further. The WTO proposed that notifiable activities be restricted to no more than 40,000 troops, that no more than three separate activities can take place at once on the territory of one state and must be limited to 40,000 troops overall, and that only two military activities involving more than 25,000 troops can be held in any one year on the territory of each participating state. The WTO has tabled a virtually identical set of proposals at CFE except that only one military exercise involving more than 40,000 troops could be held every three years by each particpant and that participants of the same alliance could not hold more than a total of six exercises a year involving more than 25,000 troops.

In its proposal at the CSBM talks NATO made it clear that it too wished to lower the maximum number of troops to be allowed in exercises, but it dropped them less than the WTO proposed: to 50,000, rather than 40,000, notifiable two years in advance. At CFE, however, NATO did lower the limit of each participant's military activities to 40,000 troops, with the exception of one occasion every two years when a larger number of troops could be involved if it had been notified 12 months ahead. The neutral and non-aligned nations' proposal would reduce the size of activities notifiable in the annual calendar to 30,000 and that notifiable two years in advance to 60,000.

Considerable progress has been made during the negotiations. The present aim is to have a package of CSBM agreed and ready for signature at the planned November 1990 summit, the same time as for the CFE treaty. It is a goal that the participating countries expect to meet.

'Open Skies'

In May 1989 President Bush proposed a new 'Open Skies' initiative, based on a proposal originally made by President Eisenhower in the 1950s, which would allow unarmed aircraft from NATO and WTO nations to overfly each other's territory. The scheme would open the US, Canada and the USSR east of the Urals to a form of verification and transparency beyond that planned for CFE.

A conference was held in Ottawa from 12 February 1990, at which a wide range of issues was addressed by the attending foreign ministers (including arranging discussion on German unification). The discussion of Bush's proposal was rather unrewarding. While there appeared to be general support for the broad concept, agreement on details proved elusive and the conference ended with the two sides far apart on some issues, most notably on the method of operation. The WTO argued for a common surveillance system with all data acquired passed on to all 23 nations, while the US maintained that each nation should collect its own data. There were also differences concerning the type of sensors to be fitted to the aircraft, the number of flights to be allowed (the USSR preferred only 30 for each side, while the US proposed around 120). Equally controversial was the Soviet desire to exclude from overflight such areas as chemical plants, rocket test ranges and nuclear power stations, and to forbid low flying over major built-up areas. A follow-on conference will be held in Budapest in late April 1990.

Controlling Chemical Weapons

Much of the year's activity in the chemical-weapons (CW) area centred around the bilateral US–Soviet discussions rather than the multilateral negotiations in the 40-nation Conference on Disarmament in Geneva which aim to achieve a comprehensive ban on chemical weapons. Within the bilateral discussions the major emphasis was on verification experiments and bilateral reductions in US and Soviet CW stockpiles. While much controversy arose over a reported US decision to maintain the option of continued production even after the conclusion of a multilateral treaty banning CW, by the end of 1989 it was clear that some progress at least in respect of agreements to reduce US and Soviet stocks was being made.

As part of its more general policy of testing arms-control verification provisions, the US proposed in July 1989 that Washington and Moscow agree to a prior exchange of CW data and limited forms of on-site inspections. A memorandum of understanding (MOU) to this effect was signed at the Wyoming ministerial in September. It detailed a data exchange in two phases and various forms of inspections. In the first phase the two sides would exchange general data on their CW capabilities and carry out a series of visits to relevant facilities. The data to be exchanged include the total CW capability in agent tons; types of chemicals used in the CW arsenals; the percentage of declared chemicals stored in munitions and devices and the percentage stored in bulk form; and the location of CW storage, production and destruction facilities. Each side could visit some of the other's CW facilities as well as make two visits to industrial chemical production plants. This first data exchange was completed in December 1989.

More detailed data exchanges are to be undertaken in the second phase, including data on the precise inventory of chemical weapons stored at declared facilities and the production capacity of all CW facilities. This data is to be verified by up to five inspections at declared facilities and up to ten challenge inspections of non-declared sites. At the insistence of the Soviet Union, the agreement states that the data exchanges and inspections take place not less than four months before a CW convention is to be concluded.

The overall significance of the chemical-weapons MOU is open to question. While the Bush Administration's aim in proposing these various measures was both to reconcile Soviet declarations regarding their CW stocks with US intelligence estimates and to test verification provisions that are to be included in the multilateral convention, neither may be possible. Since the data exchange in the first phase will not actually be verified through on-site inspection, the Soviet declaration that it possesses no more than 50,000 agent tons cannot be tested against US estimates, some of which are considerably higher. In any case, much of the data to be exchanged in the first phase has already been released publicly, raising questions about the significance of a private exchange. With regard to phase two, the Soviet insistence that actual on-site and challenge inspections take place only four months prior to the signing of a CW convention reduces their experimental utility since it will be difficult to incorporate the lessons learned into the final treaty text.

Discussions about the significance of the MOU were soon overtaken by new US proposals in a 25 September speech by Bush to the UN, in which he reiterated his pledge that the US seeks a comprehensive CW ban. He authoritatively challenged the notion that such a ban could not be adequately verified by saying that 'the knowledge we have gained from our recent arms-control experience and our accelerating research in this area make me believe that we can achieve the level of verification that gives us confidence to go forward with the ban'.

The central points of Bush's speech, however, focused on the timing and extent of possible reductions. As a first step, he proposed that the US and USSR reduce their respective CW stocks to about 20% of the current US level (believed to be between 25,000 and 30,000 agent tons) even before a multilateral treaty is signed. While a significant reduction, this proposal appeared to make a virtue out of necessity since Congress already required the US to undertake a reduction of at least 90% of its current stocks by 1997. On the other hand, if accepted by the USSR this provision would effectively force Soviet reductions of an even greater magnitude, given that its current CW stocks exceed those of the US. The second point of the Bush proposal, provided the USSR was a party to the convention, was a pledge to accelerate the reduction of CW under a multilateral treaty by eliminating all but 2%, or 500 tons, of current US stocks by the eighth year of the ten-year period. Bush, however, declared that the remaining 500 tons would only be eliminated in the following two years if 'all nations capable of building chemical weapons sign the treaty'.

This last provision proved to be the most controversial. Not only was its meaning somewhat unclear – for any state with a civil chemical industry would, in principle, be 'capable of building chemical weapons' – but its impact on the successful conclusion of a total CW ban was uncertain. Administration officials claimed that it would provide the US with much-needed leverage to persuade recalcitrant states to join the treaty regime. In addition, it would be difficult to achieve Senate ratification of a convention that required the total elimination of US stockpiles while states such as Libya and Iraq retained a CW capability. Others, however, feared that in practice the chemical disarmament process would come to an effective halt by year eight, leaving many nations with a significant, albeit reduced CW capability. In addition, the provision gives a single country which is unwilling to join the CW regime an effective veto over the disarmament process. It could also encourage those countries at present not prossessing CW to acquire them before a treaty is signed in order to ensure that they too would maintain a limited CW capability after a treaty enters into force.

In response to widespread criticism of the idea that production might continue during a transition period, Bush suggested at the Malta summit that if the USSR accepted his UN proposals the US would no longer insist on keeping open the option of continuing CW production under a treaty. The Soviet position, first enunciated by Shevardnadze in his September UN speech following Bush's appearance there, was that while the US proposals were certainly a step forward, their significance would be increased if they were accompanied by, among other things, a concomitant halt in American CW production. Since the USSR had announced in April 1987 that it had stopped producing CW, it argued that the US ought now to follow suit.

During the February 1990 ministerial, the USSR accepted Bush's UN proposal concerning the destruction of a large percentage of US and Soviet CW stocks. It was hoped that an agreement to that effect, which would also establish a co-operative programme on destruction technology, could be signed at the May 1990 summit. Among the outstanding issues to be decided before signature is a Soviet demand that reductions be accompanied by a cessation of production and a renunciation of CW use under any circumstances.

Although some form of bilateral reduction agreement may well be concluded in May 1990, its immediate significance is still unclear. The US will not be in a position to start full-scale CW destruction until mid-1991, even assuming that the current testing programme of the facilities at Johnston Island demonstrates that destruction can be done in a safe and environmentally-sound manner. Even if all goes well on Johnston Island, it will take years to complete the actual destruction of the contemplated 80% of the US stockpile. The USSR faces even greater problems, for its only destruction facility in Chapayevsk was forced to close due to local environmental concerns. It will therefore be several years before destruction of Soviet CW can begin.

Nuclear Testing

Of all the arms-control negotiations currently taking place, the US–Soviet discussions on nuclear testing are likely to bear fruit the earliest. Verification protocols to the 1974 Threshold Test Ban Treaty (TTBT), which banned tests exceeding 150-kiloton (kt) yields, and the 1976 Peaceful Nuclear Explosions Treaty (PNET), are to be signed at the May summit, thereby enabling their ratification by the US Senate. With the successful conclusion of these negotiations, however, pressure is likely to emerge in favour of more comprehensive limitations on nuclear testing, limitations which Moscow has championed but which Washington continues to oppose.

While negotiations on the PNET protocol were essentially completed by December 1988, discussions on the TTBT protocol were postponed pending completion of the Bush Administration's strategic review. After a six months' hiatus, formal negotiations reopened in June with the US reaffirming its previous positions: that both sides be allowed to conduct hydrodynamic measurements (using the US-preferred CORRTEX method) whenever planned nuclear tests were to exceed

50kt in yield, and in any event to conduct at least two hydrodynamic measurements a year.

The Soviet position at the negotiations was that the joint verification experiments conducted in 1988 had demonstrated that seismic measurements were more accurate than the hydrodynamic method preferred by the US (See *Strategic Survey 1988–1989*, pp. 56–7). In March 1989 Moscow therefore proposed that the data compiled from the 1988 experiments be released publicly. Despite a US refusal, the USSR continued to insist that seismic monitoring rather than hydrodynamic measurements should be used to verify compliance with the testing limits of both treaties. The CORRTEX method could be used a number of times a year, it argued, to calibrate the seismic measurements.

When the testing negotiations opened in June 1989 it therefore appeared that both sides were no closer to an agreement on verification than they had been two years before. At the end of the first session, however, Moscow proposed a compromise that moved towards the US position. It indicated that it would allow the use of CORRTEX for tests that were planned to be in excess of 75kt if the US would allow seismic monitoring at three US stations of Soviet choosing. In addition it proposed that both sides be allowed to make geological on-site inspections after the tests. While the Soviet suggestion was positively received by the US negotiating team, some in the Administration were adamantly opposed. The Departments of Defense and Energy believed that the use of seismic monitoring would constitute a slippery slope towards a comprehensive or low-yield test ban agreement.

The White House apparently overruled these objections, for by the time Baker and Shevardnadze met at Jackson Hole a compromise agreement had been worked out, with both sides making important concessions. The US agreed to allow geological on-site inspections for any test in excess of 35kt and agreed that either seismic monitoring or hydrodynamic measurements could be used for tests over 50kt. The USSR both agreed to the 50kt level for hydrodynamic measurements and to allow at least two additional on-site hydrodynamic measurements per year for the first five years and one measurement a year thereafter. These agreements and later ones in February 1990 on how to verify non-standard test configurations, meant that Bush and Gorbachev will be able to sign the verification protocols at the May 1990 summit.

REFUGEES: STRAINING COMPASSION, THREATENING SECURITY

When the historic moment finally arrived, no more appropriate image could have captured the fate of East European communism than that of great crowds of ordinary East Germans, on foot and in traffic jams of Trabants, pushing aside the rusting prison gates around their society. By some ironic twist, it seemed as if the refugee, so long the victim of history, was at last helping to make it; his very existence a final proof that communist regimes had never achieved the transition from a police to a political state. But if refugees brought about a turning point here, one could point to a vast army of refugees throughout the rest of the world for whom 1989 was just one more year of civic limbo.

Who Are They?

Statistics which describe the problem are at best questionable: to begin with, much depends on how one defines 'refugee'. It is certain, too, that many of the world's refugees go untabulated – particularly if one considers the 'internal refugees' who have not crossed their national borders. If the figures are ambiguous in detail, however, there is no doubt about the scale of human misery they represent. Since the early 1950s, once the 'displaced persons' of the Second World War had been relocated, the worldwide total of refugees remained relatively manageable until the late 1970s when it soared to between ten and 12 million and stayed there. Today it stands at some 15 million individuals, a stateless mass of humanity more populous than many countries. Some idea of the growth of the problem is reflected in the budget of the UN High Commissioner for Refugees (UNHCR), which has ballooned from only $7m in 1971, to $280m in 1979, and on to over $478m in 1988, which is, nevertheless still felt to be woefully inadequate. This figure does not include the funds spent by countries providing asylum. In Fiscal Year (FY)1988, for example, the United States alone spent $770m on refugee resettlement programmes, and different estimates put the total figure worldwide in any given year anywhere from $2 to $5bn.

It is understandable, then, that 1989 has been called the 'Year of the Refugee'. Refugees have, however, played a part in the history of mankind since the very beginning: Adam and Eve, the first expellees condemned to find their way in an alien world, serve to remind us that we are all spiritual refugees, awaiting eternal repatriation. The word 'refugee' first appears in English in connection with the estimated 400,000 French Protestants who fled in 1685 after the revocation of the Edict of Nantes, although they were not, of course, the first who could claim that unhappy title. Since then, the storms of war and revolution have regularly washed up the losers and the unlucky on the shores of foreign exile, from Irish Stuart supporters to German liberals and Russian revolutionaries – the complete list would be the historian's index of religious and political turmoil.

In the US, memories of rejection and hardship associated with the refugee Pilgrims are fondly preserved as motifs of national self-consciousness. And well they might be, for the United States went on to become the first of a completely new phenomenon in modern history – a great power built from scratch, not by its indigenous population, but by a continuous stream of immigrants and refugees – indeed, its immigration law did not distinguish between the two until 1980. European countries also extended a comparably generous welcome to each other's outcasts. With that mixture of solemn generosity and self-importance that characterized the imperialist style, some European states even bestowed the title of citizenship on distant populations like a badge of membership, and politicians of the time enjoined a freedom of movement within the empire which their successors have since found impossible to sustain.

With the turn of the last century, however, movements of population became possible on a scale unknown before, and refugees increasingly came to be seen as a threat to a country's social identity. Such movements, *en masse*, ceased to be solely a reflection of religious and political turmoil, and persecution, but increasingly came to include those driven by the search for greater opportunity and a better way of life. The economic migrant was born. Frontiers were closing – or were thought to be – and labour supply often seemed to have caught up with demand. Immigrants no longer arrived in trickles, but in torrents. Between 1880 and 1910, for example, some 17.6 million arrived in the US alone: restrictive legislation, notably the 1915 Immigration Act, was the predictable response. Following the First World War, 1.5 million Russian refugees were driven from their homeland by the Revolution and a comparable number from neighbouring areas. The problem of refugees was placed high on the world's agenda, and has remained there ever since.

Refugees became one of the first concerns of the League of Nations. Fritdtjof Nansen, appointed High Commissioner on behalf of the League, gave his name to a travel document which asylum countries could grant to the stateless. Despite these humane initiatives between the wars, however, the international community signally failed to head off the catastrophic refugee crises precipitated by Nazi Germany, leaving unanswered the painful question of whether a more organized, co-operative approach might not have saved many more lives.

In the aftermath of the Second World War the sad legions of 'displaced persons' greatly multiplied, and wandered through a broken land incapable of supporting them. Some ten million Germans expelled from Eastern Europe found refuge in Western Germany. But now there was a new factor: the Iron Curtain, at a stroke, had incarcerated the entire population of Eastern Europe, converting its inhabitants overnight into potential, and, as events were to prove in many cases, prospective refugees (before the construction of the Berlin Wall in 1961, 2.1 million fled from the German Democratic Republic to West Germany). The UN took over responsibility for refugees from the defunct League, creating an International Refugee Organization and the post of High Commissioner for Refugees. In 1951, an international convention was adopted, defining a refugee as one who 'as a result of events occurring before 1951 and owing to a well-founded fear of being persecuted for reasons of race, religion, nationality, membership of a particular social group or political opinion, is outside the country of his nationality and is unable or. . . unwilling to avail himself of the protection of that country...'. The convention did confirm the principle of *non-refoulement* – that a refugee should not be returned to face persecution – but did not grant the right of asylum as such. It was also limited with regard to time and location: it did not apply to events after 1951 which might give rise to refugees, and allowed signatories to restrict its application to Europe. (Both such limitations were removed by subsequent protocol.)

As with most attempts to draft general principles for a world made up of exceptions, the language of the convention was, in time, overwhelmed by a flood of special cases and emergency situations. 'Persecution', for example, would suggest harassment of a group or individual. Yet the refugees of post-war years have normally been those who rejected their political system, rather than were rejected by it; individuals risking their lives to escape from their homelands, rather than risking their freedom by remaining there. Legal distinctions, moreover, provide little moral difference between a refugee escaping political persecution and a family fleeing communal violence or warfare. Humanitarian realism, consequently, has repeatedly led the UN to stretch a point by authorizing *ad hoc* action to meet pressing cases of distress which might not fit precisely the legal framework of refugee support.

As a Threat to Security

The distressing plight of refugees, removed from their ancestral homes, deprived of their livelihoods and condemned to live on the charity of strangers, understandably gives them a claim on the conscience of the world. What is often less appreciated is that, by their very numbers, today's refugees are something of a political force in their own right, personifying irredentism and, in some areas, complicating the prospects of regional stability. Although undeniably the victims of great deprivation, they can place a heavy burden on host societies which are themselves often among the poorest in the world. When repatriation proves impossible, their pressure for resettlement presents many states with difficult choices between their moral obligation to those in need of asylum, and protection of what their domestic opinion regards as its own best interests. The prospect of a potential flood of refugees has become a major consideration in the security affairs of all states.

Palestinians exiled by the creation of the state of Israel, for example, form the second largest and one of the oldest refugee populations in the world. Some 950,000 of them in 1950 have now swelled to 2.34 million refugees, mostly housed in refugee camps in Jordan (some 890,000 alone), Lebanon, Syria, the West Bank and the Gaza Strip. The very origins of their situation – whether they were driven from their homes by Israel or chose to leave rather than accept the state of Israel – is part of the dispute in which they are caught up. In the long years since 1948, however, they have never relinquished their demand for return. Many today, in fact, reject the idea of a separate Palestinian state proclaimed by Yasser Arafat in 1988, fearing it will consign their homes and villages to Israel and leave them with nowhere to return. There is some question, moreover, whether such a separate state could provide an economic base to support the sudden return of all the refugee population. Others recognize that the passage of time must dim any realistic hope of turning the clock back to 1947; the reabsorption of this large, hostile population within its territories is not the kind of concession one may expect Israel to make. Meanwhile, a dispossessed population, united in its sense of grievance, provides both a source of manpower for military (and paramilitary) operations and a school of bitterness for future generations.

Table 1: Principal sources of Refugees (over 100,000)

Afghanistan	5,934,500	Cambodia	334,166
Palestinians	2,340,500	Iran	270,100*
Mozambique	1,354,000*	Rwanda	233,000*
Ethiopia	1,035,000*	Burundi	186,500*
Iraq	508,000*	Western Sahara	165,000*
Angola	438,000*	Vietnam	124,779
Sudan	435,000	China (Tibet)	112,000
Somalia	388,600*	Sri Lanka	103,000

* Reported totals vary significantly.
SOURCE: US Committee for Refugees, *World Refugee Survey – 1989 In Review.*

While conscious of this refugee problem both poised on its borders and impatiently waiting in Arab lands further away, Israel faces a refugee problem of its own, with as many as 750,000 Soviet Jews expected to arrive in the country in the next three years. Committed to receive all Jews who wish to come, Israel may find it difficult to integrate so many newcomers whose background differs substantially from that of previous arrivals. The two refugee problems – Jewish and Palestinian – are, moreover, interwoven, for Prime Minister Shamir (much to Western and Arab objection) has claimed that the expected influx from the USSR is an argument for holding on to the West Bank and the Gaza Strip.

To the East, the world's largest refugee population – 5.93 million Afghans who fled their country after the Soviet invasion in 1979 – represent a different type of destabilizing presence. In addition to 2.35 million based in Iran, there are some 3.58 million in Pakistan's North-West Frontier Province, near the border with Afghanistan. Most of them are peasants, some settled down on land that the local population would like, some now cultivating poppies and selling drugs, others existing in large camps out of Pakistan's direct control, but a massive drain on scarce Pakistani state aid, as well as receiving large amounts of UN and foreign aid. (Pakistan estimates it carries about half of the annual relief effort of $340m, while $1.7bn is projected as the total bill for implementing the UN's plan for eventual repatriation and resettlement.)

A significant minority are fighting men, with access to weapons and support from the West. These refugees are, in fact, a population in exile, and one which has carried on a resistance struggle against the Kabul government for ten years. Armed and experienced in guerrilla warfare but divided sharply among competing factions, dependent upon Pakistan's goodwill but clearly able to wield influence of their own in Islamabad, it is a resistance force that will play a significant – if, at this moment, unpredictable – future role. For Pakistan, they represent not only a continuing drain on resources, and a source of friction with Kabul, but a potential for well-armed in-fighting among themselves which, in turn, could threaten Pakistan's own internal stability. Meanwhile, after so many years in exile, the refugees must wonder what daunting reconstruction work awaits them when they return to their destroyed villages and neglected fields, and what bitterness may surface when they rejoin the population which chose to stay behind.

Table 2: Refugees by area

Africa	4,524,800
East Asia and Pacific	574,100
Europe and North America	1,670,600*
Latin America and Caribbean	152,800
Middle East and South Asia	9,141,600
Total	15,093,900

* Includes an estimated 720,000 Germans and 250,000 Turks who emigrated during 1989.
SOURCE: US Committee for Refugees, *World Refugee Survey – 1989 In Review.*

The vast majority of the world's refugees – around 95% – are from the Third World and are harboured by countries which adjoin the states they fled. But the refugee problem is no longer seen as yet another affliction peculiar to the Third World: its effects are felt increasingly in the advanced countries as well, and hence it has become everyone's problem. An exponential growth of mass air transport (not to mention the booming trade in false documentation) enables some Third World refugees to leapfrog neighbouring countries and present their claims directly in Paris, Rome or Vienna, where they are much harder to dispose of.

The wealthy nations represent the promised land for refugees – as they have throughout history. Requests for asylum in the United States, Canada and Western Europe have quintupled from 1983 to 1989 and the backlog has risen almost six-fold. On arrival in Europe, legal processes normally ensure the immigrants months or even years of residence, and governments, usually reluctant to grant formal asylum which carries legal status, will often allow them to remain without it. Refugee resettlement has become interwoven with immigration policy, a subject which has always been politically sensitive as 'foreign' communities are perceived as a threat to the cultural identity, linguistic homogeneity, or employment opportunities of the host country. The modern industrialized state, moreover, is no longer a place where the immigrant is left to sink or swim; today it provides a complex network of social services, the costs of which have led some experts to express concern whether governments will be able to meet their statutory obligations to their own aging, indigenous populations, much less to large numbers of newcomers. Thus, while declaring that they are still committed to the principle of *non-refoulement*, and are prepared to accept those who qualify as legitimate political refugees, the wealthy countries are all tightening up their controls on immigration, either informally or by statute, to deny entry to those who do not.

This, they have discovered, is not always easy to do, and the handling of immigration problems has already begun to generate political controversy. Economic migrants and purely political refugees are often difficult to distinguish in practice, and rapid decisions, perhaps on slim information, as to which are which, often means taking liberties with procedures, or risks with the lives and well-being of innocent individuals: few bureaucracies are likely to emerge with much credit. The matter is complicated by the fact that the decision to leave a communist state is no longer grounds enough, in itself, to claim asylum. (Vietnamese boat people in Hong Kong being processed for involuntary repatriation, for example, are not likely to receive the kind of screening once accorded to Nureyev or Rostropovich.) As Europe deliberates a common Community policy towards immigration, demography and politics combine to suggest the kinds of challenge which such a policy will face. The continued population growth anticipated along the southern Mediterranean, outstripping economic development and employment opportunities, raises the question whether that long watery border will prove any more of an obstacle than the one separating the US and Mexico. Recent events in Eastern Europe also suggest the possibility of massive voluntary shifts of population comparable, perhaps even exceeding, the upheaval which accompanied the break-up of the Ottoman Empire, when millions of Greeks, Armenians, Turks and others fled or were forcibly transported from their homes. Europe has already seen West Germany become one of the world's leading asylum centres, accepting some 842,227 refugees in 1989 alone, more than 120,000 of non-German origin. Most (720,909) were ethnic Germans, but it is interesting that the number entering the Federal Republic from the GDR (343,854) was exceeded by ethnic Germans returning from long exile in other countries, such as Poland, the USSR and Romania (377,055). Like Israel, West German law binds the country to accept all Germans seeking resettlement, but with the flow of immigration from East Germany still running at over 2,000 a day through the opening months of 1990, questions were raised whether such an influx could continue indefinitely in the face of a sustained level of two million unemployed predicted for the mid-1990s. The emigration, of course, proved an even greater headache for the GDR, no longer able to bottle up its constituency. The continued drain on its workforce sabotaged any hopes there were of a new start for a reformed GDR and helped hasten unification by the unlooked-for and unusual method of population transfer.

West Germany, while the most directly involved, is not the only country in Europe with refugee problems on the horizon. Greece is preparing for the arrival of around 100,000 ethnic Greeks from the Soviet Union. Bulgaria's policies provoked the flight of 330,000 Bulgarian Muslims to Turkey in 1989. But these may merely be a prelude to even more spectacular upheavals further east. With each day it becomes more difficult for the USSR to preserve the fiction that its nationalities policies have succeeded where Russification failed: the powerful solvent of ethnic diversity is beginning to attack the adhesive which held the Soviet jigsaw together. The dispute between Armenia and Azerbaijan has already generated its own refugees, and more may well follow, either as a result of efforts to suppress ethnic separatism or because successful separatists, from Estonia to the Trans-Caucasus, may turn on other communities, notably in Central Asia.

Some Mitigating Factors

The future, however, is not without its hopeful side. To begin with, there is the obvious truth that the overwhelming majority of refugees did not leave their homes willingly and would like nothing better than to return to them. What is more, many of them already have done so through repatriation of their own volition, which is clearly the best and usually the preferred solution for most refugees. For those whose repatriation is not possible, nor likely, international co-operation has shown that successful resettlement programmes are possible on a large scale. On 30 April 1989, for example, some 165,333 Indochinese refugees still remained in first asylum camps awaiting disposition – but these must be compared with some 1.4 million who over the years have been permanently resettled in third countries, more than half in the US which was preparing to accept as many as 50,000 more in 1990. To these must be added the millions more of Hungarians, Cubans, Russians, Czechs, East Germans and others who have lived to see their children grow up as Americans, Canadians, Britons, French and Australians.

Refugees will, of course, certainly continue to be on the world's conscience, and a tax on its resources, for the indefinite future. Tribal and communal hostility, often intertwined with boundary disputes in Africa and the subcontinent, will remain a source of trouble in those regions. Coups from the left and the right in Latin America, each producing its own crop of political refugees, will certainly disturb the hemisphere's peace from time to time. The political refugee will be with us, no doubt, as long as societies are formed into states, and their populations compete for power among themselves or with their neighbours. So, too, will the other refugee – the economic migrant fleeing the oppression, not of political forces, but of poverty.

Still, there is the natural tendency of people everywhere to remain amidst their own people and surroundings – and this tendency is as much fortified by the hope of jam tomorrow, or even the day after, as by the reality of jam today. The recent contagion of democracy in the world, too, must have its positive impact on the refugee problem. Nothing so varied in its origins as that problem is can be safely summarized or easily accounted for. But it is clear that it has been exacerbated today – where it has not been generated – by the export of Cold War geopolitical rivalry and the use of the Third World as a Cold War battlefield. The 5.9 million Afghan refugees created by the Soviet invasion, added to the 1.1 million spawned by the Ethiopian regime, alone account for almost half of the present world total – and this is not to take account of the refugees from the Nicaraguan and Angolan civil wars; the steady stream of border-crossers from Eastern Europe since 1948 and from Cuba since its revolution, the hundreds of thousands who fled Tibet, Laos and Cambodia; the more than two million Vietnamese who have left their homes since 1975 or even the one million North Vietnamese who fled south when the communists took control in Hanoi. Taken together, this vast crowd victimized by ideology easily equals, if it does not outnumber, those who have been made refugees by communal warfare, natural catastrophe, border disputes or homegrown despotism. Although the process of change in the Soviet Union may well create new refugees from ethnic strife, the least benefit to be expected from the 'Sinatra Doctrine' may be that the great powers will no longer feel a need to confront each other over the world chessboard, ready to turn any local, commonplace tumult in the Third World into full-blown catastrophe.

Chronologies: 1989

THE UNITED STATES AND CANADA

January
9 President Reagan proposes $1.15-trillion budget for FY 1990.
19 Senate confirms James Baker as Secretary of State.
20 George Bush inaugurated as 41st President of the US.
31 Japanese Premier Takeshita visits US to promote US–Japan relations.
February
14 White House defers decision on building MX or *Midgetman* missile.
21 Trial of Lt Col Oliver North, arising from Iran–*Contra* affair, begins.
21 Pentagon reveals deal to sell military parts worth $13m to Argentina, first Argentinian arms deal since 1977.
March
9– US Senate refuses to confirm John Tower as Secretary of Defense by 53 to 47; unanimously approves Richard Cheney for position (17).
10 US Treasury Secretary Nicholas Brady outlines new Third World debt strategy, combining reduction and forgiveness.
13–17 During Israeli Foreign Minister Moshe Arens' visit to Washington, US proposes series of confidence-building measures in Occupied Territories.
24 Bush proposes giving *Contras* $45m in non-military aid for year.
April
2 G-7 endorses Brady Third World debt proposals; World Bank endorses them (4).
3– Egyptian President Mubarak visits Washington to discuss peace proposals; Israeli Premier Shamir visits Washington (4); presents own peace plan (6); Jordan's King Hussein arrives for 2 days of discussion (19).
13– Congress approves $45-m *Contra* aid bill.
26 Canada cancels plans to purchase nuclear submarines.
28 Bush announces new agreement with Japan on FS-X fighter development.
May
2– Bush gives 3 major foreign policy speeches: Latin America (2); East–West relations (12); superpower relations (24).
4 Oliver North convicted on 3 charges but cleared of 9 others.
16 Israeli Foreign Minister Arens begins 3-day visit to Washington seeking support for Israeli peace proposals.
25 US Trade Secretary names Japan, Brazil and India as unfair traders under 301 clause of 1988 Omnibus Trade Act.
June
5– Bush suspends arms sales to China as Chinese dissident Fang Lizhi takes refuge in US embassy, Beijing; all high-level Sino-US government contacts suspended as further protest of Chinese disregard for democracy (20).
5–9 In US, Pakistan Premier Bhutto makes $1.14-bn deal for F-16 fighters.
July
6 Bush announces US will write off 20% of its loans to 16 African countries.
20 Bush proposes 3-stage US space programme for 21st century.
August
2– First sea-launch of *Trident* II missile is success; second sea-trial fails (15).
25 US announces $65-m military aid package to help Colombian drug war.
September
5 Bush announces $7.86-bn anti-drug programme.

18–   Shevardnadze visits US; presents arms-control proposals (21); discusses them with Secretary of State Baker at Jackson Hole, Wyoming (22–3).
28   Senate approves $4.3-bn funding for SDI in 1989–90 budget.
October
2   Bush meets Mubarak, endorses his plan for West Bank elections.
2–   Soviet Defence Minister Yazov begins week-long visit to US.
9   Yugoslav Premier Markovic, seeking $1-bn loan, begins 6-day visit to US.
17   South Korean President Roh Tae Woo begins 6-day visit to US.
November
7   US agrees to unfreeze $567m in Iranian assets.
14–15 Israeli Premier Shamir visits Washington for talks on peace process.
19   Congress approves 3-year $938-m in aid for Poland and Hungary.
December
2–3   Presidents Bush and Gorbachev hold successful Summit meeting off Malta.
19   Bush removes some of the sanctions imposed against China in June.
19   Bush signs budget bill for 1989–90, cutting federal deficit by $14.8bn.

THE SOVIET UNION

January
4   President Gorbachev meets Iranian delegation in Moscow.
11–   Communist Party leaders from Armenia and Azerbaijan meet Gorbachev to settle dispute; direct rule from Moscow imposed on Nagorno-Karabakh (12).
18   Gorbachev announces cuts in Soviet budget and defence production of 14.29% and 19.5% respectively.
22   Demonstrators in Moldavia demand that Moldavian be made the official language of the republic.
February
2   Gen Pyotr Lushev appointed C in C of Warsaw Pact forces.
16–   200,000 Lithuanians mark Independence Day for first time since 1940 in officially-sanctioned celebrations; rallies held demanding Estonian independence (24); and Georgian independence (25).
20–23 Gorbachev tours Ukraine; in Kiev speech suggests 'autonomous regions' like Nagorno-Karabakh be made 'national regions'.
March
14   Soviet authorities publish draft plans giving more power to the republics.
15–16 During Central Committee meeting, Gorbachev details farm reforms.
26   In first multi-candidate elections for Congress of People's Deputies; 44% of unopposed CP nominees are defeated after failing to get 50% of votes cast.
30   USSR announces end of student conscription.
April
7   USSR SSN catches fire and sinks off Norwegian coast, 42 die.
9–   Troops kill 20 people in Tbilisi in Georgian autonomy demonstrations, curfew imposed; Georgia's leaders resign (14); curfew lifted (18); new Georgian leadership confirms that gas killed some demonstrators (24).
9–   Run-off elections to fill 64 seats in new Soviet parliament held; Dr Andrei Sakharov elected to parliament by Academy of Sciences (20).
25   At Central Committee plenary session, 110 Party officials, including former President Andrei Gromyko, replaced.
May
3–   Strikes begin in Nagorno-Karabakh in protest at Moscow rule over the area; tanks sent in after ethnic fighting erupts (10).
14   Estonia, Latvia and Lithuania declare common position on sovereignty.

25	Inaugural session of Congress of People's Deputies elects Gorbachev as President of reconstituted Supreme Soviet.
30	Gorbachev reveals Soviet defence expenditure of 77.3m roubles for current fiscal year.

June

4–	10 days of ethnic fighting between Uzbeks and Meskhetian Turks begins in Uzbekistan; economic reforms for the region announced (19); Islam Karimov replaces Rafik Nishanov as Uzbekistan Party leader (24).
9–	Official Supreme Soviet commission investigation into 9 April rioting in Tbilisi, Georgia, condemns defence ministry role.
16–	Ethnic rioting erupts in Kazakhstan; military curfew imposed (19).
20–23	Visiting USSR, Iranian parliamentary speaker Hashemi Rafsanjani signs economic, political and defence co-operation pacts.

July

2	Former Foreign Minister and President, Andrei Gromyko, dies aged 79.
10–	Siberian coal-miners strike; spreads to the Ukraine (17); Siberian miners gain concessions, return to work (21); Ukrainians follow (25).
15–	16 killed in ethnic fighting in Sukhuni in Georgia over Abkhazian demands for secession; State of Emergency declared (18).
26–	Russian minority in Estonia strike opposing draft Estonian autonomy laws; return to work after commission set up to examine grievances (28).

August

8–	Estonia passes election law barring non-Estonians from voting; Russians strike in Estonian capital of Tallinn (9); President of Supreme Soviet declares law unconstitutional (16); strike ends (18).
14	Azerbaijan Popular Front calls 1-day strike, demands greater autonomy.
24–	Non-Moldavian workers in Moldavia begin strikes in protest at draft laws making Moldavian the official language; proposal enacted into law (31).

September

11	Azerbaijan Popular Front ends 7-day strike with promise of recognition.
20–	In CP Politburo reshuffle, 5 members dropped.
23	Lithuanian parliament declares its 1940 annexation into USSR invalid.

October

5	Estonian parliament suspends discriminatory election law of August.
6	First supply trains break month-long Azerbaijani blockade of Armenia.
8	Latvian Popular Front adopts programme advocating independence.
9–	Parliament bans strikes in transport, energy and defence industries; Vorkuta coal-miners strike when promised reforms ignored (26).
23	Foreign Minister Shevardnadze admits Soviet violation of ABM Treaty and promises dismantling of Krasnoyarsk radar.

November

3	Lithuanian parliament passes law restricting voting rights.
12–	Troops airlifted to Moldavia after clashes between police and nationalist demonstrators in Kishinev; peacekeeping troops withdrawn (20).
20	Republic of Georgia votes itself the right to secede from USSR.
27	Parliament grants economic autonomy to Lithuania, Latvia and Estonia from 1 January 1990.
28	Parliament ends direct rule of Nagorno-Karabakh.

December

1	Armenian parliament votes to unite with Nagorno-Karabakh, denouncing Moscow decision that it be ruled by Azerbaijan.
7–	Lithuanian parliament abolishes leading role of Communist Party; Lithuanian CP Congress endorses proposals for Party to separate from Moscow and for republic to become independent (20).

EUROPE

January

10– FRG tightens export controls on sensitive materials and bans participation in manufacture of chemical or nuclear weapons abroad; concedes that West German companies helped build Libyan CW plant at Rabta (18).

15– 20th anniversary of suicide of Czech student over 1968 Soviet invasion of Czechoslovakia begins 6 days of protests in Prague.

17 FRG extends national service to 18 months.

19– Ante Markovic named Yugoslav premier; Central Committee meeting fails to resolve conflict in Party and adjourns (31 Jan–1 Feb).

19– Polish government proposes direct talks to end ban on trade unions; Solidarity accepts (22).

February

11–17 US Secretary of State, Baker visits Europe, meets all European NATO foreign ministers.

11– Hungarian CP Central Committee authorize multi-party system; new constitution abrogates CP's leading role (20).

16– Slovene League of Social Democrats, first independent party since 1945, founded in Yugoslavia; Kosovo miners end 8-day strike with resignation of 3 Albanian Party officials who condoned increased Serbian control over Kosovo (27); resignations rejected by state presidency in Belgrade after Serb protest march (28).

March

5–7 124-nation international conference on the ozone layer held in London; 24-nation environmental conference later held in Holland (10–11).

9– Polish government and Solidarity agree political reforms and Solidarity participation in June elections; CP Central Committee approves (31).

11– Hungarian CP unveils election manifesto advocating multi-party system; Hungary Democratic Forum holds first national convention (12).

15– EFTA Summit in Oslo pledges co-operation with EC; confirmed during EC–EFTA meeting in Brussels (20).

23– Albanians riot in Kosovo to protest Serbian rule; curfew imposed (27).

April

4 NATO's 40th birthday marked with low-key ceremony in Brussels.

5–7 During Gorbachev visit to UK, 3 Anglo-Soviet trade deals signed.

5–8 Resumed GATT talks in Geneva sanction 15 accords liberalizing trade.

5– Polish government and opposition sign accords creating 2-chamber parliament and reserving 35% of lower house for opposition delegates; parliament approves reforms (7); Solidarity declared legal (17).

12– Hungarian CP Politburo reformed, 4 sacked; creation of a breakaway party called for (15); Premier Nemeth replaces 6 ministers (26).

19 FRG announces postponement until 1992 of military service extension.

20 At end of 2-day summit in Paris, Mitterrand and Kohl inaugurate Franco-German Council for Defence and Security.

23 Nicaraguan President Ortega begins 3-week 10-nation European tour.

May

2 Hungary begins dismantling iron fences along Austrian border.

6 Bulgaria begins expelling ethnic Turks after they protest government suppression of their cultural identity.

8– Former Hungarian leader Kádár loses last party post; 3 Politburo members create reform bloc within HCP advocating withdrawal from WTO (21).

8– Slobodan Milosevic appointed president of Serbian republic.

24 France cuts 4,160 million francs from its defence expenditure for 1990 and 1991 by delaying current weapons programmes.

27–   President Bush begins European tour in Italy; attends NATO summit in Brussels (29–30); in FRG Bush calls for destruction of Berlin Wall (30–31).

June

4&18   In Polish parliamentary elections, Solidarity wins all 161 independent *Sejm* seats and 99 of 100 independent Senate seats.

12–15   In Bonn, Gorbachev endorses concept of 'Common European Home' in joint Soviet–FRG declaration.

16–   Imre Nagy and other leaders of 1956 Hungarian uprising reburied as statesmen; HCP appoints 4-man presidium to rule until Party Congress in October; Rezsö Nyers made Party President (24).

22–   South African president-elect F.W. de Klerk begins European tour in FRG; also visits UK (23), Italy (24) and Portugal (25).

27–   USSR accepted as mediator in dispute over expulsion of Turks from Bulgaria; respective ambassadors in Sofia and Ankara return home (28).

July

2–   In Greece coalition government sworn in with Tzannis Tzannetakis as premier; Greek parliament votes to investigate former Premier Andreas Papandreou for a financial scandal (19).

9–   Bush begins European tour in Poland; offers $100-m economic aid (10); meets Solidarity leader Lech Walesa (11); visiting Hungary, Bush offers small-scale economic aid (11–12); visits Paris for G-7 summit and bicentennial celebrations (13–16); ends tour in Holland (17).

19–   Polish parliament elects Gen Jaruzelski president; he resigns as Communist Party leader and is replaced by premier Mieczyslaw Rakowski (29).

23   After 64 days without a government, Girlio Andreotti, heading 5-party coalition, sworn in as Italian premier.

25–28   Gen Dimitri Yazov makes first visit to UK by Soviet Defence Minister.

August

2–   In Poland, Czeslaw Kiszczak appointed premier at head of coalition government; resigns after losing parliamentary support (17); Solidarity member Tadeusz Mazowiecki elected prime minister by Polish parliament (24).

5   In Hungary, Democratic Forum bumps communists in run-off by-elections.

8–   FRG closes its embassies in East Berlin and Budapest (14) because of overcrowding by East German refugees; 900 East Germans flee to Austria from Hungary (19); FRG closes Prague embassy because of refugees (23); Budapest embassy refugees allowed to go to Austria (24).

September

11   Hungary opens its borders with Austria for East German refugees.

12–   Polish parliament approves Solidarity-led cabinet; economic co-operation pact signed with EC (19).

18–   After 3 months of negotiations Hungarian CP and opposition groups sign agreement for free elections and amended constitution.

18   Hungary restores full diplomatic relations with Israel.

21–   UK agrees to limit army exercises in FRG; West German government cuts low-flying time of military jets in 7 districts by 45% (28).

27–   Slovenian votes to secede from Yugoslavia; federal parliament orders constitutional changes in republics be reviewed in federal courts (28).

30   East German refugees in West German embassies in Prague and Warsaw allowed to leave for the West.

October

3–   GDR suspends visa-free travel to Czechoslovakia; anti-government demonstrations in East Berlin and Leipzig (7); Egon Krenz replaces Erich Honecker as head of state (18); government opens talks with opposition groups (26).

7–   At Hungarian Party Congress, CP dissolved and reformed as Socialist Party; Rezso Nyers re-elected President and Miklós Németh Premier (9); opposition parties formally legalized (10).

17–19   At bilateral talks in Madrid, Argentina agrees to end hostilities with UK and re-establish consular relations.

26–27   Warsaw Pact foreign ministers' meeting formally abandons Brezhnev Doctrine and pledges non-interference in each other's affairs.

28   Czech riot police break up pro-democracy marches in Prague.

30   In Yugoslavia, trial of former Kosovo Communist Party president, Azem Vlasi, on charges of instigating Albanian riots in Kosovo, opens.

31   Turkish Premier Turgat Ozal elected President.

November

5–   Conservatives win Greek election but fail to secure absolute majority; national unity government sworn in until fresh elections in April 1990 (23).

7–   East German government resigns; new 11-man cabinet formed (8); free travel to West Berlin approved (9); dismantling of Berlin Wall begins (10); parliament selects Hans Modrow as Premier (13).

10   Bulgarian Communist Party leader Todor Zhivkov resigns and is replaced by Petar Mladenov; Mladenov dismisses 10 of Zhivkov's Party allies (16); Mladenov chosen as President (17).

21   Czechoslovak regime meets opposition for first time, promises power-sharing; after 8 days of anti-government demonstrations, leadership resigns, Karel Urbanek becomes Party leader (24); parliament votes to end leading role of CP (29); dismantling of Czech-Austrian border fences begins (30).

22–   Hungarian parliament rejects proposed 3-year austerity plan; national referendum votes to postpone January presidential election and to choose president by parliament (26).

28   Chancellor Kohl announces 10-point German unification plan.

29–   Gorbachev begins 3-day state visit to Italy; trip ends with first meeting between the Pope and a Soviet leader (1 Dec).

December

1   Hungarian Premier Miklós Németh announces that armed force will be reduced by 25% and restructured.

3–   GDR CP leader Egon Krenz and Politburo resign; Krenz forced to resign as head of state and is replaced by non-communist Manfred Gerlach (6); emergency CP congress elects Gregor Gysi party leader (9).

5   Soviet Foreign Minister Shevardnadze rejects Kohl's reunification plan.

7–   Czech premier Ladislav Adamec resigns after failure to form acceptable coalition government; replaced by Marian Calfa; President Gustáv Husák resigns after swearing in coalition government with minority of communists (10); parliament elects Alexander Dubček as chairman (28) and Vaclav Havel President (29).

7–   In Bulgaria, Union of Democratic Forces founded; CP Congress renounces Party's right to rule (13); parliament approves constitutional reform package (15); government agrees to reform talks with opposition groups (27); reverses assimilation campaign against ethnic Turks (29).

17–   Hundreds killed as anti-Romanian government demonstration in Timişoara crushed by force; demonstrations spread to other cities (21); army joins demonstrators, overthrows President Ceauşescu, power assumed by Committee for National Salvation (22); Ceauşescu and wife tried by military tribunal and executed (25); provisional government named with Ion Iliescu as President, and Petre Roman as Premier (26).

18   EC and USSR sign 10-year trade and co-operation agreement.
24   Poland signs $725-m IMF loan package.

THE MIDDLE EAST

January
1   Israel deports 13 Palestinians from Occupied Territories on *Fatah's* 25th anniversary; Israeli troops and Palestinians clash in ensuing demonstrations (2)
4   US Navy downs 2 armed Libyan MiG fighters over Mediterranean.
9   Syria and Morocco agree to resume diplomatic ties.
23–   Iran and Syria meet in Damascus to mediate end of Lebanese Shi'ite militia war; cease-fire announced (25); peace deal signed giving Syrian-backed *Amal* militia control of south Lebanon (30).
30–31 Dr al-Hoss and Gen Aoun, rival Lebanese premiers, individually meet Arab League members in Tunis; no agreement on government reached.

February
4–   Israeli soldiers kill 5 Palestinian guerrillas in south Lebanon security zone; Israeli air force bombs PLO stronghold near Beirut (28).
5–6   French Foreign Minister Roland Dumas makes first visit by French minister in 10 years to Iran to improve bilateral relations.
8–   UN extends Military Observer Group mandate to 30 September; Iranian Foreign Minister Velayati and Iraqi counterpart, Tariq Aziz, meet in New York, agree to resume Gulf War peace talks in March (10).
9–   *Hizbollah* militia withdraw from south Lebanon; fighting erupts between Lebanese army and Lebanese forces militia for control of East Beirut (15); truce negotiated by Christian church leaders (16); Arab League begins talks with Lebanese religious leaders to resolve Lebanese impasse (20).
14–   Ayatollah Khomeini sentences Salman Rushdie to death; declares his book, *The Satanic Verses*, blasphemous; EC recalls diplomats from Iran (20); Iran recalls diplomats from EC countries (21).
15–16 Iraq, Egypt, Jordan and North Yemen form Arab Co-operation Council.
17–   Soviet Foreign Minister Shevardnadze visits Syria at start of Middle East tour in pursuit of an international peace conference; visits Jordan (19); in Egypt (20–23) meets Israeli Foreign Minister Moshe Arens and Yasser Arafat (22); ends tour in Iraq (23–24) and Iran (25–26).
19   3-day strike by Palestinians begins in Occupied Territories.

March
6–   Gen Aoun blockades areas of West Beirut run by rival Muslim government; fighting erupts between Christian and Muslim forces (8); Muslim militias block Aoun's territory (21); cease-fire takes effect (29).
7   Iran formally breaks relations with UK over Rushdie controversy.
7–8   In south Lebanon, Israel blockades UN peacekeeping troops for 15 hours after being refused entry to Ebel as Saqi to pursue Palestinian guerrillas; Israeli air force bombs 2 PFLP centres in east Lebanon (20).
13–16 Islamic Conference Organization's annual meeting in Saudi Arabia turns down Iranian demands for execution of Salman Rushdie.
22   2nd formal US–PLO meeting in Tunis fails to agree priorities for further Middle East peace discussions.
27–   At end of 3-day visit to Baghdad, King Fahd of Saudi Arabia signs non-aggression pact with Iraq; travels to Egypt to confirm formally Cairo's return to Arab world (27–31).

April

1–   Fighting between Christian and Muslim forces in Lebanon resumes; Syria bombs Jounieh port to block Christian militia exit (21); Arab League foreign ministers in Tunis propose immediate cease-fire and despatch Arab observer force to Lebanon to monitor it (26–27).

5–   Israel releases 474 Palestinians detained during *intifada*; Israeli border police kill 5 Palestinians during raid on West Bank village of Nahalir (13).

6–   In US, Israeli Premier Shamir presents 4-point peace plan; PLO rejects it (20); Palestinians in Occupied Territories follow suit (26).

8   Israeli Navy kills 4 Palestinians attempting to infiltrate south Lebanon.

8–   Iraqi government orders Kurdish population in villages of Qala Diza and Ranya (13) to relocate to south Iraq.

18–   Price rises provoke anti-government riots in southern Jordan; premier Zeid al-Rifai resigns (24); replaced by Sharif Zeid Bin Shaker (27).

20–   Gulf War peace talks resume in Geneva; end in stalemate (23).

May

3–   Rival Lebanese governments agree to suspend blockade of Beirut ports; cease-fire collapses (6); another imposed (11); car bomb in Beirut kills Grand Mufti Sheikh Hassan Khaled (16); Arab League establishes committee to mediate (26).

5–   West German aid worker kidnapped in south Lebanon; British resident kidnapped (11); West German freed (14).

14   Israeli cabinet approves peace plan involving elections in Occupied Territories; PLO rejects proposal (15); US and UK guardedly welcome it (22).

15–   Israel imposes indefinite curfew on Gaza Strip; leader of Islamic faction group, *Hamas*, arrested in Gaza Strip (18–19); in first armed clash of *intifada* 3 Palestinians and 1 Israeli soldier shot dead (19).

25–26   Arab League Summit in Casablanca re-admits Egypt, endorses PLO role in peace process; implicitly recognizes Israel by endorsing UN Resolutions 242, 338.

June

3–   Iranian leader Ayatollah Khomeini dies; Ali Khamenei replaces him as supreme spiritual leader (4); presidential election moved forward to July (19).

6–   Palestinians in Gaza Strip issued identity cards; curfew lifted (11); 8 Palestinian leaders of *intifada* deported to Lebanon (29).

12–   Kurdish population forcibly removed from Iraqi town of Clara Diza; Iraq announces intention to depopulate 20-mile buffer zone along its Turkish and Iranian borders (26).

July

4–   Lebanese Muslim militia reopen crossing points into Christian Beirut after 4-months; Arab League announces failure to mediate cease-fire (31).

28   Hashemi Rafsanjani elected President with 94.5% of votes.

28–   Israel kidnaps Iranian *Hizbollah* leader Sheikh Abdul Karim Obeid from south Lebanon; US hostage Lt Col William Higgins, kidnapped in 1988, killed in retaliation (31).

August

10–   In Lebanon Syrians begin attack on Soukh el-Gharb; France begins diplomatic attempts to end fighting (12); builds up flotilla in eastern Mediterranean as Syrian and Iranian-backed militia unite to oust Gen Aoun (15); UN calls for cease-fire ignored (16); France reduces its flotilla from 8 vessels to 5 (24); French peace plan involving cease-fire and political reforms presented to Syria (28).

16– Mehdi Karoubi elected speaker of Iranian parliament; parliament endorses proposed 22-man cabinet (29).

17 700 people die in explosion at Al-Hillah military complex in Iraq.

September

2 Iranian President Rafsanjani resigns as leader of armed forces.

6– US evacuates its embassy in Beirut after anti-US demonstrations; Arab League ministers reveal 7-point peace plan (16); proposals accepted by both sides (22); cease-fire takes effect (23); blockade lifted on Beirut airport and seaport (24); Lebanese parliament begins meeting in Taif, Saudi Arabia, to discuss Arab League proposals for political reform (30).

15– Egypt formally presents 10-point peace plan to Israel; Israeli cabinet postpones decision (17); PLO accepts proposals (21).

15 Israel successfully test-fires *Jericho* II ballistic missile.

25–26 Arab Co-operation Council meets in North Yemen to sign economic, cultural and commercial agreements.

October

6– Israeli cabinet rejects Egyptian September peace plan; US presents amended 5-point peace plan to Israel and Egypt (10); PLO rejects US idea of direct Palestinian–Israeli talks (16).

6– 2 Red Cross workers kidnapped in Sidon, south Lebanon; Lebanese parliament, meeting in Taif, accepts Arab League peace plan (22).

November

1– US Secretary of State Baker offers Israel a modified version of October peace plan; Israel accepts the proposals (5).

5– Lebanese parliament elects René Mouawad President who asks Selim al-Hoss to form national unity government (13); Mouawad killed by car bomb (22); Elias Hrawi elected his successor (24); Gen Aoun replaced as Armed Forces Chief by Gen Emile Lahoud (28).

8– In first Jordanian elections for 22 years, Muslim fundamentalists win most seats; parliament opened by King Hussein (27).

December

1– PLO accepts US October peace proposals provided they are directly represented at talks; Egypt accepts proposals in principle (6).

4– Jordanian King Hussein names Moudar Badran premier; Badran abolishes 14-year old martial law (19).

5 Israel kills 5 suspected Palestinian guerrillas crossing from Egypt.

6– Beirut cease-fire broken as battles break out around Green Line; 6 killed in PLO attack on Syrian checkpoint in south Lebanon (14); Israel launches 3 raids against *Hizbollah* guerrillas in south Lebanon (26–27).

7 Iraq announces successful test launch of 2 separate types of surface-to-surface missiles.

AFRICA

January

4– Polisario rebels hold first direct talks with King Hassan of Morocco; announces cease-fire (27).

10 Cuban soldiers begin withdrawal from Angola.

13– Zaire ends 2 friendship and co-operation treaties with Belgium and suspends debt repayments; Belgium halts development plans in Zaire (14).

19 South African President Botha suffers stroke.

28 Sudanese government announces that SPLA rebels have captured garrison town of Nasir after 7-month siege.

February

2– In South Africa F.W. de Klerk replaces P.W. Botha as leader of ruling National Party; Progressive Federal Party, Independent Party and National Democratic Movement form the Democratic Party (4).

6–8 Algerian President Chadli Benjedid visits Morocco to improve relations.

14– Sudanese Foreign Minister Hassan al-Tarabi offers rebels an immediate cease-fire and peace conference; Defence Minister Abdul Maged Hamed Khalil resigns over government failure to support peace attempts (20); 150 army officers in letter to Sudanese premier Sadiq al-Mahdi demand political and economic change (22).

15 Cease-fire between UNITA and Angolan government, mediated by Ivory Coast President Houphouët-Boigny, takes effect.

15–17 Meeting in Morocco, Libya, Algeria, Tunisia, Mauritania and Morocco create Arab Maghreb Union.

16 UN Security Council authorizes Namibian independence plan and the UN Transition Assistance Group (UNTAG).

17– In Ethiopia, EPLF and Afar Liberation Front capture towns of Adigrat (17) and Enda Selassie (19); government troops driven completely out of Tigray Province when capital Mekele is seized by rebels (28).

23 National referendum in Algeria votes end to one-party socialist state.

March

4– All Sudanese political factions except National Islamic Front (NIF) adopt peace pact to end civil war; premier Sadiq al-Mahdi proposes new broad-based government (5); cabinet resigns (11); 23-man coalition government excluding NIF formed (22).

13 Polisario announces resumption of hostilities in Western Sahara.

15– South African President Botha resumes his duties after illness.

April

1 In Chad, coup attempt by civilian and army leaders fails.

1– As UN Namibian peace plan comes into effect, SWAPO guerrillas cross border from Angola to Namibia; peace proposals involving UN-monitored SWAPO withdrawal into Angola approved (6); guerrillas begin withdrawal (10); South Africa returns its troops to barracks (26–29).

8– In South Africa, Democratic Party formally launched; elects Zach de Beer its parliamentary leader (10).

9– Mauritanian border guards kill 2 Senegalese, causing racial violence in Mauritania and Senegal; Mauritania begins airlift of nationals from Senegal (25); Senegal declares State of Emergency (28); Morocco, France and Spain begin repatriation of refugees from both countries (30).

12 South African press reveals recent visit to the country by USSR Deputy Foreign Minister Anatoly Adamishir, first by a USSR official in 30 years.

13–14 Senior Zimbabwean politicians resign in corruption scandal; Zimbabwe Unity Movement launched by Edgar Tekere (30).

May

1– In South Africa, anti-apartheid campaigner David Webster assassinated; first major policy speech by National Party leader F.W. de Klerk outlines racial reform plans (12).

1– SPLA declare 1-month unilateral cease-fire in Sudan; reject government offer to establish a committee to impose permanent truce (8).

3 Nigerian President Gen Babangida ends 5-year ban on political activity; anti-government riots in Benir City (24); spread to Lagos (31).

16– Military coup to overthrow Ethiopian President Mengistu foiled in Addis Ababa; rebel troops claim control of Eritrean capital (17); mutiny crushed (18); Mengistu replaces entire military high command (24).

June
1– Mozambican Defence Minister announces all Soviet military advisers to leave within 2 years; government reveals 12-point peace plan (23); RENAMO accepts the proposals (28).
5– Ethiopian government proposes unconditional peace talks with Eritrean and Tigray rebels; offer accepted by TPLF (13) and EPLF (29).
8– In South Africa President Botha renews State of Emergency; ruling National Party's 5-year plan for racial reforms revealed (29).
18 In Sudan, coup attempt to restore former President Nimeiri to power fails; coup led by Gen Omar Hassan al-Bashir ousts government and abolishes constitution in favour of a Revolutionary Council (30).
22– 4-point Angolan peace plan agreed by President dos Santos and UNITA at summit of 18 governments at Gbadolite; cease-fire begins (23).

July
4– Sudanese Premier Gen Bashir declares 1-month unilateral cease-fire and offers amnesty to rebels; former Premier Sadiq al-Mahdi arrested (6).
5 South African President Botha meets jailed ANC leader Nelson Mandela.
5– Angolan government suspends peace talks after UNITA breaks cease-fire; talks resumed in Kinshasa (16).
14– 23 killed in anti-government riots in Mogadishu, Somalia; in resulting arrests army massacres 46 people (16).
19 National Party leader F.W. de Klerk meets Mozambican President Chissano in Maputo.
24–26 At annual OAU Summit, Egyptian President elected chairman.

August
7– Zimbabwean President Mugabe and Kenyan President Moi meet in Nairobi to discuss ending Mozambican war; during peace talks between rebels and Mozambican church officials, rebels present 16-point peace-plan but talks end inconclusively (8–11).
14– South African President P.W. Botha resigns; F.W. de Klerk sworn in as acting president (15); visits Zaire (24–25) and Zambia (28).
19–20 Talks between Sudanese rebels and government collapse.
21 Senegal and Mauritania sever diplomatic relations.
24 UNITA rebels end 2-month truce in Angola.
31 Libya and Chad sign agreement referring disputed Aouzou Strip to an international court if settlement not agreed within 1 year.

September
6– South Africa's ruling National Party wins election but loses 30 seats; government allows previously-banned protest marches through Cape Town (13) and Johannesburg (15); F.W. de Klerk inaugurated as president (20).
4– In Ethiopia, TPLF capture Alele Susula after 10-day offensive; government and EPLF begin peace talks in US mediated by former US President Carter (7); US peace talks end in agreement to further meeting in November (19).
12 White SWAPO lawyer Anton Lubowski assassinated in Namibia; SWAPO President Nujoma returns after 30 years exile (14).
18– UNITA leader Jonas Savimbi boycotts African summit in Zaire attempting to revive Angolan peace; proposes own 5-point peace plan (27).

October
7– Moroccan King Hassan cancels peace talks with Polisario after they attack Guelta Zennour; Polisario capture Moroccan positions at Hawza (11).
15 In South Africa, 8 ANC members including Walter Sisulu and a Pan Africanist Congress member, released from jail after 25 years.

15   Ethiopian government troops abandon northern city of Dessie to rebels.

15–17   Peace talks between UNITA leader Savimbi and Angolan government resume in France.

November

3–   Israel re-establishes diplomatic ties with Ethiopia; Tigray rebels meet Ethiopian government in Rome (4); Premier Selassie resigns (7); replaced by Hailu Yemew (9); second round of preliminary EPLF-government peace talks in Nairobi schedule further talks for 1990 (20–29).

7–   SWAPO wins first free Namibian election but fails to secure two-thirds majority; last South African troops withdraw (23).

16   Speaking to President's Council, President de Klerk announces desegregation of all South African beaches.

December

1–   Sudanese government and rebels open peace talks in Nairobi; end in disagreement over basic issues (5).

12–   Second round of talks between Tigrayan rebels and Ethiopian government begins in Rome; rebels capture town of Rabel in Shoa Province (21).

24   Attempt by National Patriotic Front guerrillas to depose Liberian President Doe fails.

ASIA AND THE PACIFIC

January

2–   Soviet negotiator Yuli Vorontstov meets *Mujaheddin* in Tehran; travels to Islamabad for talks with Pakistan government (4); and main rebel alliance (6–7); *Mujaheddin* refuse further direct talks with USSR (9).

2–   Ranasinghe Premadasa sworn in as Sri Lankan President; lifts State of emergency (11); Indian peacekeeping troops begin withdrawal (5).

7   Emperor Hirohito of Japan dies, Crown Prince Akahito becomes Emperor.

14–   Dinh Nho Liem, Vietnamese First Vice Foreign Minister visits Beijing; agrees on Vietnamese troop withdrawal from Kampuchea by September 1989.

February

1–   Seoul establishes full diplomatic relations with Hungary; vice-ministers from North and South Korea meet in Panmunjom; North Korea boycotts talks aimed at convening joint parliament sessions until end of US–South Korean 'Team Spirit' exercises (8).

1–4   Shevardnadze visits Beijing to organize first Sino-Soviet summit in 30 years, agrees date (15–18 May).

10–   *Mujaheddin Shura* meets in Rawalpindi, Pakistan to appoint interim *mujaheddin*-led government; collapses over number of places to be allocated to Iran-based Shi'ite groups; *Shura* resumes (14); interim government announced in Pakistan with Seghbatullah Mujjaddedi as President and Abdur-Rasul Sayaf as Premier (23).

12   Prince Sihanouk resumes leadership of Cambodian resistance coalition; 4 resistance factions and leaders of ASEAN countries meet in Indonesia, fail to reach agreement on a political settlement (16–21).

15   Last Soviet troops withdraw from Afghanistan.

15   In first general election in Sri Lanka for 11 years, the ruling United National Party wins 6-year term, taking 125 out of 225 seats in Parliament.

24–   President Bush joins representatives from 163 foreign nations at Emporor Hirohito's funeral in Japan; visits China (25–27); and South Korea where holds talks with President Roh (27).

23   Indonesian President Suharto and Chinese Foreign Minister Qian Qichen
          meet in Japan, announce intention to resume diplomatic relations.

March

5–   Anti-Chinese riots break out in Tibet; martial law imposed (7); Beijing
          expels non-residents to deter further independence demonstrations (21).

6–   Afghan *Mujaheddin* launch offensive on Jalalabad; capture Samarkhel (8);
          Najibullah offers rebels local autonomy if they cease fighting (27).

14   3 Kampuchean resistance factions establish a unified military command
          with Prince Sihanouk as head.

20–   South Korean President Roh indefinitely postpones the referendum
          assessing his government's performance; orders police not to end 3-month
          strike in Hyundai shipyard at Ulsan (29).

20–4   Chinese National People's Congress meets, Premier Li Peng announces aus-
          terity budget cutting economic growth to 7.5%.

23   India closes 13 of the 15 transit points to Nepal on expiry of Indian–
          Nepalese trade treaties.

April

1–   Sri Lanka offers rebels parliamentary seats if they surrender; offer refused
          (2); government begins week-long cease-fire which is immediately broken
          (12); President Premadasa accepts Tamil rebels' offer of peace talks (16).

5–   Vietnam announces it will unconditionally withdraw troops from
          Kampuchea by September; Kampuchean resistance leader Prince Sihanouk
          calls on France to organize an international peace conference (6).

9–   In first attack on US facilities in Philippines since 1987, New People's Army
          destroy communication equipment; assassinate Col James Rowe of US
          Advisors Group in Manila (21).

15–   Death of former Chinese Party General Secretary, Hu Yaobang, sparks
          student demonstrations in Beijing demanding democratic reform; after
          Yaobang's funeral, protests spread to Xian and Changsha (23); students
          begin boycotting lectures (24); talks with government fail (29–30).

25–   Japanese Premier Takeshita resigns over Recruit scandal; his close associate
          Ilei Aoki commits suicide (26).

May

3–   Sri Lankan government demands Indian troops leave by end 1989; first
          round of official Tamil Tigers–Sri Lankan government peace talks are incon-
          clusive (11–29); Sinhalese rebels agree to hold official peace talks (11).

4–   In Beijing students march on Tiananmen Square commemorating 4 May
          movement; students demanding democracy occupy square and begin
          hunger strike (15); Beijing workers join pro-democracy marches (16); mar-
          tial law imposed but army attempt to enter Beijing to clear Tiananmen
          Square thwarted by protestors' blockade (20).

7–   Afghan army breaks *Mujaheddin* siege of Jalalabad; government announces
          major rebel offensive on Khost (16); at Grand Assembly, President
          Najibullah offers 11 *Mujaheddin* leaders local autonomy in return for peace
          (21); *Mujaheddin* reject offer·(23).

15–   In Beijing first Sino-Soviet summit since 1959 begins; full relations restored
          (16); final communique restates differences over Cambodia (18).

24   Hong Kong indefinitely suspends work on post-1997 constitution due to
          unrest in China.

28   Former Japanese Premier Nakasone resigns from Liberal Democratic Party
          over Recruit scandal; official investigation into scandal ended (29).

June

2   Foreign Minister Sosuke Uno elected Japanese premier.

4–   Hundreds of students killed as Chinese troops forcibly clear Tiananmen

Square; (6); authorities begin executing political protestors (21); Jiang Zemin replaces Zhao Ziyang as Party leader (24).

19   Burma officially changes its name to Union of Myanmar.

20–   Sri Lankan government declares State of Emergency; Tamil Tigers end insurgency, agree to aid withdrawal of Indian peacekeeping troops (28).

22   Indefinite State of Emergency imposed on Bougainville Island by Papua New Guinea as separatists demand mining compensation.

July

5–6   Afghan army offensive retakes *Mujaheddin* gains of past 4 months including Samarkhel; 30 guerrilla leaders killed in sectarian fighting in Fakhar valley (9); *Mujaheddin* claim recapture of Samarkhel (13); superpower talks on Afghan settlement open in Stockholm (31).

18   Sri Lanka–Tamil Tiger peace talks end in discord; government confirms that Velupillai Prabakarar, leader of Tamil Tigers, killed by dissident followers (24); India begins withdrawing peacekeeping troops (29).

20   Vietnam and UK reach agreement on repatriation of Vietnamese boat people from Hong Kong.

21–   Burmese opposition leaders Aung San Suu Kyi and Gen Tin Oo placed under house arrest; 42 Burmese troops killed in unsuccessful assault on rebel base at Kaw Moo Ra (22–23).

23–   Japanese ruling Liberal Democratic Party retains power but loses majority for first time in Upper House elections; Premier Uno resigns (24).

24   Indian parliamentary opposition resigns, calls for Rajiv Gandhi's resignation over Bofors arms scandal.

25–   2-day talks in Paris between Cambodian government and 3-party resistance coalition ends in disagreement; international peace conference co-hosted by France and Indonesia begins in Paris (30).

August

9   Toshiki Kaifu becomes Japanese premier.

22–   Afghan President Najibullah proposes new peace plan, including cease-fire, international peace conference and elections; *Mujaheddin* reject plan (23); *Hezb-i-Islami* withdraws from *Mujaheddin* interim government (29).

28–30   Reconvened Cambodian peace conference in Paris fails to agree.

September

13–   In Sri Lanka, peace conference of all political factions except JVP adjourned until October to enable individual consultations; government offers JVP truce if it attends October meeting (17); Indian government agrees to cease operations against Tamil Tigers and withdraw all remaining troops by end 1989 (18); cease-fire takes effect (20).

26   Vietnamese troops complete withdrawal from Cambodia, *Khmer Rouge* opens attack on Pailin.

27–   US and Philippines formally agree to reopen base negotiations in December; former Philippines President Marcos dies in Hawaii (28).

October

1–   Pakistan is readmitted to Commonwealth after 17-year absence; Commonwealth summit in Malaysia selects Chief Emeka Anyaoku as next Secretary-General (18).

1–   Sri Lankan Tamil Tigers agree to regional elections if Indian peacekeeping troops withdraw; government offers concessions to JVP rebels if they surrender arms (1); 807 JVP rebels surrender after 6-day government cease-fire (3).

4–   Cambodian government garrison of Sisophon surrenders after 5-day guerrilla offensive; rebels claim capture of border towns (22–28); government imposes overnight curfew on Phnom Penh (30).

5   Dalai Lama awarded Nobel Peace Prize.
31   China expels 2 Hong Kong liberals from Basic Law Drafting Committee.
31   Afghan government troops regain control of Salang Highway.
November
4   Deng Xiaoping resigns his last official Chinese Party post.
19   President Aquino loses in national referendum on her autonomy plan for
         southern Philippines.
22–   Ruling Congress Party fails to secure a majority in Indian general election;
         Premier Rajiv Gandhi resigns (29).
December
1–   Philippine President Aquino survives sixth coup attempt by mutinous
         troops; rebel leader Lt Col Galvez surrenders in Manila (16); remaining 400
         rebels surrender at Cebu airbase (9).
2   Taiwan's ruling Nationalist Party retains power in first multi-party election,
         but opposition Democratic Progressive Party wins 21 seats.
2   V.P. Singh becomes Indian premier as head of coalition government.
2   Communist Party of Malaya signs peace treaty with Malaysia and Thailand,
         ending 41 years of conflict.
12   Hong Kong begins involuntary repatriation of Vietnamese boat people.
20–   Sri Lankan Tamil Tiger rebels register as a political party under name of
         People's Front of the Liberation Tigers; government troops capture and kill
         last rebel leader of Sinhalese People's Liberation Front (28).

CENTRAL AND LATIN AMERICA

January
11   Colombian government signs peace accord with M-19 guerrillas, who prom-
         ise to maintain country-wide truce.
15   Brazil introduces new economic plan to halt inflation.
24–   In El Salvador, rebels offer 12-point peace plan for their participation in gen-
         eral elections; President Duarte rejects the proposal (25).
February
2–   Carlos Andrés Peréz sworn in as Venezuelan President; reforms liberalizing
         the economy announced (16); after 2 days of rioting over price rises, consti-
         tutional rights suspended and curfew imposed (28).
3–   In Paraguay President Stroessner deposed after coup by Gen Andrés
         Rodríguez; Stroessner goes into exile in Brazil as government announces
         general elections within 90 days (5).
7–   El Salvador rebels propose 30-day cease-fire either side of a presidential elec-
         tion; they meet representatives of 9 political parties in Mexico to discuss
         plan (20–21); Duarte presents peace proposals (26); rejected by rebels (27);
         El Salvador Army announce unilateral cease-fire until 1 June to allow further
         peace talks (28).
13–14   In El Salvador, Presidents of Costa Rica, El Salvador, Guatemala, Honduras
         and Nicaragua request UN military observer forces to monitor Arias peace
         plan; agree to disband and repatriate Honduran-based *Contras*.
March
1–   El Salvador armed forces begin unilateral cease-fire; ARENA Party candi-
         date Alfredo Cristiani wins presidential election (19).
4–   In Colombia, Patriotic Union Party withdraws from government-promoted
         peace talks following assassination of senior leaders; President Barco meets
         M-19 guerrillas to arrange further peace talks (30).
10–11   At G-8 meeting in Venezuela, finance ministers from Argentina, Colombia,

Mexico, Peru, Uruguay, Venezuela and Brazil approve a regional debt plan snubbing recent US debt proposals.

15 Interior Minister Carlos Cacares, head of opposition Christian Democrats Patricio Aylwin and 2 other opposition leaders meet to discuss constitutional reform in Chile.

31 Argentinian Economy Minister Juan Sourrouille resigns and is replaced by Juan Pugliese after austerity measures fail.

April

2– In Haiti, army-led coup fails; leader, Lt Col Himmler Rebu exiled to US (4); 2nd military coup mounted against Haitian leader Gen Avril (5); coup thwarted after Dessalines infantry barracks overrun by loyal troops (8).

2–4 During first visit by Soviet leader to Cuba in 15 years, Gorbachev meets Castro, speaks to parliament, attacks export of revolution or counter-revolution.

11 Mexico signs $3.6-bn loan deal with IMF to restructure its foreign debt.

16 In national referendum, Uruguay votes to maintain 1986 law giving amnesty to military officers accused of human rights abuses.

26 In Chile proposals for constitutional reform presented by Interior Minister Carlos Caceres after consultation with opposition, rejected by Gen Pinochet who demands resignation of the cabinet; in ensuing reshuffle only 2 ministers replaced (27); government presents own reform proposals involving 19 constitutional amendments (28).

May

1– In Paraguayan elections, Gen Andrés Rodríguez wins presidential race and ruling *Colorado* Party secure a majority in Congress.

7 Ruling MNR party wins congressional elections in Bolivia, no candidate secures majority in concurrent presidential election.

8– Peruvian Premier Armando Villanueva and his cabinet resign after increased guerrilla violence; *Sendero Luminoso* guerrillas enforce armed strikes in 3 provinces (10–12); new cabinet headed by Luis Alberto Sánchez sworn in (15).

9 Coup attempt by Guatemalan Air Force to oust Defence Minister, Gen Morales, fails.

11– Panamanian leader Noriega annuls 7 May presidential elections following defeat of his candidate; Bush sends 2,000 more troops to Panama (11); visit by OAS delegation fails to solve political impasse (25–27).

14– Peronist candidate Carlos Menem wins Argentinian presidential election; President Alfonsín appoints new cabinet (26); announces emergency austerity measures (28); following food riots, State of Emergency declared (29).

31 Chilean government and opposition agree series of constitutional reforms after 2 months of negotiation.

June

1– In El Salvador, Alfredo Cristiani sworn in as President; his Chief of Staff José Rodríguez Porth killed by unidentified guerrillas (9).

12– In Cuba, Gen Arnaldo Ochoa Sanchez and 6 others arrested on drug smuggling charges; Interior Minister José Abrantes replaced by Gen Alberto Colome for failure to stop smuggling (29).

13 World Bank agrees $1.1-bn loan to Mexico, a quarter of which is allocated to debt reduction.

July

2– In Mexico PRI loses state election for first time since 1929; Mexican debt successfully renegotiated in line with Brady debt initiative (23).

6– Chilean opposition nominates Patricio Aylwin as presidential candidate; national referendum approves group of constitutional reforms (30).

8–   Carlos Menem sworn in as Argentinian President; austerity plan revealed by
          Finance Minister Miguel Roig (9); Menem offers to end Falklands hostilities
          if UK removes exclusion zone (12); Roig dies of heart attack (14); replaced
          by Nestor Rapanelli (15).
13–   4 Cuban officers including Gen Sanchez executed for drug smuggling; for-
          mer Interior Minister Abrantes, arrested on drug-trafficking charges (31).
16–   In Panama, talks between government and opposition begin; OAS proposes
          fresh elections (20); idea rejected by Noriega's supporters (21).

August
1–   Argentina lifts trade restrictions with UK; at end of first direct talks for 5
          years, both sides agree to meet again in October (16–18); diplomatic visits
          exchanged for first time since 1984 (31).
4–   Nicaraguan President Ortega signs political accord with opposition guaran-
          teeing free elections and dismantling of *Contras*.
18–   Colombian anti-drug campaigner Senator Luis Carlos Galán murdered;
          President Barco announces emergency measures against drug cartels includ-
          ing extradition to US (19); 100,000 people arrested in drugs raid (21); drug
          cartels threaten to kill 10 judges for each suspect extradited (25); govern-
          ment imposes curfew in Medellín after bomb attacks (30).
21–   In Panama, government/opposition talks end in failure; OAS admits failure
          to resolve crisis (23); Francisco Rodríguez named provisional president by
          Noriega as mandate of Manuel Solis Palma expires (31).

September
1–   US breaks off diplomatic relations with Panama as unelected provisional
          government of President Rodríguez sworn in; US announces further econ-
          omic and trade sanctions (12).
7   Drug cartel accountant Edwardo Martinez Romero extradited to US; former
          Medellín mayor Pablo Pelaez Gonzalez assassinated in retaliation (11); Jus-
          tice Minister Monica de Grieff resigns after death threats (22); M-19 guer-
          rillas and Colombian government sign peace treaty (26).
13–   FMLN rebels in El Salvador offer 11-day unilateral cease-fire as they begin
          talks with the government; agree to re-meet in October (15).

October
3   Panama army coup attempt against Noriega fails.
4–   M-19 guerrillas in Colombia vote to lay down arms and form political party;
          Carlos Pizarro selected as their presidential candidate (6); Roberto Salazar
          Manrique sworn in as new Justice Minister (8); 3 drug traffickers extradited
          to US (14); judge murdered in retaliation (17).
6   Argentinian President Menem pardons 280 civilians and members of armed
          forces for human-rights abuses in 1970s.
16–18   Peace talks in Costa Rica between El Salvador government and rebels fail.

November
2–   *Contras* agree to peace talks with *Sandinista* government; at opening of talks
          in New York, *Contras* spurn government offer of cease-fire (9); talks end in
          disagreement (21).
2–15   Judges in Medellín, Colombia, strike in demand for greater protection from
          drug traffickers.
11–   In El Salvador, FMLN guerrillas begin attack on San Salvador; 6 Jesuit
          priests killed by government troops (16); rebels seize hotel containing US
          military advisers (21); all hostages released unharmed (22); El Salvador gov-
          ernment rejects cease-fire offer from rebels (23); President Cristiani sus-
          pends relations with Nicaragua for supporting the FMLN attacks (26); US
          begins evacuating its citizens (29).

26   In presidential and parliamentary elections in Uruguay, Luis Lacalle and the National Party defeat ruling *Colorado* Party.

December

6   Suspected drug traffickers bomb Colombia's security and intelligence agency, killing 50.

11–   Argentina launches 2nd austerity programme in 5 months; Finance Minister Raparelli resigns (15); Antonio Erman Gonzalez named replacement, launches another emergency economic plan (18).

14   Patricio Aylwin elected President of Chile, ending 16 years military rule.

17   Fernando Collor de Mello elected President of Brazil.

20–   US troops invade Panama, install Gullermo Endara as President; Noriega takes refuge in Papal Nuncio's residence (24).

EAST–WEST ARMS CONTROL

January

7–   World conference on CW opens in Paris; USSR announces it will unilaterally destroy its CW during 1989 (8); final communique bans CW use and condemns user nations (11).

15–   Concluding document of CSCE review meeting in Vienna announces Conventional Stability Talks to begin March; Shevardnadze announces unilateral withdrawal of some SNF in Europe (19).

23–   GDR and Poland announce reductions in their armies; Czechoslovakia and Bulgaria follow (27); Hungary also agrees to cut forces (30).

February

2   MBFR talks in Vienna formally concluded after 16 years.

7   Geneva Conference on Disarmament, discussing CW ban, resumes.

20   EC Foreign Ministers ban export of chemicals used to manufacture CW.

March

2   FRG Foreign Minister Hans-Dietrich Genscher demands immediate start to East–West SNF talks.

6–   As CFE talks open in Vienna, NATO and WTO submit separate and contrasting prosals for future discussion; talks go into recess (23).

9–   At start of CSCE review conference in Vienna, WTO attempts to include naval and air forces on the agenda, is rejected by NATO; talks recess (23).

April

7   In UK Gorbachev announces USSR will cease production of weapons-grade uranium in 1989.

27   UN Disarmament Conference in Geneva recesses.

May

5–   CFE talks resume in Vienna; Warsaw Pact proposes equipment ceiling (18); proposes troop cuts of 1 million on each side (23).

10–11   In Moscow Secretary of State Baker rejects USSR offer to dismantle Krasnoyarsk radar if US strictly interprets 1972 ABM Treaty.

29–30   At NATO summit in Brussels Bush outlines 4-point conventional disarmament plan; compromise reached on NATO nuclear modernization; decisions on SNF deployment deferred until 1992.

31   Pentagon officials reveal 1,269 missiles destroyed by US and USSR in first year of INF Treaty.

June

19   11th round of US–USSR START talks resume in Geneva.

26–   US and USSR resume talks on partial test ban treaty in Geneva; US, USSR

and UK hold separate talks also in Geneva to consider a conference to ban all underground nuclear testing (27).

29 40-nation Conference on Disarmanent in Geneva recesses.

July

6 Speaking to Council of Europe in Strasbourg, Gorbachev offers unilateral SNF reductions if NATO agrees to talks on elimination of such weapons.

13– At CFE talks in Vienna NATO presents new proposals for conventional force reductions, with cuts twice as large as old; talks recess (14).

August

2 USSR presents new arms reduction proposals at CFE talks in Vienna.

7 After 7 weeks of talks, START session recesses.

8 Superpower nuclear test talks recess in Geneva after 6 weeks.

31 UN Conference on Disarmament in Geneva ends 1989 session.

September

7– CFE talks resume in Vienna; NATO presents proposals covering information exchange, stabilization and verification measures (21); WTO agrees to inclusion of tactical aircraft in talks (28).

19– Chemical industries agree global CW ban at 3-day 67-nation talks in Australia; speaking to UN, Bush proposes 80% cut in US CW stock (25); at UN, USSR proposes total ban on CW (26); US rejects proposal (27).

19– Secretary of State Baker announces US agreement to include mobile ICBM in START; START talks resume in Geneva (28).

October

2 US and USSR resume nuclear test ban verification talks in Geneva.

19 CFE talks recess while NATO studies WTO proposals on inspection and verification.

26 In Finland Gorbachev pledges to withdraw 4 remaining USSR nuclear subs from Baltic and repeats desire for nuclear-free zone there.

November

9 CFE talks resume in Vienna.

December

8 START talks recess in Geneva.

14 Tenth round of US–USSR bilateral talks on CW ends in Geneva.

14 NATO and WTO table separate draft treaties for reducing conventional forces at CFE talks in Vienna.